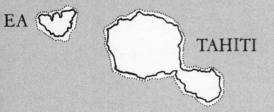

TETIAROA

EA

TAHITI

MEETIA

ANCIENT TAHITIAN SOCIETY

The *Resolution* and *Adventure* at Tahiti. Painting by W. Hodges, Cook's second voyage. National Maritime Museum, Greenwich, England.

ANCIENT TAHITIAN SOCIETY

VOLUME 3   RISE OF THE POMARES

DOUGLAS L. OLIVER

THE UNIVERSITY PRESS OF HAWAII
HONOLULU

Copyright © 1974 by The University Press of Hawaii
All rights reserved
Library of Congress Catalog Card Number 73–77010
ISBN 0-8248-0267-5
Manufactured in the United States of America

Book design by Roger J. Eggers

VOLUME 3 *CONTENTS*

VOLUME 3
RISE OF THE POMARES

CHAPTER 25 *TRIBAL POLITY AT BEGINNING OF EARLY EUROPEAN ERA*

[The] prime duty of the historian [is] a willingness to bestow infinite pains on discovering what actually happened. (Collingwood 1946:55)

Chapter 23 was concerned with Maohi social relations insofar as they were affected by considerations of residential proximity in combination with coercive force. The attempt was made to depict these kinds of social relations before they began to undergo radical change as a direct or indirect result of European influences.[1] Moreover, events were dealt with largely in terms of modes, and persons in terms of statuses; this course was followed partly by design, but it was also necessitated by the nature of the available data.

The present chapter will be concerned with the same kinds of social relations, but will focus upon the changes they underwent during the first five decades after Europeans appeared on the scene. The focus will be upon specific individuals and events rather than upon generalized statuses and typical occurrences. Such a reconstruction may serve to provide some corrective, and an additional footnote or two, to current notions about this minor but intriguing chapter of colonial history. But my main object is to add some flesh and movement to the skeleton of pre-European Maohi politics hitherto assembled; for, it is my firm opinion that although Europeans wrought radical changes in some phases of Maohi life — via their steel tools, their diseases, et cetera — and although European influence also had the effect of encouraging and facilitating certain developments in Maohi polity, the motives and instrumentalities of such developments remained basically Maohi, and hence directly relevant to my reconstruction of pre-European Maohi society.

The developments I refer to comprised the consolidation of coercive authority over all Tahiti and Mo'orea into the hands of one individual — or, in labels current to the era, the emergence of a "monarchy" out of what had been a number of more or less autonomous tribal chiefdoms. Besides the general ethnological and sociological interests attached to this topic, which I consider to be of major theoretical importance, it deserves attention for some special, local reasons. To begin with, of all the matters touched upon in the journals and other writings of the early European visitors to these Islands it is the one they were most crucially concerned with, and about which they wrote most fully. Second, these developments encompassed more aspects of Maohi life than perhaps any other configuration of events. And finally, they have occasioned more scholarly controversy, perhaps, than any other aspect of Maohi life (except, possibly, for the question concerning the origins of stratification).

The differences among scholars who have concerned themselves with these matters have tended to polarize. At one extreme is the implication that indigenous Maohi society was fundamentally and immutably multitribal, and that the monarchy which emerged resulted solely or mainly from European influences (e.g., Handy 1930:77ff.). At the other extreme is the conclusion set forth by other scholars that the trend toward consolidation of political authority was intrinsic to Maohi society — that monarchy was undoubtedly hastened by European intervention but would in time have culminated even without that intervention (e.g., Newbury 1967a). The general theoretical implications of this issue, which reach far beyond the confines of Tahiti, or even of Polynesia, have been largely overlooked in most writings on the subject, or obscured by parochial advocacy of this or that competing dynastic claim (Gunson 1963). For example, one question that arises in regard to societies like this one has to do with the inevitability of political consolidation: inasmuch as most types of Maohi groups were pervasively hierarchical, and because in most such hierarchies there was only one status endowed with final decision-making authority, was it inevitable that the top status-holders of the various tribes would vie for overall supremacy when population increase, aided by ease of communication, brought them into more frequent interaction with one another? And if so, what were the other factors that served, in the long run, to promote or frustrate such consolidation? Because of the "exogenous" factors represented by the European presence, the events I am about to describe do not constitute a "pure" case study of this kind of development, but they nevertheless provide some suggestive clues.

There are undoubtedly many ways of looking at changes in a society's administrative structure and politics. The present focus is on *tribal chiefly authority*, which I view mainly as command over certain kinds of services and certain material products of services. The nature of such services and objects will of course vary from society to society. I trust that the nature of services and objects comprising such authority in Maohi society has been described sufficiently in previous chapters, so that I now concentrate on the campaigns waged by certain chiefs to extend their domains of command. Assuming (justifiably, I believe) the absence of any significant regional differences with respect to cognitive inventory and social values, I will devote most attention to the resources and strategies of the principal campaigners themselves.

Tahiti

When H.M.S. *Dolphin* anchored in Matavai Bay in 1767 the island of Tahiti appears to have been divided into several tribes, or closely knit tribal coalitions, of various orders of complexity:

Teva i tai (Seaward Teva), a unit of fifth-order complexity (see chap. 23) that made up the whole of the Taiarapu Peninsula and numbered about 14,000 to 15,000 inhabitants.[2]

Teva i uta (Landward Teva), a unit of fifth-order complexity occupying the southern quarter of Greater Tahiti and numbering about 7,000 inhabitants.

Mano rua (or Pa'ea), a unit of fourth-order complexity.

Mano tahi (or Puna'auia), a unit of fourth-order complexity.

Throughout the era under study, and possibly for some decades prior thereto, these last two tribes (which I shall henceforth call by their more familiar territorial labels of Pa'ea and Puna'auia) were on many occasions so closely allied that their inhabitants and territories came to be known collectively as Te Oropa'a and Atehuru, respectively. This union, which had a population of about 2,100, was, however, an alliance of near-equals rather than one unified hierarchically to the degree that Seaward Teva was.

Te Fana, a unit of probable third-order complexity whose 1,000 or so inhabitants occupied an area known as Tetaha or Fa'a'a.[3]

Te Poreonu'u, a fourth-order unit of about 4,200 inhabitants that occupied the major territorial divisions of Pare and Arue as well as the atoll Tetiaroa (Wilson 1799:380).

Te Aharoa was the name applied collectively to the inhabitants of the five major territorial units of Tahiti's thinly populated northeastern side: Ha'apape (or Mahina), Ha'apaiano'o (or Papeno'o, or Vavau), Tiarei, Mahaena, and Hitia'a. Little, however, is known about their interrelations beyond the fact that Hitia'a's principal people figured more prominently in events elsewhere on the island than did the chiefs of the other units. This may signify that Hitia'a's chief also exercised some authority — or at least weightier influence — over other Te Aharoa chiefs.[4] But lacking evidence of such authority I tentatively classify these populations into five separate tribes of third- or fourth-order complexity. They numbered about 6,300 people.

Something has already been said of the topography and natural resources of these various regions of Tahiti island, so I turn to the principal dramatis personae of the events about to be described.

Seaward Teva

By 1767 the Seaward Teva, comprising the population of Tahiti's Taiarapu Peninsula, had become a relatively stable tribal unit, of fifth-order complexity, under the firmly entrenched and only occasionally challenged chieftainship of the members of a dynastic line whose official incumbent bore the Title of Vehiatua i te Mata'i (see fig. 25–1, foldout), traditionally associated with marae Matahihae of Teahupo'o, but later established also at marae Vaiotaha of Tautira, by virtue of Teahupo'o's defeat of Tautira in the Rahui War described earlier. After Taiarapu was politically unified, Vaiotaha became its most important marae, and Tautira its main center of tribal activity, probably because of the localization there of the cult of 'Oro.

The first Vehiatua to "enter history" was the one seen by Cook during his circumnavigation of Tahiti in 1768. Cook met this Vehiatua briefly at Tautira; he labeled him "King," or "Ari'i Rahi of Taiarapu," and described him as "a very old man with a white beard, not at all attended by a crowd of people." At the same time Cook encountered Vehiatua's elder son, Ta'ata Uraura, who was about thirteen at the time and who, according to Cook, "seem'd to have much influence." (Beaglehole 1955:108–109.) We learn from other sources that the spouse of Vehiatua was Purahi (or Pura'i?) or Te Vahine Moeatua,[5] a firstborn child of a couple combining high-ranking Titles from Papara, Hitia'a, Vairao, and Ha'apape (Adams 1901:32). Cook's "Old King" Vehiatua died about 1771 and does not figure prominently in the visitors' accounts of this era; but the fierce old chief's violent attack against Mo'orea (described in chap. 12), left a residue of ill will there and among Mo'orean partisans on Tahiti, particularly in Poreonu'u. And as for his spouse, it is claimed that she was one of the principal instigators of the War of the Ahu Ra'a Reva, which served to curb the political pretensions of Papara, of which more anon. After the death of her husband, Te Vahine Moeatua took as her consort Ti'itorea of Mo'orea, whose kin-Title evidently ranked below that of his mate's. He served as "prime minister" to his mate's sons (Corney 1919:270) and was identified by Morrison as "Chief of Towtirra [Tautira]" (1935:93).[6] It is not clear whether their relationship was ever institutionalized by a contractual rite of "marriage."

When the curtain of written history rises over Taiarapu there is revealed an autonomous tribe, called the Seaward Teva, whose various subdivisions were more or less united under the political supremacy of the individuals named in figure 25–2. The numerals I, II, III are my notations for purposes of identification. The Maohis themselves did not use such notations as far as I know, and even the person designated as Vehiatua I was not the first to bear that Title.

The relationships of these principals to others elsewhere will be described as the story unfolds; meanwhile it will be useful to reproduce some of what has been recorded about their personalities.

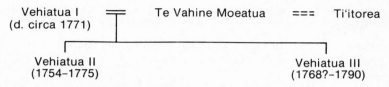

FIGURE 25–2. Kin relations among principals of Seaward Teva.

Vehiatua I, whom Cook and Banks met in 1769, had been in his prime a fierce and relentless warrior. An account of his war against Papetoai was reproduced in chapter 12; the same document provides an additional picture of his character in an account of his treatment of a "rebel" chief, Mae:

Vehiatua seeing Mae in the hands of a warrior and about to be slain, gave orders to spare, and secure him as a prisoner. According to usage a few captives were taken to be offered at the marae, these, with the captive chief, were marched to Taiarabu, the inferior prisoners were immediately offered in sacrifice to the gods. But Mae who was considered as a rebel was reserved for a more fearful end, as a warning to other chiefs on the peninsula. When this savage conqueror was surrounded by his warriors, he ordered the captive to be brought before him, pinioned his arms, ordered the scalp to be cut off, the eyes to be drawn from the head of the living victim and the body otherwise mutilated. During this diabolical process, the savage warriors ridiculed the agony and mimiced the contortion and dying struggles of the victim, and seemed to derive the greatest pleasure from the whole scene. To complete the disgusting tragedy the skull of the unhappy victim was carefully cut off, and made into a cup from which Vehiatua quaffed his frequent draughts of the inebriating ava, prepared by a process worthy of the cup from which he drank. (Thomson, History, pp. 24–25)

Vehiatua II, elder son and successor to Vehiatua I, was a wholly different kind of man; perhaps the clearest description of him is by G. Forster, who met him in 1773:

O-Aheatua, the king of O-Taheitee-eetee, (Little Taheitee) which is otherwise called Tiarraboo, was a youth of seventeen or eighteen years of age, well-made, about five feet six inches high, and likely to grow taller. His countenance was mild, but unmeaning; and rather expressed some signs of fear and distrust at our first meeting, which suited ill with the ideas of majesty, and yet are often the characteristics of lawless power. His colour was of the fairest of his people, and his lank hair of a light brown, turning into reddish at the tips, or being what is commonly called sandy. He wore at present no other dress than a white sash, (marro) round the waist to the knees, made of the best kind of cloth, and his head as well as all the rest of his body was uncovered. On both sides of him sat several chiefs and nobles, distinguishable by their superior stature, which is the natural effect of the immense quantity of food which they consume. One of them was punctured in a surprising manner, which we had never seen before, large black blotches of various shapes, almost covering his arms, legs, and sides. This man, whose name was E-Tee, was also remarkable for his enormous corpulence, and for the deference which the aree (king) paid to him, consulting him almost upon every occasion. The king, during the time he sat on the stool, which was his throne, preserved a grave or rather stiff deportment, scarce to be expected at his years, though it seemed to be studied and assumed, only to make our meeting more solemn. (1777:I, 305–306)

The young chief was to die in 1775, after a lingering illness, which was described in almost daily reportorial detail by the Spaniard Rodriguez (Corney 1919).

Vehiatua IIII (also, Tetuaunumaona), younger brother of Vehiatua II, succeeded the latter to the office of chieftainship of Seaward Teva at the tender age of about seven and continued in office until his death some fifteen years later. I have found no direct description of his personality and only indirect and marginal references to his actions. In any case, he appears, like his brother before him, to have been strongly influenced if not actually dominated by his strong-willed mother, the famous Vahine Moeatua, or Purahi.

Hitia'a

As noted in chapter 3 the most outstanding Maohi of Hitia'a at the opening of this era was its tribal chief, *Reti*, who bore the kin-Title Teri'itua associated with marae Hitia'a. Reti is introduced to us in Bougainville's account of his short visit to Tahiti, specifically to Hitia'a, in April 1768. At that time Reti seems to have been in authority, but his father was still alive and active. Reti and his principal people conducted themselves hospitably toward the Europeans and were evidently pleased to have them there, after an understanding had been reached that the visit would be brief. From this and other evidence the impression we gain from this encounter is of a Maohi chief whose authority was benevolent and firmly established — that is, one who, unlike some other chiefs we shall meet, had no need or wish for European aid in maintaining or increasing his authority. According to the Spaniards who met Reti in 1774 he was at that time between forty-five and fifty years old. Gayangos described him as being "of good presence, full of humour active in body," adding ʌhat "he made himself more easily understood by all of us than did any other" (Corney 1915:133). To this evaluation Rodriguez added that Reti was "brown in hue, tall, very active, and has a large and deepish scar on the forehead; he is a man of proved bravery, and quick understanding" (Corney 1919:10). Even the more laconic English subscribed to this favorable evaluation:

Could I have prevailed on my self to have again altered My Conduct, and make choice of a Tyo [*taio*] or Friend, as is the Custom here, it should have been Ereti the Friend of *M. Bougainville*; not that he was less importunate & craving than others; but because he was much more sensible and inteligent . . . than any others were. (Wales, in Beaglehole 1961:799)

G. Forster wrote of him as follows:

O-Rettee was a fine grey-headed man, but very healthy and vigorous, as the old people of Taheitee in general seem to be; his countenance was the picture of a lively, chearful, and generous man. He told us he had been in many battles, and shewed us several wounds he had received, particularly a blow with a stone on his temple, which had left a deep scar. (1777:II, 85)

Boenechea's journal describes a meeting in 1774 with Teinui, a young man of eighteen or twenty, who was said to be the son of Reti (Corney 1913:314). Teinui also asserted that he himself was chief of Hitia'a, and, according to normal rules of succession, he may indeed have succeeded his father to kin-Titles and their ceremonial prerogatives. But the descriptions of his relations with his father indicate that the latter was at that time still very much the wielder of tribal political authority. According to Rodriguez, Reti also had daughters (Corney 1919:10); however, I have sought in vain for clues to Reti's other kin relations. Nor can I find any references to Teinui in accounts of subsequent events, or identify Teinui with any other name that appears later on. Reti himself was still alive during Cook's last visit, in 1777 (Beaglehole 1967:1344), but how much longer he survived I cannot discover.

In any case, Reti was at one time an ally of Tutaha, tribal chief of Pare-Arue, during the latter's war against the Seaward Teva in 1773. Earlier evidence of this relationship occurred during Bougainville's visit to Hitia'a, when Tutaha was afforded a friendly reception there (Bougainville 1772:229). And he seemed quite at home at Matavai at the time of Cook's last visit (G. Forster 1777:II, 85; Beaglehole 1967:1063). More puzzling is the connection between Reti and the Leeward Islands, for it was to the chief of Porapora (and conqueror of Ra'iatea) that Reti made a present of an anchor lost by one of Bougainville's ships off Hitia'a.[7]

Writing in 1769, Cook described Hitia'a ("Whidea") as having two chiefs, Reti ("Orrette") and "Teemehinnee" (Te Mahinau?) (Beaglehole 1955:105); but I can find no other reference to the latter, or to "Fanaue," whom Henry identified as "under chief" of Hitia'a (1928:71). Names of still other Hitia'a "chiefs" are introduced into the historical cast by later writers (e.g., "Marre marre" and his son, "Oeehaitaih Otee" by Bligh in 1789, and "Teehu" by missionaries in 1801 through 1808),[8] but I am unable to connect these with Reti or with anyone else.

Mahaena, Tiarei, Ha'apaiano'o, Ha'apape

No individuals from the tribal territories of Mahaena, Tiarei, and Ha'apaiano'o were prominent enough on Tahiti's political stage during the first part of the "historical" era to draw Europeans' attention; but some Ha'apape personages figured in the chronicles of that era, not only because European vessels made a practice of anchoring at Matavai Bay, but also because of the historical importance of certain individuals associated with Ha'apape's marae Fareroi.

In Emory's Ha'apape genealogy (reconstructed by him from notes of Brander[9]) the entries coming within the purview of this era are related, as shown in figure 25-3.

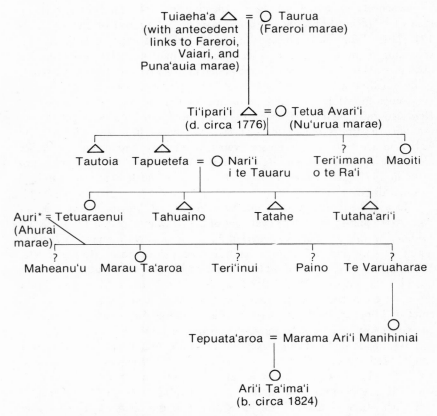

*Auri was brother of Purea and of Pomare I's wife's father.

FIGURE 25-3. Kin relations among principals of Fareroi.

Reckoning back from the approximately accurate birth date of Ari'i Ta'ima'i (the famous Papara dowager immortalized by Henry Adams), the Ti'ipari'i ("Little Ti'ipa") here listed would have been born between 1700 and 1715, and his eldest son, Tautoia, between 1720 and 1735. (According to Henry, Ti'ipa and Tuteia (Tautoia?) were names (or Titles?) of Ha'apape's high chief and underchief, respectively.) In 1774 Cook was met by a "chief" named "Tee," whom he described as an "Uncle to the King [i.e., Pomare I] and one of his prime ministers" (Beaglehole 1961:384).[10] "Tee," who made himself helpful to Cook throughout this visit, was reportedly one of the "Principal People." Although "Tee" may have exercised some local influence he was clearly overshadowed by other notables from elsewhere who turned up at Matavai, and he seems not to have possessed the authority one might expect of the chief of an autonomous tribe, despite his distinguished connections.[11] "Tee" died some months before Cook's last visit, in 1777, when his preserved corpse was still on view (Beaglehole 1967:208).

The middle-aged woman who was seen in Matavai and whom Wallis took to be "Queen" of Tahiti was Purea — who was not "queen" of any place, and whose main connections with Ha'apape derived from the marriage of her brother Auri to Tetuaraenui (see fig. 25–2), and from her husband Amo's mother, Teroro e Ora. Purea's ancestral home was Fa'a'a, and she resided at Papara, the home of her husband; the respectful consideration shown to her at Matavai was based on these other connections, and probably also upon her notoriously imperious bearing in whatever company she happened to be.

When H.M.S. *Bounty* was at Matavai in 1788 the local chief was one called "Poeno" ("Poenu," "Poe'eno"); such was also the case during Vancouver's visit (December 1791 to January 1792) and during Bligh's return visit some months later.[12] The nearest name to "Poeno" I can find on the Ha'apape genealogy (fig. 25–2) is Paino, who would have been a greatgrandson of Ti'ipari'i — a not impossible identification, if the genealogy may be trusted. In any event, by this late date Matavai, and possibly all Ha'apape, had become at least intermittently subordinate to Pare, whose situation we will consider.

Poreonu'u

By 1767 the inhabitants of Pare-Arue constituted a unified and fairly stable tribe known as Te Porionu'u. Inasmuch as it was the principal personages of this tribe who succeeded eventually in consolidating political authority over all Tahiti and Mo'orea, we need to look very closely into the genealogical connections on which their political pretensions were founded. It goes without saying that it is unrealistic to hope for historical reliability; Maohi genealogies were no less subject to manipulation than were other forms of verbal "documentation." The extent to which the genealogies in question were thus manipulated is evident in statements attributed to the two most "authoritative" Maohi historians of post-European times: Mare and "Queen" Marau. The former mobilized genealogical evidence reaching back to the Maohis' most venerable *ari'i* marae in order to "prove" the supremacy

in rank of the Poreonu'u chiefs' Titles over all others throughout the archipel-
ago. In striking contrast, Marau (in the words of her amanuensis, Adams)
characterized the Poreonu'u chiefs as having been "an inferior chiefdom"
with their principal roots in the savage, "Manahune," Paumotus. (Handy
1930:79; Adams 1901:84.)[13] With respect to their genealogical evidence,
and insofar as that evidence is "authentic" (in terms of Maohi admissibility,
which is the criterion most relevant to our present concerns), both these
authorities were of course "right," for like most Maohi notables the
Poreonu'u chiefs had antecedents reaching in all directions and back to the
gods themselves. But rather than reproduce any of these genealogies in full,
my present purposes will be amply served, first, by summarizing some fairly
consensual traditions regarding the beginnings of this chiefly line in Pare-
Arue, and, second, by identifying in detail the eighteenth-century representatives of that line.

According to Adams, Arue and Pare formerly constituted separate tribes
(1901:77ff). There may have been other eras during which they were allied
with one another, or even joined together into a single tribe, but some traditions have it that the unity manifested during the era now under study was
established in consequence of the settlement there of a chiefly personage
from Fakarava (Paumotu) named Tu. Here is the Ari'i Ta'ima'i-Adams
version of this episode:

> Aimata's son, Pomare V, the last king, wanting to establish his title to lands
> in the Paumotus, had naturally to acknowledge the connection and to prove his
> descent. The genealogy adopted for the occasion made the first Tu, who came from
> the Paumotus, grandfather to Taaroa manahune, who married Tetuaehuri i Taiarapu,
> as I have told in Chapter III. Tu of Faarava, having undertaken a visit to the distant
> land of Tahiti, came in by the Taunoa opening, which is the eastern channel into
> what is now the harbor of Papeete. Landing at Taunoa a stranger, he was invited
> to be the guest of Mauaihiti, who seems to have been a chief of Pare. Tu made
> himself so agreeable, or so useful to his host, that Mauaihiti adopted him as *hoa*,
> or brother, with the formal ceremonies attached to this custom, which consist in
> a grand feast, and union of all families, and offering of all the rights and honors
> which belong to the host. Tu accepted them, and at the death of Mauaihiti he became
> heir and successor in the chief's line. He gave up all idea of returning to the Paumotus,
> and devoted his energy to extending his connections in Tahiti. He himself married
> into the Arue family, which gave his son a claim to the joint chiefery of Pare Arue;
> and at last his grandson, or some later generation, obtained in marriage no less
> a personage than Tetuaehuri, daughter of Vehiatua of Taiarapu. The received
> genealogy represents the son of Taaroa manahune and Tetuaehuri as Teu, who was
> known as Hapai or Whappai to the English, and lived into this century, but Tahitian
> genealogies have a perplexing way of dropping persons who do not amuse them,
> and there may well be a leap of one or two generations in that of Pomare. (Adams
> 1901:85)

Another version, derived from Ari'i Ta'ima'i's daughter, Marau, exem-
plifies the last sentence in the above passage and also reverses the positions
of Pare and Arue:

According to Marau, the Tu or Pomare family of Pare were descended from a Taumotuan chief name Tu who came from the atoll of Fakarava in the 17th century. Tu was adopted (*fa'a taua*) by an *iatoai* named Mauaihiti, in Arue. Later it is said, he married a daughter of the chief of Arue. Their son was Taaroa-Manahune, to whom this anomalous name, or nickname, came as a result of an insult sustained in reference to his Taumotuan derivation. Taaroa-Manahune married Tetua-e-huri, daughter of Vehiatua of Teahupoo. Their son was Teu, who was married in the middle of the eighteenth century to Te-tu-paia, chiefess of Opoa, Raiatea. The son of this marriage was Tu (Cook's "Otoo"), later known as Pomare I. (Handy 1930:76)

To further complicate matters, a reconstruction put together from various sources by Newbury and labeled "Origins and Genealogy of the Pomare Dynasty" derives the Paumotuan link from a marriage between a Pare chief and a Paumotuan woman in the latter part of the seventeenth century (1961: Appendix I). And the famous Puna'auia genealogy, the one publicly adopted by the Pomares themselves (Emory, Marae Traditions), traces the "official" Pomare line some forty generations back from Vaira'atoa, the first in the line to bear the name Pomare, showing links to the most venerable and highly respected marae of Tahiti and Mo'orea, and with no mention whatsoever of any Paumotuan forebear.

Without attempting to decide which, if any, of these accounts is the "true" one, we can rest assured that the enemies of this chieftainship selected the versions that imputed the most recent and socially inferior origins to it.

Be that as it may, the eighteenth-century representations of this chiefly line included some forebears of sufficiently high kin-titular rank to secure for them almost universal acknowledgment of their rights to certain preeminent ceremonial privileges. For purposes of this narrative I use the eighteenth-century phase of the "official" Puna'auia genealogy (Emory, Marae Traditions), beginning with a Tutaha (whom I shall designate "Old" Tutaha), who appears to have been born about 1680 and who is described as having resided both in Puna'auia and in Pare-Arue (near marae Tarahoi).

As several members of this set of kin played such key roles in the events we are concerned with, I should attempt to identify them; but this is easier said than done. Not only is identification obscured by Europeans' inconsistencies in transcribing Maohi names, and by individuals having had multiple names, but there are some significant differences among the various recorded family inventories with respect to numbers of offspring and (a crucially important factor) to order of birth.

"Old" Tutaha, who evidently died long before 1767, affects the story mainly in having provided his descendants with consanguineal links with Tarahoi, his primary ancestral marae in Pare-Arue, and also with important marae in Ha'apape, Fa'a'a, Afareitu (Mo'orea), Fa'ahiti, and so forth. To this array of potentially useful kin connections, his wife, Tera'iatua, added her own immediate connections with marae Tepotuarai of Papararau (Puna'auia).

Tutaha (m)   married   Tera'iatua, of Te Potuari
 Born 1680   marae (Puna'auia)

  offspring:
    1. (m) Ta'aroa Manahune. Born circa 1705?
    2. (m) Tutaha (Banks' "Hercules"). Born circa 1708?
    3. (f) Te Vana'a o Tane.
    4. (f) Te Reiatua.

Ta'aroa Manahune, married   (first wife) Tetuaehuri of
 (resided at Matahihae   marae Matahihae (Teahupo'o)
 and Tarahoi)

  offspring:
    1. (m) Teihamoeroa i Matahihae (or Fa'atupuai i te Ra'i o Vehiatu
     i te Mata'i). Also called Teu and Hapai. Born circa 1728.
    2. (m) Mauaroa (or Teri'i Hinoi Atua). Called "Mowroah" by
     Bligh, who viewed his corpse in 1792.
    3. (f) Teri'i ae Atua.

         (second wife) Tetua Umeretini
          i Vairao (also called
          Mataitatia) of marae Nu'utere.

  offspring:
    4. (m) Te Fana Mua i Tarahoi.
    5. (f) Tetua Umeretini.
    6. (f) Uratua.
    7. (m) Te Aha Huri Fenua.

This couple's oldest child, Ta'aroa Manahune, who evidently also expired before 1767, extended the family connections to Teahupo'o and Vairao through his marriage to high-ranking women in these districts; but it is his younger brother, Tutaha, who engages our interest as a living participant in the events under study. Tutaha has also been identified as "brother" of Teu (see G. Forster 1777:II, 92 and Gunson 1964:68), but I am inclined to accept the Puna'auia genealogy in this particular, especially since it was confirmed by that punctilious investigator, Bligh (1789:II, 62).[14]

  According to my calculations Tutaha ("Tootaha," "Tutuhah," "Tuteha," "Dootahah") was born about 1708; he died in battle in 1773. Banks dubbed him "Hercules," whom he seems to have resembled in physique (Beaglehole 1962:I, 258). Being only a second-born son, Tutaha's

kin-Title evidently ranked lower than that of his elder brother, Ta'aroa
Manahune (and of the latter's eldest son, Teu); but there is no question
whatsoever that it was Tutaha who exercised the chiefly authority over Pare-
Arue during Cook's first visit to Tahiti.

> Of all these Courts Dootahah's [in Pare] was the most splendid, indeed we
> were almost inclined to believe that he acted as Locum tenens for *Otou* [Tu, Pomare I]
> the *Earee rahie* [*ari'i rahi*], his [great] nephew, as he lived upon an estate belonging
> to him and we never could hear that he had any other publick place of residence.
> (Beaglehole 1962:I, 385)

Indeed his influence was so powerful in that part of the island that in neighboring Ha'apape, through a grandparent's connections there, he was able to
interdict the local residents' trade with Cook:

> Early this Morning the Master went to the Eastward in the Pinnace to try if
> he could not procure some Hogs and Fowls from that quarter, but he returnd in
> the evening without success, he saw but a very few and those the Inhabitants pretended
> belonged to Tootaha: so great is this mans influence or authority over them that
> they dare part with nothing without his consent, or other wise they only make use
> of his name to excuse themselves from parting with the few they have, for it is
> very certain these things are in no great plenty with them. (Beaglehole 1955:92;
> see also Beaglehole 1962:I, 274.)

And his connections and influence in Fa'a'a and Puna'auia were such as
to entitle him to receive the Europeans there with all the formality of a
visit of State.[15] In fact, so evident was this man's authority and influence
that Cook described him as "the Chief man of the Island" (Beaglehole
1955:85).[16] In any case, whatever the extent of his personal influence, or
of his kinship connections, Tutaha's *tribal* domain was Pare-Arue, and his
principal marae was Tarahoi, on Pare's Cape Utuhaihai (Cook's Marae
Point).

By my calculations Teu (Hapai) was born about 1728; he lived until
1803, and although he was close to the events that shaped these Islands'
political history, he seems to have played a relatively minor role in them.
In fact, his most notable actions were his marriage to Tetupaia ("Oberroah"),
the eldest offspring of Tamatoa III, Ra'iatea's highest-ranking kin-Titleholder
and sovereign chief, and his siring of Tu, or Pomare I. Cook and Banks
do not even mention Teu during H.M.S. *Endeavour*'s visit in 1769. In
the journal of his second voyage Cook mentions him briefly, as Tu's father,
and as having interdicted local trade with the English on one occasion;
but that is all. Here is G. Forster's description of an encounter with Teu,
in 1773:

> As this visit was merely a visit of ceremony, we soon got up to return to
> our boat, but were detained a little longer by the arrival of E- Happai the father
> of the sovereign. He was a tall, thin man, with a grey beard and hair, seemed

to be of a great age, but was not yet entirely worn out. He received the presents which our captains made him, in a cold careless manner, which is natural to old people whose senses are considerably impaired. The accounts of former voyages had already apprised us of that strange constitution, by virtue of which the son assumes the sovereignty in his father's life time, but we could not without surprize, behold the aged Happai, naked to the waist in his son's presence, conform to the general custom. Thus the ideas universally annexed to consanguinity, are suppressed in order to give greater weight to the regal dignity, and I cannot help thinking that such a sacrifice to political authority, argues a greater degree of civilization than has been allowed to the Taheitians by our former navigators. However, though Happai was not invested with the supreme command, his birth and rank entitled him to deference from the common people, and to a proper support from the king. The province or district of O-Parre, was therefore under his immediate orders, and supplied not only his wants, but those also of his attendants. (1777:I, 330–331)

In 1788 Bligh described Teu as follows: "I found this Old Cheif, who I suppose is about 70 Years of Age, lying under a Small Shed . . . He is a tall Man with weak Eyes and his Skin is much Shrivell'd and Dryed by drinking of that punicious [pernicious] Root the Ava" (1789:I, 382).

In 1803, when Teu died, the Davies *History* described him as "probably the oldest man on the Island," and as having been for some time "quite childish" (Newbury 1961:59).

Most of Teu's offspring played key roles in the events herein chronicled. To begin with, however, we must attempt to resolve some discrepancies in the sources concerning the number and birth-order of these offspring. Putting together information from various sources (including eyewitness accounts by G. Forster and Bligh), I propose the following list in order of birth:[17]

1. Te Ari'i na Vaho Roa, also Tetua Nihura'i; a girl born circa 1749.

2. "Tedua Towrai" (Tetua te Ahurai?), also Ari'ipaea Vahine and Fataua; a girl born circa 1750.

3. Tu Nui e A'a i te Atua, also Vaira'atoa, Pomare I, and Tina; a boy born circa 1751.[18]

4. "Tedua Tehamai" (Tetua te Ahamai?); a girl born after Tu, died young.

5. Te Ari'i Fa'atou, also Ari'ipaea; a boy born circa 1758.

6. Te Tupuai e te Ra'i, also Vaetua, Maioro, and Paiti; a boy born circa 1763.

7. Auo, also "Erreretua"; a girl born circa 1768.

8. Te Pau; a boy born circa 1770.

Teu's eldest child, Te Ari'i na Vaho Roa, is something of a mystery. According to several sources she was married to Teri'irere, chief of Papara, who was some thirteen years younger than she; but she bore him no children. She died sometime prior to 1789 (according to Bligh) without having actually figured in any way in the stormy events of the time. The obscurity surrounding the existence of this eldest member of an otherwise politically active set of siblings is particularly puzzling in view of the status of her next younger sister, Tetua (te Ahurai?), "Towrai," also called Fataua and Ari'ipaea Vahine.[19] The latter, whom G. Forster described as having "almost as great authority among the women, as the King her brother [i.e., Pomare I] had in the whole Island" (1777:II, 96), removed to Ra'iatea at what must have been an early age (probably because of her mother's connections there). She does not enter the story until 1789, when she returned to Tahiti on a visit; on this occasion Morrison wrote of her as follows:

This woman being the first Born has the right of the Sovereignity of Taheite but having no Child she had Transferd the right to her Brother [i.e., Pomare I] during her Absence, and now Continues it to his son [Pomare II]; tho she is not out of Power herself by it when she visits Taheite, being always honor'd and respected. . . . (1935:101)

I am at a loss to explain Morrison's identification of her as "first Born" in the face of Forster's and others' assertions that that position belonged to Te Ari'i na Vaho Roa. However, Ari'ipaea Vahine was more politically active and influential than her elder sister.

This Homage [i.e., of being uncovered to] is due to Otoo [Tu, Pomare I] as Earee dehie of the isle, to Tarevatou [Te Ari'i Fa'atou] his Brother and [blank] his second sister, to the one as heir and to the other as heir apparent [blank] his eldest Sister being married, is not intitled to this Homage. (Beaglehole 1961:409–410)

According to Morrison's report, which is contradicted by no other that I know of, Ari'ipaea Vahine was childless. G. Forster, writing in 1774, described her as unmarried; whether she remained so thereafter cannot be ascertained, but the circumstance of childlessness and postponed marriage (or no marriage at all), when considered in connection with her activities and influence, suggests that she may have been a leading member of the Arioi — a status that may have outweighed the social superiority ascribed to her elder sister by birth.

The first son of Teu and Tetupaia is our principal character. Tu Nui e A'a i te Atua ("Tu," "Otu," "Otoo"), also known as Vaira'atoa, later became Pomare I, and — after this newly assumed Title passed to his son — ended his days mainly as Tina ("Tynah"). This individual, whom I shall continue to call Pomare I (for the sake of clarity, even though the Title Pomare was not assumed until his adult years, and even though he retired from that Title upon his son's succession), must have been born between 1748 and 1752; he died in 1803. I shall have much to say later on about his character and actions, but can point out now that he was a very large man (according to G. Forster, he was the tallest man on Tahiti [1777:I, 326]; see fig. 25–4). He may also have been physically powerful, but his talents were better suited to political maneuver than to physical combat. He began his career as chief of the relatively small tribe of Poreonuʻu (Pare-Arue), but possessed in addition the less tangible but immensely important asset represented by kin connections with several high-ranking and/or tribal chiefly persons elsewhere, including principally a link through his mother with Raʻiatea's highest-ranking dynasty.

FIGURE 25–4. Pomare I. "O Tu-Nui-e-Aʻa-i-Te-Atua, Lord Paramount of Tahiti (1747–1803)." Drawn from life by W. Hodges in 1773. Greenwich Hospital, Greenwich, England.

Of the number of women who shared Pomare I's sleeping mat from time to time,[20] there were three whose relations with him had some degree of institutionalized "permanence." One of these was his official "wife." Although I can find no account of the performance of their nuptials, I conclude that there must have been such, inasmuch as the offspring this woman bore Pomare I were generally recognized as his successors and heirs. (While recognizing the fact of their "marriage," some Tahitian factions did, however, cast doubt upon the biological paternity of the principal successor, Pomare II.) Another of these women, who is generally acknowledged to have been a sister of the first one, seems to have been accorded as much "queenly" ceremonial deference as the first, and considerably more husbandly attention; but I can find no indications that her relations with Pomare I were ever institutionalized in terms of nuptial rites (a circumstance which turned out to be irrelevant, since — as I shall attempt to demonstrate — this woman bore no children to Pomare I). Finally, the third of these women was described by Turnbull as Pomare I's "supplementary wife."

The first of these consorts may have begun living with Pomare I as early as 1774; in any case the two were almost certainly "married" before 1780, when their successor-to-be was born. (According to Morrison the marriage itself took place shortly after Cook's departure, in 1773 [Morrison 1935:173].) Thereafter, this woman bore Pomare I four surviving children, and one who was strangled at birth — the parents being Ariois at the time. Until Pomare I's death in 1803 this woman was generally regarded to be his principal consort.

The name usually given to this first and most "official" of Pomare I's consorts was 'Itia ("Iddeah," "Edea," "Edeea," etc.), or Tetuanui Rei i te Ra'iatea, and her kinship connections were very distinguished indeed. Her father was Teihotu, whose closest consanguineal connections are shown in figure 25–5 (based on Emory, Marae Traditions).

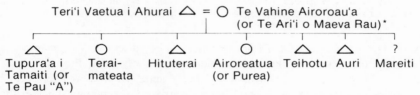

*According to Gunson's undocumented assertion (1964:61–62), Teri'i Vaetua was the *wife* and Airoroau'a the *husband*, but this is contrary to both Adams and Emory.

FIGURE 25–5. Some kin relations of 'Itia's father.

Ahurai was the principal marae of the Fa'a'a district, and Teihotu's eldest sibling, who held the Title Te Pau i Ahurai, was *ari'i rahi* of that tribal district. This important chief was named Tupura'a i Tamaiti. In addition, Teihotu's sister, the famous Purea, was the wife of the chief of Papara, and Teihotu's younger brother, Auri, married into the principal families of Puna'auia and Vaiari. 'Itia, through her mother, Vavea,[21] had other connections no less distinguished (fig. 25–6).

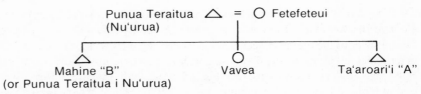

FIGURE 25–6. Some kin relations of 'Itia's mother.

This family was associated with Mo'orea's preeminent marae, Nu'urua, and, as I shall show, 'Itia's uncle Mahine was Mo'orea's most powerful chief during the 1760s and 1770s. Through her maternal grandmother, Fetefeteui, 'Itia traced connections with high-ranking Titleholders of Pa'ea and elsewhere. Vancouver provided a description of her:

> The queen-mother, although destitute of any pretensions to beauty, and having in her person a very masculine appearance, has yet, in her general deportment, something excessively pleasing and engaging; free from any austerity or pride, she is endued with a comparative elegance of manners, which plainly bespeaks her descent, and the high situation in which she is placed. Although her figure exhibited no external charms of feminine softness, yet great complacency and gentleness were always conspicuous; indicating, in the most unequivocal manner, a mind possessing, and alone actuated by those amiable qualities which most adorn the human race. All her actions seemed directed to those around her with an unalterable evenness of temper, and to be guided by a pure disinterested benevolence. Self, which on most occasions is the governing principle in the conduct of these islanders, with her was totally disregarded; and indeed, such was her very amiable disposition, that it counterbalanced any disadvantages she might labour under in a deficiency of personal attractions. (Vancouver 1801:320–321)[22]

The second consort of Pomare I was, as noted above, a younger sister of 'Itia. In referring to this woman the sources apply three different names to her: Pateamai (Emory, Adams), Vaiareti/Vaieriti (Bligh's "Whyerredee," Vancouver's "Fier re te"), and Teano (Morrison); but putting together the circumstantial evidence provided by these sources, I am fairly certain that they all refer to the same person. Vaiareti (for so I shall call her) was first married to the sovereign chief of Taiarapu, Tetua Ounumaona, the younger brother and successor of the Vehiatua who died in 1775, during the Spaniards' stay at Tautira. Tetua Ounumaona, who also bore the Title Vehiatua, died in 1790, without issue. Vaiareti, shortly after having been widowed, must have joined her elder sister, 'Itia, in Pomare I's household. This timing accords with Bligh's statement, in 1792, that he was "surprised . . . to find Tynah [Pomare I] to have another Wife while Iddeah was living" (1792:130). In other words, when Bligh left Tahiti at the end of his previous visit, in 1789, the new "wife" was not yet in evidence. As we shall see, these connections provided additional rationale for the subsequent political union of Pare-Arue and Taiarapu.

Apparently, the new arrangement was a congenial one all round. Bligh described Vaiareti as being "a Woman of Iddeah's Stature, but [having] a much handsomer Countenance," and he added that "the Women were on the best of terms with each other" (1792:130). Indeed, so close was their relationship that 'Itia expected Vaiareti to look after her ('Itia's) own offspring:

> Tynah and his Wives as usual dined with me to day. He took an opportunity to sollicit the attendance of the Surgeon on his youngest Child Oro(a)oh, who he said was very ill. We found it under the care of an Old Man, for what is strange, Women are not permitted to be attendants on any of the Royal Family, so that Male or Female, the Children are unnaturally nursed by Men. The Complaints of the Child was said to be in his bowels, — the belly was much distended; but the Scorfula (?) seemed the most alarming symptom, for in one groin it had broke out, & in the other were swellings which convinced us of the deploreable state this poor infant was in. I told Iddeeah to take better care of her Child, and altho I disputed the propriety, she insisted that Whyerreddee's attention should be engaged towards it & not particularly hers. (Bligh 1792:155b)

Vancouver, writing a few months earlier, provided a sharper contrast between the sisters, along with a description of their mutually shared position of privilege:

> The portrait of *Fier re te* on canvas would most probably be generally thought intitled to a preference; yet she appeared by no means to possess either mental endowments, or other excellent qualities, in the same degree with the queen-mother; if she had them, they were latent, and required some particular exertion to bring them into action. Her softness and effeminacy afforded her some advantage over her sister; yet there was a shyness, want of confidence and manner in her general demeanor, that evinced her motives to be less disinterested. We were however led to believe, that she was not destitute of the amiable qualities, though to us they did not appear so conspicuous as in the character of the queen-mother. Of the two ladies, *Fier re te* was now the favorite of *Pomurrey*, at least we had every reason to think so by the general tenor of his conduct.[23] Notwithstanding this preference, he was observed in several instances to abide implicitly by the advice and opinion of the queen-mother, and to treat her with great affection and regard; who in return never appeared jealous or dissatisfied at the marked attention, or evident partiality, with which her sister *Fier re te* was treated by *Pomurrey*. (1801:321–322)

The third woman to have had more than a casual connubial relationship with Pomare I was Pepiri ("Pepeere"), described by Turnbull in 1802 as one who "attended him [Pomare I] in the double capacity of mistress and servant" (1813:140). Pepiri was a daughter of Piha, a man of Vaiuriri, whose rank, or at least tribal authority, entitled him to a polite formal relationship with Pomare. In other words, Pepiri herself was of some social consequence; but there is no evidence that her connection with Pomare I was ever institutionalized by formal marriage rites. Nor does Pomare's connection with her appear to have had any political intent; Pepiri's father was a minor notable, at most, and he ended up among the enemies of Pomare I's successor and was slain and sacrificed by the latter's supporters in 1807 (Newbury 1961:99).

Vaiareti's incumbency seems to have been short lived; she was Pomare I's favorite during the early 1790s, but had dropped out of the picture by the time the missionaries arrived, in 1798. She was succeeded, it appears, by Pepiri. Of the three, 'Itia was most consequential by far. She bore all of Pomare I's acknowledged children, and she remained his ally and solicitous aide to the end of his days. Perhaps even before she bore him his last child she began to maintain her own separate establishment, which she shared with a succession of paramours, but this seems not to have affected her nonsexual relations with Pomare I.

The second son of Teu and Tetupaia was Ari'ipaea ("Oreepyah"), or Te Ari'i Fa'atou, who was born circa 1758 and who played a very active part in the events to be described.[24] As noted earlier, Ari'ipaea's wife was the famous Vahine Metua ("Inomedua," "Inna Madua"), or Teri'itua i Hitia'a. (She is not to be confused, however, with the Teri'itua i Hitia'a, or Reti, who was chief of Hitia'a.) I am at a loss to describe this woman's antecedents. Adams listed her as a daughter of Aromaiterai (of Papara and Mataoa) and of Tetua Unurau (sister of Papara's chief, Amo), and hence a sister of Te Vahine Moeatua, the widow of Taiarapu's Vehiatua I (1901:32). This may be so, although as Gunson pointed out, it was unusual for uterine siblings to be so far apart in age — that is, Te Vahine Moeatua was born circa 1736 and Vahine Metua circa 1762 (1964:63). In any case, the younger woman's antecedents were superior enough to warrant her marriage to the high-ranking Ari'ipaea, and the position assured her by pedigree was reinforced by virtue of a strong personality.

The next offspring of Teu and Tetupaia was a son, Te Tupuai e te Rai, also known as Paiti (which I shall call him), Maioro, and Vaetua ("Whydooah," "Whytooa," "Wyetua," "Widouah"). Paiti, who was described by Mortimer in 1789 as "a very impudent, dissolute young man," much addicted to kava (1791:45), also acquired a reputation as a bold warrior. He wielded great influence in Ha'apaiano'o, where he resided most of the time — why, I do not know, but possibly because of marital connections there (Bligh 1789:I, 411; Vancouver 1801:300ff). He was also given to homosexual practices, as witnessed by a missionary. According to Wilson, Paiti was an Arioi "of the first rank" (1799:179).

After Paiti was a daughter, born about 1768, named Auo ("Wowwo"), also called "Terrerree" (by Cook), "Erreretua (by G. Forster), and "Whyerreddee" (by Bligh). The Puna'auia genealogy places Auo *before* Paiti in birth order, but Bligh (1792:141), G. Forster (1777:II, 96), and Henry (1928:249) placed her after him, with which I am inclined to agree; in any case, the question is not structurally crucial, as is the one regarding

Ari'ipaea Vahine noted above. Auo's chief significance derived from her marriage to Metuaro Mahau (or Ta'aroari'i), a high-ranking kin-Titleholder and influential tribal chief of Mo'orea, of whom I shall say more later on.

The last-born child of Teu and Tetupaia was a son, Te Pau Ari'i i Tarahoi ("Teppahoo," "Tuppahoo," "Tepaow"), of whom Vancouver wrote the following in 1792, when this Te Pau (there were several of that name or Title) was about twenty-two years of age:

> There is yet a fourth brother whose insignificance has hitherto precluded his name, which is *Tapahoo*, from appearing in any of our transactions with these worthy people. Although in the possession of a very considerable property, *Tapahoo* seems little regarded by his family, and less esteemed by his people. This want of respect is greatly, and possibly wholly, to be attributed to a natural imbecillity of mind; as, to all appearance, he is a young man of an exceedingly weak and trifling character. (1801:325)

Evidently, however, his shortcomings did not stand in the way of his political advance, for he succeeded to the chieftainship of Fa'a'a upon the death of that tribe's chief, also named Te Pau. Bligh's explanation for this succession was that the elder Te Pau (i.e., Te Pau "B" in fig. 25–1) had married a sister of the younger Te Pau's (Te Pau "C") mother, Tetupaia (Bligh 1792:135). It is in fact possible that Te Pau "B" had no son of his own, and moreover that Te Pau "C" was his namesake, and perhaps even adopted son.

When the *Dolphin* anchored in Matavai Bay, Pomare I was between fifteen and nineteen years old, and his youngest sibling, Te Pau "C," was still unborn. Although Pomare I was accorded the deference due a successor to the de jure chieftainship of Pare-Arue, and the ceremonial respect to the incumbent (through his mother) of a *maro ura* kin-Title from Opoa, he was very decidedly under the de facto tribal authority of his great-uncle Tutaha. In fact he was so overshadowed by the latter that Wallis evidently did not even know about the young man's existence. Even Cook, writing in 1769, knew no more about him than that there was somewhere nearby a sovereign *ari'i rahi* "which was not Tootaha from what we could learn, but some other person we had not seen, or like to do, for they say that he is no friend of ours and therefore will not come near us" (Beaglehole 1955:104). According to Banks, "The *Earee ra hie* [*ari'i rahi*, i.e., Pomare I] is always the head of the Best family in the countrey; to him great respect is paid by all ranks but in Power he seemd to us inferior to several of the Principal *Earees*, nor indeed did he once appear in the transacting of any part of our business" (Beaglehole 1962:I, 384).

Fa'a'a (Te Fana)

The triangle-shaped area between Pare and Puna'auia known as Tetaha, or Fa'a'a, was occupied by a unified tribe known as Te Fana i

Ahurai — Ahurai having been the marae of the tribe's highest-ranking kin-Titleholders and tribal chiefs. Handy included this population among the Oropa'a, along with Puna'auia and Pa'ea (1930:71) [25] and such an alliance undoubtedly existed from time to time; but during parts of the Early European Era the chiefs of Te Fana acted independently, and entered into intertribal coalitions to suit their own purposes. Adams characterized this tribe's position in the following terms:

The district of Faaa, though it contained only about seven miles of seacoast, was for many reasons very important. It stood, as an independent little nation, between the great Teva alliance in the south, the Porionuu and te Aharoa in the east, and the large island of Eimeo or Moorea, some twelve miles to the west. As Tefana leaned toward Papara or against it, the chiefs of Papara were apt to be less anxious about their enemies or more anxious to win friends. (1901:41)

I listed, earlier in this chapter, the members of the leading family of Fa'a'a who were alive during the first years of the era now under study. Their various kin connections and ties of sentiment indicate how central was the part played by this small tribe in Tahitian-Mo'orean history. The senior member of the family, and its tribal chief, was Te Pau i Ahurai (also called Tupura'a i Tamaiti), who appears in the sources as "Toobouratomite," "Tipouro," "Teppahoo," and "Lycurgus." [26] During Cook's first visit, this chief, who was most hospitable and helpful to the visitors, appeared to be as much at home in Pare-Arue as in his own home district, and he was evidently on the best of terms with the Pare-Arue chief Tutaha. His younger brother, Teihotu, does not figure in the recorded events of that era; but, as we have already seen, the latter's wife, Vavea, was a member of Mo'orea's leading family, and his daughters married the chiefs of Pare-Arue and Taiarapu, respectively. Still another brother of Te Pau's, Auri, acquired affinal connections with leading families of Puna'auia and Vaiari; and a sister, Purea, was principal consort of the chief of Papara. Te Pau himself (Te Pau "A" in fig. 25–1) was killed in 1773, along with his ally Tutaha, in their joint expedition against the Seaward Teva. Thus, it is his successors who are of more direct relevance to subsequent events, but the identity of these successors is puzzling.

During Cook's second and third voyages, of all the individuals met by the captain and his aides, the one whose presence was most commanding, and whose influence and authority was most extensive in Tahiti's northwest quadrant, was one whose name was first recorded as "Towha" ("T'tewha," "Tettewah," "Tetewha," "Tewha," etc.). It was he who was "Admiral" of the impressive assembly of war canoes reviewed by Cook in 1774, who orated so eloquently and commandingly when occasion demanded, and who was in fact so superior to Pomare I — in probity, in courage, in qualities of leadership, and so forth — that even the Pomare-serving English came in time to acknowledge the contrast. (Beaglehole 1961:389; Beaglehole 1967:219n)

"Towha" seems to have been equally at home in both Fa'a'a and Pa'ea. Adams identified him as having been leader of the "family" of Ahurai (1901:94), but his name does not appear on any Ahurai genealogy that I know of, and he was almost certainly not the titular successor to the Te Pau i Ahurai mentioned above, who died in 1773. Adams also stated that Towha's other name was "Tahua," but I can find no confirmation of this in any journal or genealogy. My own conclusion is that "Towha" is the Te To'ofa, whom Henry listed as having been an "underchief" of Pa'ea, the same Te To'ofa perhaps whose Title, Taura Atua i Patea, was associated with one of the three marae which made up that district's Maraeta'ata temple complex. This is confirmed by such statements as J. Forster's, naming him one of the two "joint-chiefs" of Atehuru (1778:354). Cook described "Tewha" as having been "Chief of the district of Tettaha" (Cook 1784:30),[27] and he undoubtedly wielded authority over that tribe, but his Ahurai kin-Title (if indeed he held one) ranked inferior to that of the titular successor of the Te Pau i Ahurai named Tupura'a i Tamaiti (Tepau "A") who ruled in Fa'a'a until 1773.

According to J. Forster the successor to the Te Pau i Ahurai kin-Title was "Toomataroa" (Tu Mataroa?). This distinction between the titular offices of "Towha" and "Toomataroa" is sharpened by the passage from J. Forster that specifies the former as having been a joint chief of Atehuru and the latter, chief of Fa'a'a (1778:354). In other words, the situation in Fa'a'a paralleled for a time the one in Pare-Arue, where the highest-ranking local kin-congregation Title was held by Teu (and subsequently by Pomare I), while tribal authority actually rested in the hands of a lower-ranking relative, Tutaha. "Toomataroa," who also held the Title Te Pau, was evidently so eclipsed by "Towha" that little is recorded about him save that he was married to "Terrano" (or "Tettoohow-deeah"), a sister of Teu's wife, Tetupaia; he was friendly toward Pomare I, and he died sometime between Bligh's visits of 1789 and 1792.[28] Having died childless, he was, as noted earlier, succeeded by his wife's sister's son (Pomare I's youngest brother), who then himself assumed the Title Te Pau (i.e., Te Pau "C").

Puna'auia (Mano Tahi)

Due to the proximity of Ha'apape, Pare-Arue, and Fa'a'a to the Europeans' ship anchorage in Matavai Bay we are relatively well informed about personalities and events of that region. And because of Paparan pride and its nineteenth- and twentieth-century historian champions, we have been provided with some fairly detailed — though not necessarily wholly accurate — accounts of leading personalities and important events in that region. But written chronicles about the region between these two, generally known as Atehuru, are scant and confusing — due in part to the region's distance from Matavai and in part to its leaders' hostility to the European-backed Pare-Arue regime. Nevertheless, a few essentials of its political land-scape may be reconstructed, including the circumstance that it consisted of two autonomous but fairly consistently allied tribes, Mano Tahi (or Puna'auia) in the north, and Mano Rua (or Pa'ea) in the south.

During the Early European Era politically significant ceremonial activities in Puna'auia took place mainly at a large coastal marae called Taputapuatea. The marae ruins in Puna'auia now called by that name are located on Puna'auia Point; assuming the two to be the same — a likely but not absolutely certain identification — the marae was founded, according to tradition, by Titihauri, a high-ranking kin-Titleholder of Opoa, to com-memorate his marriage to the daughter of a Puna'auian chief (Emory, Marae Traditions). During the era now under study it was a major center of 'Oro worship, although of course not the only one; and, according to Rodriguez, it was the marae "whereat they swear [Pomare I] in as *arii*" (Corney 1919:170). Like other Taputapuatea marae — that is, those serving as repositories of an 'Oro image — it was the locale for human sacrifices to that god. (Rodriguez and his editor, Corney, appear to have assumed that *this* Taputapuatea was the "senior" one of its kind on the island [Corney 1919:155n], but it had not always been so, and would not so remain.) On the other hand, the district's most venerable marae was marae Tahiti (or Te Ara e Tahiti, or Puna'auia), a small, unpretentious structure located in the Punaru'u Valley about a mile inland. This marae was second only to Vaiari's Farepua in social preeminence, having been established (according to one tradition) by the fabled Puna'auia chief Te Manutunu and his Vaiari wife, Hotutu (see chap. 16). In 1797 marae Tahiti was also a repository of an 'Oro image and hence was a "Taputapuatea" — which seems not to have been the case during the 1760s and 1770s (Wilson 1799:208). The principal kin-Title associated with this marae was Tetuanui e Marua i Te Rai, one of Tahiti's highest-ranking ones, whose incumbent during the first part of this era was Pohuetea ("Potatow," "Pottatea," "Poatateu").[29] Pohuetea's main Title is said to have bestowed upon its bearer the right to don a *maro ura*; as far as I can discover (and for reasons I cannot fathom) Pohuetea did not assert this privilege for himself, but he did exercise exten-sive authority and influence, as chief of a populous and warlike tribe.

The first mention of Pohuetea in any of the sources occurs in Gayango's account of his circumnavigation of the island, in 1772 (Corney 1913:322–323). Cook first referred to him in the *Journal* of 1773, but he had evidently known Pohuetea during his earlier visit to Tahiti, for he refers to him as "my old friend Potattou the chief of that district [Atehuru]" (Beaglehole 1961:210–211). Pohuetea was described by Pickersgill as having

. . . carried great command over his teritories and had allways a number of men exerciseing and seemingly kept stricktly to military Duty; he is one of the stoutest men I ever saw, his thigh would measure more round in the Middle then any part of my Body he is very proportionablely made, and his natural Powers are so great that his vast bulk is no impediment to his agility. (Beaglehole 1961:769)

To this may be added G. Forster's comment:

. . . his features were so mild, comely, and at the same time majestic that Mr. Hodges immediately applied himself to copy from them, as from the noblest models of nature. . . . His ample garments, and his elegant white turban, set off his figure to the greatest advantage, and his noble deportment endeared him to us, as we naturally compared it with the diffidence of O-too. (1777:I, 360–361)

In 1773 Pohuetea was evidently one of Tahiti's most powerful tribal chiefs. He was also one of her most durable ones, politically, for Bligh was able to report, fifteen years later, that Pohuetea was one of the island's three greatest chiefs, along with Pomare I and Vehiatua III (1789:II, 77). Indeed, he was still alive and active in January 1792, when he visited Vancouver — having meanwhile assumed the new name of "Hidiea" (Hitiea?) (Vancouver 1801:275–276), but he died shortly thereafter, or so Bligh reported in June of 1792 (1792:165b).

Pohuetea was unquestionably a man with noble consanguineal antecedents, but what those were I am unable to discover. Individuals bearing the name (or Title?) Tetuanui e Marua i Te Rai appear in the Puna'auia genealogy, the more recent having been the great-grandfather (father's father's father) of Ta'aroa Manahune and Tutaha (Emory, Marae Traditions), but what Pohuetea's kin relationship was to that individual, if any, is not known to us.

We are provided with descriptions of Pohuetea's first wife, and of his subsequent marital arrangements, but no information about the genealogical connections of these women. The first wife was Purutihara ("Polatehara," "Polotheara") about whom G. Forster wrote:

Polatehara . . . was so like [Pohuetea] in stature and bulk, that we unanimously looked upon her as the most extraordinary woman we had ever seen. Her appearance and her conduct were masculine in the highest degree, and strongly conveyed the idea of superiority and command. When the Endeavour bark lay here, she had distinguished herself by the name of captain Cook's sister (tuaheine no *Toote*;) and one day, being denied admittance into the fort on Point Venus, had knocked down the sentry who opposed her, and complained to her adopted brother of the indignity which had been offered to her. (1777:I, 361)

In due course Pohuetea and Purutihara separated and took new mates — the amicability of which arrangement was reported on earlier (chap. 19, section on semi-marriage).[30] According to Bligh, when Pohuetea died, in 1792, he left no child to succeed him, ". . . in consequence [of which] the present Minor Chief, some relation, is not firmly fixed in his Government" (1792:165b).

Pa'ea (Mano Rua)

Mano Rua, or Pa'ea,[31] the district south of Puna'auia, was made up of
three divisions, each with its own marae complex — namely 'A'ou'a (marae
Maraeta'ata), Natu'oha (marae 'Utu'aimahurau), and Mara'a (marae Tuitui).
These divisions were eventually under the same regime whose high chief
and underchief bore the Titles Te Vahitua i Patea and Te To'ofa, respectively.
(Henry 1928:78–79)

Only two of Pa'ea's marae complexes figure importantly in events of
this era, but these two were very important indeed. One of these was
Maraeta'ata, situated about 460 yards inland and consisting of four separate
marae units, three enclosed and one detached rectangular platform.[32] According to Adams (1901:75), Maraeta'ata had three "heads": "Pouira, the
Tevahitua i Patea; Tetooha, the Taura Atua i Patea; and Punua'aitua." I
interpret this to mean that each of the three enclosed units in this complex
had its own proprietary kin-Title, as given. As noted above, Henry names
only two chiefly Titles for this division of Pa'ea (and by direct implication,
for the division marae); but her designations are otherwise the same as those
of Adams.

Elsewhere Adams represented his informant, Ari'i Ta'ima'i, as asserting
that Maraeta'ata "belonged to" Tutaha, the powerful Pare-Arue chief
(1901:109); but I consider this wholly unlikely. Like most Maohis of his
social status Tutaha could probably trace — or contrive — connections with
any important marae, anywhere; and for someone of his great political authority such claims would probably have been acknowledged, willingly or under
coercion, by all but his most active enemies. In fact, Tutaha could have
made quite credible claims to Pa'ea connections, but to identify Maraeta'ata
as "his own" marae, as Adams so stated, is an unwarranted assertion as
far as I can tell — indeed, it stands in direct contradiction to another of
Adams' statements, just quoted, naming "Tevahitua," "Tetooha," and
"Punua'aitua" as "heads" of the marae. The importance of this point should
become clear as I begin to chronicle the events of this era.

Marae 'Utu'aimahurau was situated directly on the lagoon shore and
about five kilometers south of Maraeta'ata. After 150 years of neglect and
dismemberment it is now no longer possible to identify its original form,
but various descriptions of it during its heyday, including a sketch by Webber,
indicate that it was a complex structure similar to Maraeta'ata,[33] and even
more important in terms of politically significant ceremonials.

According to Henry, Tevahitua and Te To'ofa, two of the proprietary
kin-Titles connected with Maraeta'ata, were the same in the case of
'Utu'aimahurau, and partial confirmation for this is found in a Pa'ea
genealogy reproduced by Emory, which is labeled "Genealogy of Te-To'ofa,
chief of Teoropaa. Outuai was his marae." (Marae Traditions.) I am led to

conclude that these two marae complexes were closely connected, ceremonially, by reason of common proprietorship. Under such circumstances, as loci for certain kin-specific ceremonies, they may well have been interchangeable, which may account in part for the confusion between them in some sources.[34] On the other hand, it appears that 'Utu'aimahurau was the preferred location for performance of those rites involving the presence of 'Oro. According to Thomson one of the principal images of this god was installed at 'Utu'aimahurau about the middle of the eighteenth century; the incident is described in a tradition recorded in Henry and said to have been taken from the priests Tamera and Pati'i. After establishing a foothold of 'Oro at Tautira, in the form of a marae and an image for that god,

> . . . the priests of 'Oro went to the body of Tahiti, the fish, with a sacred stone from the marae they had just made. They landed at 'Utu-'ai-mahu-rau (Cape-eating-many-mists), at Pa'ea, then called Atahata or Ata-huru (Fleeing-clouds).
>
> There they were allowed to take possession and were also aided in building their marae, which was called 'Utu-'ai-mahu-rau. 'Oro-hu'a-manu ('Oro-of-the-bird-feathered-body) became master there; the image was woven the size of that at Opoa and covered with red, yellow, and black feathers from the image at Tautira. (1928:130)[35]

All three of the proprietors' names (or Titles?) listed by Adams (including the two chiefly Titles given by Henry) are to be found on a genealogy reproduced by Emory — that is, the one labeled "Genealogy of Te-To'ofa, chief of Teoropaa. Outuai was his marae." [36]

I cannot discover who specifically bore the name or Title Tevahitua,[37] but, however senior that individual may have been in terms of kin-Title rank, he was clearly overshadowed in political authority and influence by the incumbent Te To'ofa. (It is, of course, possible that one individual held both Titles at some time or other, but based on a statement in Adams, which will be reproduced later on, I consider this to have been unlikely at this period.)

Te To'ofa, holder of the Title Taura Atua i Patea, is undoubtedly "Tewha," or Cook's "Admiral," et cetera, whom I have described above as having exercised chiefly authority, though holding a subordinate kin-Title, in Fa'a'a. As noted earlier, I have been unable to specify Te To'ofa's kin connections in Fa'a'a, and from the Paea genealogy he does not appear to have reached his position of tribal authority by primogenitary succession, but there can be no doubt whatsoever about the reality of that authority. Also, he seems to have been the close and consistent ally of Puna'auia's Pohuetea, and a relative of Papara's Teri'irere.[38]

In February 1789 Bligh reported that he received a visit from the widow of "Old Admiral Tet-towah" and recorded that the latter had died "many Months before I arrived" (1789:II, 35). Thus, Te To'ofa evidently died about 1787 or 1788, leaving his son as his successor, under the regency apparently of his widow, whom Bligh described as having been "considered a high personage." Bligh gave the latter's name as "Wanowoorah" (Fanau Ura?); I cannot identify this woman genealogically. Bligh had the opportunity of seeing this woman in company with Pomare I on two occasions. In 1789 he described their relationship as "affectionate"; in 1792 he wrote that "I found a shyness about our Friend Tynah [Pomare I] and his Wives to this Woman and her party" (Bligh 1792:166). Slender as this evidence is, it does suggest that Te To'ofa's widow was a woman with very high-ranking kin connections, including probably some with Pomare I. In 1789 she was described as having been "old and infirm," (Bligh 1789:II, 35) but this evidently had not discouraged her "remarriage," to a man of unrecorded origins, named "Tewryighne" (Tauriaine?) (Bligh 1792:166). In addition, Bligh recorded during his next visit, in 1792, that she was assisted in her regency by "a very clever young fellow called Terraighterree — his official capacity is that of a Priest and had great weight among the People" (1792:165b).

As for Te To'ofa's son and successor, in 1790 Morrison estimated his age to have been about twenty-two. This tall young man, who also bore the Title Te To'ofa, evidently proved to be a vigorous and politically consistent successor to his famous father, but his reign was brief, for he died ("of an ague") even before Morrison's departure, in 1791, and was succeeded by the son of his sister — subject to the latter's "regency or Guardianship" — inasmuch as the successor was only four years old at the time. (1935:106, 107)

Landward Teva

The social unit called Landward Teva (Teva i Uta) consisted of four major subdivisions, which were (from east to west) Vaiari (or Papeari), Vaiuriri (or Papeuriri), Atimaono, and Papara. For several decades prior to this era the chiefs of Papara had dominated the whole unit in terms of coercive authority and persuasive influence — although their control over the three eastern divisions was largely indirect, and at times probably quite ineffectual. At one time in the traditional, far-distant past, ceremonial preeminence over all Landward Teva (based on kin-Title rank, and possibly also decisive coercive authority) rested with the high-ranking proprietors of marae Farepua, in Vaiari. Subsequently, however, that authority (such as it was) was seized by Paparan leaders; and by the opening of the Early European Era some of the ceremonial eminence attendant upon high rank had shifted to Paparans as well. Indeed, during the early years of this era, efforts were undertaken to assert the Paparan chiefs' rank supremacy over all other Tahitian kin-Titleholders.

When H.M.S. *Dolphin* anchored in Matavai Bay the tribal chief of

Papara was Amo, or Tevahitua i Patea, a man of middle age. Few direct observations have been recorded about the personality of this man, even though he was at the center of the swirling political events of the 1760s and 1770s. The main reason for his historic obscurity probably lies in the distance of Papara from Matavai, but it may well be that Amo was in fact overshadowed, in terms of personal qualities, by such individuals as Tutaha, Te To'ofa, Pohuetea, "Old" Vehiatua, and Amo's own wife, Purea. It is also likely that Amo was deliberately discouraged from visiting the Europeans at Matavai, as was his son two decades later. Bligh wrote of the son: "I have sent a message to Tomārre, the Chief, that I shall be glad to see him. — he has hitherto been prevented from coming by a dread of my not treating him well, and I have not been able to do away his fear. I attribute it to some underhand Work of our Friends at this place, who would consider him as a Rival, and do not like him to partake of the benefits they derive from us." (1792:170b)

The fullest (though not necessarily the most accurate) genealogy I have found listing Amo's antecedents and collaterals is Emory's reconstruction (Marae Traditions) based on notes left by Tati Salmon; this takes us back only to Tavi Hau Roa of Tautira, whose estimated birth date is circa 1660. Tavi, it may be recalled, was the too-generous husband of beautiful Taurua, of Farepua marae, Vaiari. According to the traditional story, Tavi "lent" Taurua to a Paparan chief named Tuiterai ("A"), and then wholly relinquished her to the latter even after defeating him in a battle fought over her.[39] The only issue of the mating of Tuiterai and Taurua so recorded was a male, Teri'itahi, who eventually married Tau Vahine (or Tetua Umeretini) of marae Nu'utere, Vairao; the latter bore him three offspring, Te'eva Pirioi, Aromaiterai, and Amo, whose lines thereafter separated but continued in some measure to influence each other's lives.

Te'eva Pirioi, the daughter and eldest child, is recorded as having married Ari'imao, a high-ranking kin-Titleholder of Opoa. This couple resided in Ra'iatea but their son and only child, Maua, is credited with the fateful act of having transferred to Papara, circa 1760, an image of 'Oro and the *maro ura* called Teraiputata, which embodied (among other things) symbolic connections between *ari'i* of Ra'iatea and Huahine.[40] Other descendants of Te'eva Pirioi played roles, and possibly leading ones, in the stormy political events of the Leeward Islands, but do not directly concern us here.

Teri'itahi's second child and elder son was Aromaiterai ("A"), who, it will be recalled, was for reasons unstated denied the succession and exiled to Mataea. This occurred circa 1730, according to Adams (1901:37). He and his wife (a local woman named Terahi i Te Tua) had three offspring: Tetuanui (f), Vanu'u (m), and Mutuarea (m).[41] Tetuanui married a Pa'ea man; their descendants were prominent in the affairs of Mo'orea and Tahiti, but not enough so to require further description here.[42] The names Vanu'u and Mutuarea drop out of sight, but another Aromaiterai (Aromaiterai "B" in fig. 25–1), which seems to be an alternate name for one of them (Adams 1901:38), appears in another genealogy as the husband of a sister of Amo, to whose branch of the family we now turn.

After his sister's removal to Ra'iatea and his elder brother's exile to Mataoa, Tuiterai "B" (or Teri'i Tu A'a i te Ra'i, or Te Ura i te Ra'i) remained in undisturbed possession of the chieftainship of Papara, and he and his wife (Teroro e Ora of Fareroi marae, Ha'apape) are recorded as having had eleven offspring, only three of whom concern us here. The firstborn, a daughter, was Faretopa (also Teharetuanui), whose marriage to Tuva'a might have forged a useful link with Pa'ea had any offspring remained long enough alive. Tuiterai's second-born, also a daughter, was Tetua Unurau, whose marriage to her father's brother's son, Aromaiterai "B" served to join these collateral lines, genealogically — but not politically, as we shall see. The Papara genealogy reproduced by Emory credits Tetua Unurau and Aromaiterai "B" with seven offspring, the ones of immediate concern to us being Te Vahine Moeatua (or Purai, or Purahi), the wife of Seaward Teva's "Old" Vehiatua, and Vahine Metua ("Inomedua"), also Teri'itua i Hitia'a, who was the wife of Pomare I's brother, Ari'ipaea.[43]

Tuiterai's third child, and first son, was Amo, who must have been born circa 1725. As noted above, few direct observations have been recorded about this chief's personality, and inferentially the sources provide almost diametrically opposite views of him; in some accounts he is represented as having been a shrewd and active aggrandizer, in others as the timid and somewhat reluctant cat's-paw of his wife, Purea.

Purea, or Airoreatua i Ahurai i Farepua, was sister of the chief of Fa'a'a, named Te Pau i Ahurai ("A"), and could claim other kin connections reaching into some of Tahiti's and Moorea's highest-ranking and politically most powerful families. Along with these social-relational resources she possessed a forceful, imperious presence joined with great ambition. In introducing her to his readers Adams wrote, "If a family must be ruined by a woman, perhaps it may as well be ruined thoroughly and brilliantly by a woman who makes it famous" (1901:40).

Purea's entry into recorded history occurred in 1767, when she visited H.M.S. *Dolphin*: "At PM, the Gunner came off with a tall well looking Woman about forty five years old, she had a very Majestic Mein, & he seeing her paid Great respect by the Inhabitants, she being just come there, he made her some presents" (Wallis, Journal, 13 July, LMS Archives). Thereafter, Wallis referred to her as "Queen"; her manner was undoubtedly "queenly" wherever she happened to be, but what respect she commanded in Matavai derived mainly from her husband's maternal connections there (that is, Amo's mother, Teroro e Ora, was associated with Ha'apape's marae

Fareroi). Writing two years later, Banks described Purea as being
". . . about 40, tall and very lusty, her skin white and her eyes full of
meaning, she might have been hansome when young but now few or no
traces of it were left" (Beaglehole 1962:I, 266). And G. Forster, writing
in 1774, said of her: "She appeared to be between forty and fifty; her person
was tall, large, and fat, and her features, which seemed once to have been
more agreeable, were now rather masculine. However something of her
former greatness remained; she had 'an eye to threaten or command', and
a free and noble deportment." (1777:II, 100–101)

Like many such couples of high rank and extensive political authority,
Amo and Purea came in time to have separate households and sexual partners,
but there were offspring of their union — at least one and possibly as many
as nine.[44] In any case, all sources that I know of identify their firstborn,
a son, as having been Teri'irere, said to have been born about 1762. As
successor to his father's kin-Titles, including two feather-girdled ones, and
through his mother's family connections in Fa'a'a, Teri'irere's rank was
among the highest in Tahiti-Mo'orea. And his parents' ambition to enhance
his prestige even further was one of the principal motives behind events
on Tahiti in the early years of this era. But before chronicling these events
something more needs to be said about this notable, but as it turns out,
hapless young man.

The first European to meet up with Teri'irere was Cook, in 1769:

This morning a Chief whose name is Oamo, and one we had not seen before, came
to the Fort, there came with him a Boy about 7 years of Age and a young Woman
about 18 or 20; at the time of their Coming Obarea and several others were in
the Fort, they went out to meet them, having first uncover'd their heads and bodies
as low as their waists and the same thing was done by all those that were on the
out side of the Fort; as we looked upon this as a ceremonial Respect and had not
seen it paid to any one before we thought that this Oamo must be some extraordinary
person, and wonder'd to see so little notice taken of him after the Ceremony was
over. The young Woman that came along with him Could not be prevaild upon
to come into the Fort and the Boy was carried upon a Mans Back, altho he was
as able to walk as the Man who carried him. This lead us to inquire who they
were and we was inform'd that the Boy was Heir apparent to the Sovereignty of
the Island and the young woman was his sister and as such the respect was paid
them, which was due to no one else except the *Arreedehi* which was not Tootaha
from what we could learn, but some other person who we had not seen, or like
to do, for they say that he is no friend of ours and therefore will not come near
us. The young Boy above mention'd is Son to Oamo by Obarea, but Oamo and
Obarea did not at this time live together as man and wife. he not being able to
endure with her troublesome disposission. (Beaglehole 1955:103–104)

The "Boy" in this passage was successor not to the "Sovereignty of the
Island" but to his father's kin-Titles and to his de facto chieftainship over
Papara; and the "other person," still unseen by Cook, was Pomare I.

Several sources state that Teri'irere's wife was none other than Te Ari'i na Vaho Roa, the firstborn child of Teu and Tetupaia, and hence Pomare I's eldest sibling. If so, the age of the spouses was discrepant even by Maohi standards, for according to the most plausible estimates I can arrive at, the wife would have been some thirteen years older than the husband. In any case she bore him no children that we know of, and according to Bligh she had died before the latter's visit of 1789 (1789:II, 62).

Another question regarding identity concerns Teri'irere himself. According to Adams' version, Teri'irere died very young and was succeeded by a half-brother, Temari'i (or Ari'ifa'ataia), who was ten years younger than Teri'irere, and was the son of Amo by another wife (a niece of Purea's, and also from Fa'a'a).[45] But according to another version, which I accept and which seems also to have been tacitly accepted by most primary sources, including the London missionaries, and Bligh (1792:157b, 166b), Temari'i was an alternative name for Teri'irere, and not a brother of the latter's (although the latter may well have had a brother, or half-brother as well). Morrison met "Temmaree" in 1791, and described him as ". . . a Handsom well made man of about 27 or 28 years old and about 6 feet high" (1935:114); in other words, the age of Temari'i would have been the same as Cook's Teri'irere, and not of the latter's half-brother, who by Adams' birth date estimate would have been less than twenty years old at the time of his meeting with Morrison.

In any case, Temari'i Ari'ifa'ataia (formerly Teri'irere, and eventually Ari'ipaea "B") lived on for another seven years after his encounter with Morrison, during which time he played a leading role in the island's political developments.[46]

Finally, in my list of principal Paparans figuring prominently in the political history of the era, I must not overlook Tupaia, the remarkable man who accompanied Cook's first expedition homeward but who died in the Indies en route. Tupaia was first met by Wallis. At that time he was with "Queen" Purea on her visit to Matavai; he appeared to be her principal aide and advisor, but may also have been her current bedfellow as well. He was still attached to Purea during Cook's visit two years later, but left her service to accompany Cook (and more specifically, Banks) to England.

Tupaia appears to have been born circa 1725, in the northwestern region of Ra'iatea. Banks described him as "well born" (Beaglehole 1962:I, 312); but nowhere is the claim made that he was of the Hui Ari'i.[47] He was, however, trained in the priestly craft and was knowledgeable in many other fields, including particularly geography and navigation. After arriving on Tahiti — circa 1760, if he accompanied Maua and Manea, as one account implies — he joined Purea's establishment and served as her principal political advisor (and possible abettor); what his relations with Amo were, we are not informed.

Turning now to the other territorial divisions that, along with Papara, constituted Landward Teva, their populations were of course also caught up in the wars and other political maneuvers characteristic of Tahiti and Mo'orea. It is reasonable to suppose that some of their principal people were deeply and actively engaged in some of these events — but about this one can only speculate. For, either the roles of such personages were so secondary, or their distance from European observers so remote, that they figure hardly at all in the written accounts of the era. From the Europeans' vantage point of Matavai these Vaiarians, and others, were part of the Papa-ran hinterland, and to Europeans visiting at Tautira they were seen to be vaguely under the Vehiatuas' sway.

In fact, the political situation of these districts did probably correspond fairly closely to the Europeans' perspectives. That is to say, although their chiefs' traditional political loyalties were with Papara, the nearby presence of a strong and aggressive Vehiatua — or a display of overpretentiousness on the part of Papara's chiefs — probably encouraged a shift in alliance. One of the more notable aspects of this situation is of course the extent to which Vaiari itself seems to have become eclipsed. Not only had it become dispossessed of the political influence which it allegedly once exercised over all of Landward Teva, but even the ceremonial preeminence once accorded its highest-ranking Titles (of marae Farepua) seems to have shifted to kin-Titles elsewhere.

MO'OREA

If the political landscape of the island of Tahiti is in some places overclouded with uncertainty, that of Mo'orea is almost wholly fogbound. Except for a few forays, measured in hours or days, no noteworthy Europeans spent any time there during the first four decades after 1767. In fact, Cook himself did not learn until 1777 of the existence of its magnificent harbors: "It is a little extraordinary that I should have been thrice at Otaheite before and on(c)e sent a boat to this island and yet not know there was a harbour in it . . ." (Beaglehole 1967:226). Except for traditional data collected decades after the era under study, most information we have about the island's territorial divisions and leadership was obtained by the Europeans from residents of Tahiti or political exiles from Mo'orea, who could hardly have been counted on for unbiased objectivity.

Handy (after Marau) asserted that the island "anciently" consisted of eight subdivisions, but Henry listed twelve so-called districts, ranging in complexity from one small single-neighborhood unit (i.e., 'Oi'o) to one comprising most of the island's populous northern half and itself subdivided into seven divisions of at least multi-neighborhood size and complexity. In choosing between these two authorities one should take into account the possibility that Handy's version was influenced by the eight-tentacled octopus metaphor, which was used so commonly to refer to this island and others; whereas Henry's version lists for many of her "districts" the names of the conventional "tribal" designata, such as mountain, cape, marae, assembly ground, Arioi house, chiefly Title, and so forth.

The fish-anatomy names applied metaphorically to Mo'orea's various parts — The Fin in the South, The Upper Flesh of the Fish, et cetera — probably referred not to social divisions but to the island's outline and topography. Nor can I find any historical evidence of a persistent confederation of units corresponding to Handy's reported "The Four Above" (i.e., South) and "The Four Below" (i.e., North) (1930:79–80).

Traditions concerning the founding of Mo'orea's principal marae do not tell us much about tribal boundaries or political realities, nor do they indicate clearly where the island's highest-ranking kin-Titles were localized. According to these traditions, summarized in chapter 16, the four most famed marae were Nu'urua (at Varari), Te Fano (at Pape'are), Umarea (at Afareaitu), and Taputapuatea (at Papeto'ai).

During the eighteenth century the Titles (or were some of them personal names?) that figured most prominently in the accounts were Marama, Mahine, Punua Teraitua i Nu'urua, Teri'itapu nui, Tetuanuireia i te Ra'iatea, Pateamai, and Hamoa (or Ha'amo'a?). Henry listed numerous others (1928:89–94; but only the above, and certain personal names or subordinate Titles closely associated with them, play identifiable parts in the events we are considering.[48] It is important for my purposes to be able to match names, Titles, and places (including marae), but the extent to which I have failed to do so will be woefully apparent.

The Title Marama appears preeminently in traditions of Mo'orea's beginnings; according to the Handy-Marau version reproduced earlier it was a Marama (from the Leeward Islands) who first established Hui Ari'i rule at Mo'orea, with bases at Nu'urua and Te Fano marae. Later on, according to traditional accounts recorded in Adams, members of this dynastic line extended their authority or rank superiority, or both (the traditions are somewhat ambiguous), over most or all of Mo'orea (1901:161–171). However, during the five decades now under study, the holders of the Marama Title — Marama Ari'ihau and his daughter, Marama Ari'i Manihinihi — do no figure prominently in the recorded chronicles. Although according to Adams, the rank of their Title was supreme in Mo'orea, the tribe over which they ruled was less powerful, and less actively engaged in the wars of the era, than others on the island.

The Mahine who played so active a part in this half century's political events held the Title — he may also have held others — of Punua Teraitua (Te ra'i atua?) i Nu'urua (Adams 1901:95), but he was identified by Adams as chief of Opunohu (p. 107), and not of Varari "district," where Nu'urua was situated; and it was in the Opunohu area that Cook encountered him in 1777 and described him as "The Cheif" (Beaglehole 1967:226). Henry also listed a Mahine as having been high chief of Atimaha (1928:94). In any case Cook described this Mahine as being between forty and fifty years old, and bald-headed.[49] Cook stated that Mahine's wife was the sister of Papara's Amo (Beaglehole 1967:226).[50] We learn elsewhere (Vancouver 1801:323) that Mahine was an Arioi, and childless, but Morrison credited him with an adopted son, "Tayreehamoedooa" (Tairihamoetua?) (1935:173).

In 1777 and for some years thereafter this Mahine (i.e., Mahine "A") was the most powerful and perhaps the most influential tribal chief on Mo'orea, but nowhere is the actual source or domain of his authority made explicit. Cook first called him "a popular Cheif of that Island" (Beaglehole 1967:198), and "This Cheif who with a few people has made himself independant of Otaheite" (p. 227); but this opinion was based on the notion, undoubtedly mistaken, that Mo'orea had at one time been a dependency of Tahiti. Vancouver described Mahine as "the usurping chief of Morea" (1801:319), and Morrison reported him as having seized the "Government" in a revolt against his "nephew" Metuaro, the "proper king of that Island" so-called (1935:172).

The exact identity of this Metuaro (also called Motuaria and Mahau) is difficult to pin down. A genealogy of Nu'urua marae (constructed by Emory from notes of Tati Salmon and Brander) lists Mahine's closest relatives (see fig. 25–7).

Assuming that Mahine's brother had no issue (the sources mention

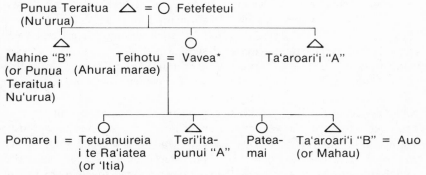

*Gunson (1964:62) identified Vavea as husband (and hence Teihotu as wife), but this does not accord with versions by Emory or Henry, or with any other genealogy that I know of.

FIGURE 25–7. Some kin relations of Mahine.

none), the nephew in question must have been a son of Vavea; but this creates another problem, since according to both Adams and Emory, Vavea had two sons, Teri'itapunui and Ta'aroari'i ("B"). Vancouver identified Metuaro with the former:

> Mahow I considered to be the same person mentioned by Captain Cook, under the name of Tiareetaboonooa; as, on our first arrival, he was introduced to me by the name of Areetaboonooa, which appellation was almost immediately dropped, and he was afterwards called Mahow; occasioned most likely by the recent alteration in their language, which has been stated to have taken place on the accession of the young king Otoo." (1801:322–323)

Adams made this same identification, at least on one genealogy; on another one Adams identified Metuaro with Ta'aroari'i ("B"), and provided a clue to the puzzle in another passage.

> Vancouver sent a boat to Eimeo for Pomare, who came over January 2, 1792, bringing with him his brother-in-law Motuaria, or Metuaro, who was supposed by Vancouver to be the same Terii tapunui that was known to Cook and Forster as chief of Varari in Eimeo. He was called commonly Metuaro Mahau. According to our records, he was Taaro-arii, a younger brother of Cook's Terii tapunui, who was dead without issue, and left his name and property to Taaro-arii, who also had no male children. (1901:106)

In any case, the importance of the problem of one Teri'itapunui-Metuaro or two is diminished somewhat, structurally, inasmuch as the second of the candidates (if there were two) was sibling and successor to the first. (I sympathize with any reader who may have become impatient at my concern with these tedious details but wish to remind him that correct identification and genealogical placement of the dramatis personae is essential for understanding the political events of this era.)

Cook mentions a Teri'itapunui, in 1777, as having been Mahine's sister's son, chief of Varari and the "lawful heir" to the kingship of Mo'orea (Beaglehole 1967:198, 231). In 1789, Mortimer visited Varari and there met "King" Teri'itapunui, whom he described as "a tall, stout, good-looking man, speaks but little, and seemed to be of a timid disposition." According to Mortimer, Teri'itapunui received him in company with his wife, who was "a very agreeable, insinuating woman, with a great deal of natural politeness about her." (1791:38) If my identification is correct this woman was none other than the youngest sister of Pomare I, one named variously Vai'io, Auo, "Wowo," "Tirrayraydooa," and so forth; and some of her poise may be accounted for by the circumstance of her earlier familiarity with Europeans at Matavai and Pare. Vancouver had much more to say about Teri'itapunui-Mahau during his 1791–1792 visit, but these events will be described later on.

Tetuanui Rei i te Ra'iatea was, of course, the famous 'Itia, Pomare I's principal consort, whom I have already identified. I have also described

Pateamai (or Teano, or "Fier rete"), as having first married Vehiatua III and, after his death, as having for a time shared her sister's connubial relationship with Pomare I.

LEEWARD ISLANDS

Tahiti and Mo'orea were closely linked with the Leeward Islands by ties of trade, cult, and kinship, some of which were of crucial importance to political developments on Tahiti-Mo'orea during the era now under study. Events on Tahiti-Mo'orea also had consequences upon those in the Leeward Islands during this era, although perhaps relatively less so until the very end of the era. In any case, interest throughout the remainder of this book will focus on Tahiti-Mo'orea; among other reasons for doing so is the fact that until about 1809 the information on the Leewards is mythical, indirect, or based on observations made during Europeans' very brief visits there. I have elsewhere reproduced mythical evidence concerning some aspects of the "prehistory" of the Leeward Islands — evidence relating mainly to the origin and spread of Opoans and their institutions (including feather-girdled kinship Titles, the cult of 'Oro, and the Arioi sect). The first recorded European visit to these islands was Cook's; after leaving Tahiti in 1769 the *Endeavour* cruised and visited among them between July 16 and August 11. Cook made brief return visits in 1773 and 1774, and again in 1777; and the *Aguila* visited Ra'iatea for about two days in January 1775. H.M.S. *Pandora* called briefly at Huahine (fig. 25–8), Ra'iatea, and Porapora in May 1791 searching for *Bounty* mutineers. The next visit was a short one by Turnbull in 1801, when the ship barely escaped seizure by Ra'iateans. Missionaries began visiting the Leeward Islands in 1807, but it was not until 1818 that a permanent mission station was established there.

Ra'iatea resembled Tahiti's fifth-order tribal units in territorial complexity. According to Henry it consisted of nine "districts" — Opoa (the district of the dynasty that traditionally supplied the island's sovereign chief) and eight others, said by Handy to have been delimited by an Opoan chief after his supporters had conquered the rest of the island's populations. ("The Arii at Opoa took his *urupiti* (cavalla fish, signifying Raiatea), cut it down the middle, and laid the two halves side by side. Each side he divided into four *mataeinaa*" [Handy 1930:90].) Nothing is reported in this or other accounts concerning the territorial organization of Ra'iatea prior to this legendary reorganization; nor can I discover any information about the orders of territorial complexity of the reorganized "districts."

The sources agree that the Opoan chiefs did in fact exercise some tribal authority over the whole island, but the western "district" of Tevaitoa, which I mentioned in another context, in chapter 16, appears to have been somewhat more independent of Opoa than were the seven others.

In addition to the tribal authority exercised by Opoans, the kin-Titles of its chiefly dynasties were, during the eras under study, ranked as high as or higher than those of any other kin-congregations in the Society Islands.

Henry designated Apu Roa as the "national marae" of Taha'a, thereby signifying that the island's four "districts" constituted a larger territorial unity of some kind, but indications are that this larger unit itself did not remain autonomous, having become a "dependency" first of Ra'iatea then of Porapora before Europeans first touched ashore there. According to the summaries of Henry, Porapora consisted of eight so-called districts, but I am unable to specify their respective orders of complexity. From time to time all or most of the island seems to have been dominated by the chiefly dynasties of one or another of these districts; this was certainly the case during the sixth and seventh decades of the eighteenth century, but otherwise, dynastic rivalries appear to have kept the island in a fairly constant state of political instability.

FIGURE 25–8. "The harbour at Huahine." Drawing by J. Webber. British Museum.

Maupiti resembled Ra'iatea in being divided into nine so-called districts — eight subordinate ones and that of the island's "high chief." From Handy's account it appears that these "districts" became firmly united, but judging from the small size of the island and of its population, it seems unlikely that it had reached an order of complexity, in terms of territorial units, much beyond what for Tahiti I labeled *multi multi-neighborhoods*.

By European times the island of Maupiti is reported to have become subordinate to chiefs of Porapora, but the precise nature of the relationship is not recorded.[51]

The territorial organization of Huahine differed somewhat from that of the other islands. By European times the island's two geographic divisions had become wholly subordinate to a chiefly dynasty residing near Lake Maeva in the north. Southern, or Little, Huahine was composed of four contiguous "districts" of unspecified complexity; before becoming subordinate to the Maeva overlords these four were united under the authority of the chief of one of them, but whether this same arrangement prevailed after Maeva domination is not recorded. As for the northern geographic division, Greater Huahine, Henry stated that it was divided into ten "districts," without specifying their nature. Other writers however listed only eight, and according to Handy these were not "districts" in the ordinary sense:

Maeva had eight sons, four by Tuaroanuihau (the last high priest of Huahine) whose ancestral marae, Orohaehaa, at Maeva, was named Tua-roa-nui-i-ae-pau and then four by Teroro Hiti, a warrior chief from Matahiva in the Tuamotus. The land at Maeva, called *aia tupuna o te ui* was divided into the eight mataeinaa, one for each son, and each land they had conquered outside Maeva was also divided among these eight sons to be added to their *mataeinaa* and to be a possession of their families and descendants. Thus Huahine, in patchwork fashion became entirely apportioned among the eight *mataeinaa*. Each *mataeinaa* was, in turn, divided into two parts, one for the *matahiapo* (senior branch), and the other for the *iato* (junior branch) of the family. (1930:96)

This Huahinean method of subdividing conquered territory was of course much more inclusive, but resembled somewhat one practiced elsewhere. I refer to the practice followed by some head chiefs of complex territorial units in acquiring and maintaining personal family estates in each of the major territorial subdivisions under their authority. Usually such chiefs established their own stewards in separate estates, and these were directly responsible to their master and not to the local chiefs in the territorial subdivisions in which the estates were located.

Little is recorded about Mai'ao's political situation, save that it was a "dependency" of Huahine (Teissier 1956:518), and that it was a refuge for survivors of canoes swept off course between Tahiti-Mo'orea and the Leeward Islands.

According to mythic evidence already cited, the various Leeward Islands were closely interlinked by numerous ties of kinship, reinforced by easy and frequent visiting, and evidently also by much intra- and interisland warfare. Opoa appears to have retained over a long period of time its cult primacy and its preeminence in terms of ranked kin-congregation kin-Titles; and inasmuch as statuses in these hierarchies sometimes, and in some respects, were backed by coercive sanctions, the principal chief of Opoa (and hence of

Ra'iatea) may be said to have exercised a kind of authority over all these islands from time to time. But, around 1750, under the leadership of a chief named Puni, Poraporans defeated most of their neighbors and imposed Puni's force-backed authority over them. Huahine evidently threw off the invaders after a while, but in 1769, the date of the first European visit, the other Leeward Islands were firmly under Puni's control. (Beaglehole 1955:153; 1962:I, 317–318)

Having heard much about this military conqueror, the English visitors were somewhat surprised at sight of the man himself:

In the evening we all went to see the great king and thank him for his civilities particularly of this morning. The King of the *Tata toas* or Club men who have conquerd this and are the terror of all other Islands we expected to see young lively hansome &c &c. but how were we disapointed when we were led to an old decrepid half blind man who seemd to have scarce reason enough left to send hogs, much less galantry enough to send ladies.[52] (Beaglehole 1962:I, 327)

On this occasion Cook also referred to Puni as appearing to be "stupit" (Beaglehole 1955:150).

Four years later, on his second visit to Ra'iatea, Cook was able to report at greater length about the political situation in these islands:

Before I quit these isles it is necessary to mention all I know concerning the goverment of Ulietea and Otaha. Oreo, so often mentioned is a Native of Bola bola, but is possessed of Whenooa's or Lands at Ulietea, which I suppose he as well as many of his Country got at the conquest. He resides here as Opoonies Lieutenant, and seems to be vested with regal authority and to be the supreme Magistrate in the island, Oo-ooroo who is the Aree by hereditary right seems to have little more left him than the bare title and his own Whenooa or district in which I think he is sovereign. I have always seen Oreo pay him the respect due to his rank and was pleased when he saw me distinguish him from others. Otaha, so far as I can find is upon the very same footing, Boba and Ota are the two Chiefs, the latter I have not seen; Boba is a Stout well made young man and we are told is, after Opoone's death, to Marry his Daughter, by which Marriage he will become Vested with the same regal authority as Opoony has now, by which it should seem that tho a Woman may be vested with regal dignity she cannot have regal power. I cannot find that Opoony has got any thing to himself by the conquest of these isles any farther than providing for his Nobles who have siezed on best part of the lands; he seems to have no demand on them for any of the many articles they have had from us. Odiddy has several times enumerated to me all the Axes, Nails &c Opoony is possessed of which hardly amounts to so many as he had from me when I saw him in 1769. Old as this famous man is he seems not to spend his last days in indolence, when we first arrived here he was at Mauraua, soon after he returned to Bolabola and we are now told he is gone to Tubi. (Beaglehole 1961:429–430)

Cook's "Oo-ooroo" [Uru], the *ari'i* of Ra'iatea "by hereditary right," was Vetea Uru, son of Tamatoa III by the latter's third wife, and thus half-brother to Pomare I's mother, Tetupaia, who was daughter of Tamatoa III by his first wife. Evidently Vetea Uru retained the tribal (now subtribal) chieftainship of Opoa district, and continued to be recognized as Ra'iatea's highest-ranking resident Titleholder, but was subordinate to Puni's deputy, Oreo, in secular matters concerning Ra'iatea's other subtribal districts.

As for Popa and Ota, identified by Cook as Taha'a's two chiefs, I cannot further identify them, nor discover whether the former did subsequently marry Puni's daughter, as Cook was told would be the case. G. Forster described "Boba" as a relative of Puni's (1777:II, 391) — a likely but not very useful identification. Vancouver reported the presence of a man named Boba on Tahiti in 1792 (1801:307), but there is no evidence of his having been the same person.

The identity of Puni is certified by Emory as having been none other than the Teihotu Mataroa, son of Teihotu Matanevaneva, the Poraporan chief whose downfall and heroic but somewhat foolhardy death is described in a mythic account reproduced earlier. In that account, it will be recalled, after the latter had been killed by his rebellious subjects and political rivals, the victors elected his infant son to chieftainship of the new regime (Hau Teraitapu), therewith changing his name to Puni. (See chap. 16; and Emory, Marae Traditions.) According to Emory's calculation Puni was born circa 1700; in 1789 it was reported to Bligh that the great warrior had died some thirty months previously, that is, about 1786. It speaks much for Puni's reputation that one of the anchors lost by Bougainville off Hitia'a was subsequently sent to Puni, presumably as a respectful gift (Beaglehole 1967:252; Lesson 1839:450).

As noted earlier, Huahine was at one time attacked and occupied by Puni's forces, but the invaders were shortly thereafter driven away. In any case, when the *Endeavour* called there in 1769 the "King" of the island was reported to be a man named "Oree" (Ori) and relations with Porapora were described as hostile:

. . . the People of this Isld are remarkably Civel and Expres'd a great Desire of our going to kill the Bollobollo Men who are their Enemies and come every month or six weeks taking away their Things and Killing all that Oppose them. (Pickersgill, in Beaglehole 1955:143n)

This view was repeated to Cook in 1773, but was evidently not shared by Ori himself:

Oree probably heard of this [i.e., requests to Cook to attack Porapora] and took an oppertunity when he was left aboard to disire that I would not, teling me that Opoone their King was his Friend, the Common people in general seem to bear an implacable hatred against the Bolabola men nor is this to be much wondred at sence they have made a conquest of most of the neighbouring iles, the little Island of Huaheine under the brave and wise conduct of Oree still preserves its independancy, not a Bolabola man have yet been able to get a footing there tho' we have been told some attempts have been made but of this we have no absolute certainty, from the great plenty of everything on the Isle one might conclude that it had injoyed the b(l)esings of Peace for many years. . . . (Beaglehole 1961:221)

As Cook subsequently learned, Ori may have possessed much authority in Huahine — or, at least, on the northern of the island's two parts — but the highest-ranking kin-Titleholder at the time of Cook's visits was a young lad named Teri'itaria, who had been born about 1763, the son of Mato and Fatuarai (Fatuarei?). In 1777 Cook found Ori to be no longer at Huahine, having removed to Ra'iatea. As for the current government of Huahine Cook wrote at the time:

Anarchy seemed to prevail more here than at any other place, the Earee rahie as I have before observed was but a Child and I did not find there was any one man or set of Men who managed the Government for him, so that when ever any missunderstanding happened between us I never knew whom to apply to to settle matters. The you(n)g Chiefs Mother would some times exert her self but I did not see she had greater authority than many others. (Beaglehole 1967:237)

As one example of this anarchy, Cook had some unhappy encounters with a Poraporan adventurer then on Huahine who had succeeded in collecting around him some other ruffians and who seemed to be a law unto himself (Beaglehole 1967:236–237).

Fatuarai, the young *ari'i rahi*'s mother, who was known also as Teha'apapa, was descended from high-ranking kin-Titleholders of Tahiti, Mo'orea, and Huahine (Henry 1928:257). Her father is described in one account as having been Huahine's "principal warrior chief" and associated with marae Tiva (Chesneau 1928:81). Mato, the boy's father (also known as Terii te Po Arei), was identified by Henry as "high priest of Opoa" (1928:257). His kinship with some other principal personages of the era is shown in figure 25–9.

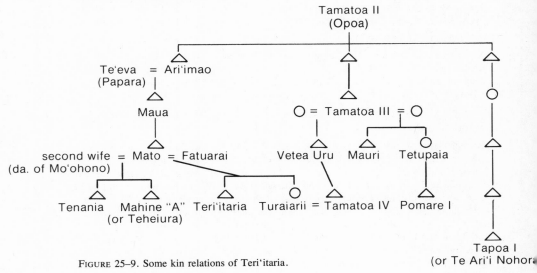

FIGURE 25–9. Some kin relations of Teri'itaria.

After siring Teri'itaria (about 1763) and Turaiarii, Mato left Fatuarai and married the daughter of Mo'ohono, identified by Chesneau as "grand-priest of Huahine" (1928:81). By this wife he sired three children, two of whom figure prominently in political developments, namely, Tenania (who "married" 'Itia after the latter separated from Pomare I) and Mahine ("A") (known also as Teheiura and Puru, who later became "king," or, with Tenania, "co-king," of Huahine). Mato was not in evidence during any of Cook's visits to Huahine; Chesneau reported that he was killed around 1775 in an interisland battle, but this date and the circumstances of this conflict are clouded with uncertainties.[53] All of this is of course most intriguing, and probably important; and I relegate discussion of the matter to a footnote only because of the paucity of data concerning it.

I shall take up the threads of this Leeward Islands history as events in Tahiti-Mo'orea warrant. Meanwhile, let us consider what ideas and objects of Leeward Island origin were exercising palpable influence upon the course of political history of Tahiti and Mo'orea at the beginning of the European era.

'ORO IMAGES AND FEATHER GIRDLES

In my accounts of myths having to do with the diffusions of 'Oro worship I reproduced (in chap. 22) one of Henry's, which described how some of the god's zealots had established the cult on Tahiti by building a marae called Taputapuatea on Taiarapu and by installing in it an 'Oro image called 'Oro Rahi To'o Toa (Great-'Oro-of-*toa*-wood). The date of this event is not given, but the description of it implies that it was the first successful establishment of the cult on Tahiti.[54] The account then continues:

Thus encouraged, the priests of 'Oro went to the body of Tahiti, the fish, with a sacred stone from the marae they had just made. They landed at 'Utu-'ai-mahu-rau (Cape-eating-many-mists), at Pa'ea, then called Atahata or Ata-huru (Fleecy-clouds).

There they were allowed to take possession and were also aided in building their marae, which was called 'Utu-'ai-mahu-rau. 'Oro-hu'a-manu ('Oro-of-the-bird-feathered-body) became master there; the image was woven the size of that at Opoa and covered with red, yellow, and black feathers from the image at Tautira.

Gradually, as the priests of the new order increased, new marae to 'Oro in the feather body were erected all around Tahiti, and finally Pepeto'ai in Mo'orea had its Taputapu-atea, which was originally Te-pua-tea (White-flower). The change of the name was occasioned by a marriage which took place between a high chief of the Manea family in Papeto'ai and a princess of Opoa. The princess brought her marae stone from the original Taputapu-atea, and she and her husband named it Tura'a-ma-rafea (Kneeling [stone] of-two-meetings). This stone raised the marae from a social to a national grade, so that it became the Taputapu-atea of all Mo'orea. (1928:130–131)

This account does not indicate whether facsimile images of "'Oro in the feather body" were made and installed in the various marae erected for this manifestation of the god, nor does it imply that a separate 'Oro image had been installed in the Taputapuatea built on Mo'orea. In fact, the only other evidence, mythical or otherwise, for the presence of any other 'Oro image on Tahiti-Moorea during the era under study derives from Thomson's *History*.

Shortly after [1730–1740] a quarrel took place between the two districts of Te oropa and Teva uta. A battle called *Ohure popoi hoa* (a name of filthy meaning) was fought at Papara in which the latter were beaten and dispersed. A party fled to the island of Raiatea, among whom were *Faanonou* the grandfather of Tati and *Teiva* [Te'eva Pirioi] a female who was soon afterwards married to Ariimao ancestor of Tamatoa and king of Raiatea, by whom [Ari'imao] she had a son called *Maua*. Faanonou became the friend of Maua, and when he resolved to return to Tahiti, through the influence of his friends, and his mother he obtained an idol made at the great marae of Oro at Opoa, and which had been consecrated by the priests there, and became a duplicate of their god. This new idol was deposited in the sacred canoe of Oro called *Te vaa roa i te matai* and committed to the care of Faanonou to be conveyed to Tahiti. The priest of Oro giving strict injunctions that it should be conveyed to his paternal marae at Papara with as little pomp and ceremony as possible. Faanonou accordingly sailed for Tahiti accompanied by Tupaia a priest of Oro and one or two canoes, arrived in safety at Papara, where in the small family marae adjoining the dwelling of the chief the god Oro found his first resting place on Tahiti probably about the year 1760. So quiet and unostentatious was the landing of Oro, that it was scarsely known for a considerable period, that such an arrival had taken place. When it at last became generally known throughout the island, he was at once adopted as the national god, the god of war, and the spirit of the new god seemed at once to have possessed the people. (Thomson, History, pp. 16–17)

Thus, we are provided with evidence — legendary but circumstantial — of the presence of *three* 'Oro images on Tahiti-Mo'orea during the eighteenth century: the Great-'Oro-of-*toa*-wood (at Taputapuatea, Taiarapu); the 'Oro-of-the-bird-feathered-body (at marae 'Utu'aimahurau, Pa'ea); and the one installed by Maua and Tupaia at Papara (which I shall call the "Papara image," in the absence of its name being given in the sources). There may have been more, but these alone are specified in the accounts about which I know.

Indeed, the only one of these three images that I can actually account for in historically authenticated reports is the so-called Papara one, which, as we shall see, became a most important element in the political strife of the era.

Of parallel and indeed interdependent importance in the political history of the Early European Era were the feather girdles, which served to symbolize and legitimatize certain of the very highest-ranking kin-Titles of Tahiti-Mo'orea. One of these was the red-feathered girdle (*maro ura*) reportedly introduced into Papara (along with the Papara image of 'Oro) as the result of Te'eva's marriage to Ari'imao. Another was the fabled yellow-feathered girdle (*maro tea*) allegedly bestowed upon the first Te'eva by his genitor, Hotutu's shark-god lover from overseas. Thenceforth, after Te'eva moved from Vaiari and settled down at Papara, entitlement to this girdle was identified with the dynastic line holding the chieftainship of Papara's principal kin-congregation, and it was the only such yellow-feathered girdle recorded for Tahiti-Mo'orea.[55] Thus, during the era now under study, there were traditions extant concerning two distinct feather girdles associated with the chiefly kin-Titles of the principal Paparan kin-congregation (and derivatively, with chieftainship of the Papara tribe). Whether these traditions were substantialized in the existence of two actual girdles — a *maro tea* and a *maro ura*, or two *maro ura* — I cannot say.

The question is further complicated by references in the sources to what Adams called ''a curious form of the Maro ura.''

Besides the ura or red feathers, which were the exclusive signs of the Arii rahi, a curious form of the Maro ura had been made the symbol of supreme authority by Purea [the Fa'a'a woman married to Amo, chief of Papara]. This was the British pennant left flying at Matavai by Captain Wallis at his departure. Purea took it to her Marae of Mahiatea, and seems to have converted it into the Maro ura with which her son was to be invested. (1901:109)

This same girdle (which I shall call the ''Wallis *maro*'') was seen in 1777 by Cook, who described it as follows:

One of the bundles was now untied and it was found, as I have before observed, to contain the Maro with which they invest their Kings with Royalty. It was carefully taken out and spread out at full length on the ground before the Priests, it was about five yards long and fifteen inches broad, and composed of red and yellow feathers but mostly of the latter; the one end was bordered with eight pieces, each about the size and shape of [a] horse shoe, with their edges fringed with black pigeon feathers; the other end was forked and the ends not of the same length. The feathers were in square compartments ranged in two rows and otherways so desposed as to have a good effect being first paisted or fixed to their Country cloth and then the whole sewed to the upper end of the English Pendant, Captain Wallis desplayed, and left flying a shore the first time he landed at Matavai, so at least we were told and we had no reason to doubt it as it was part of an English pendt. About six or eight inches square of the Maro was not compleat, that is there were no feathers upon it except a few that were sent by Waheatua as before mentioned. The Priests made a long Prayer over the Maro in different forms which, if I misstake not, they called the prayer of the Maro. When it was finished, the Maro was carefully foulded up put into the Cloth and laid upon the Morai. (Beaglehole 1967:202; see also Bligh 1792:138)

It would be useful to discover whether the British pennant in question was in fact added to one of the traditional Paparan *maro* — the ancient *maro tea* or the more recent *maro ura* introduced by Maua and Tupaia — or whether the whole Wallis *maro* had been fabricated *de novo* by Amo and Purea. Unfortunately a positive answer to this question eludes me — although I strongly suspect the first alternative to be the correct one. My interest in this question goes deeper than idle ethnographic curiosity. Such a development would carry important implications if it turned out that an entirely new *maro*, and one deriving its significance from the European presence, had been created as the symbol for Teri'irere's incumbency.

Another *maro* — this undoubtedly an ancient one — which figured importantly was the one usually deposited at Pare's Tarahoi marae and allegedly introduced by Tetupaia from Opoa, when she became the wife of Pare-Arue's chief Teu, circa 1740. (Tetupaia was the eldest child of Ra'iatea's sovereign chief, Tamatoa III.) (Henry 1928:249.) In February 1791 Morrison witnessed the investiture of Pomare II at Tarahoi with a *maro ura* that may plausibly be identified, in whole or in part, with the one introduced by Tetupaia:

> This day the Ceremony of Investing the Young King with the Marro Oora or Royal Sash took place; the Sash is of fine Network on which Red and Yellow Feathers are made fast, so as to cover the netting; the sash is about three yards long, and each end is devided into six tassels of Red Black & Yellow feathers, for each of which they have a name of some Spirit or Guardian Angel, that watches over the Young Chief while the Marro is in his Posession and is never worn but one day by any one King; it is then put into the Sacred Box and with a Hat or Shade for the Eyes Made of Wicker & Covered with feathe(r)s of the same kind and never used but on the Same occasion it is delivered to the priests, who put it Carefully by in the Sacred House on the Morai, where no person must toutch it. (Morrison 1935:116).

Two other *maro ura* figure in accounts of Tahiti-Mo'orea. One was the traditional entitlement to such associated with the principal kin-Title, Te Ari'i Nui o Tahiti, of Vaiari's Farepua marae, the other was the entitlement associated with the kin-Title, Te Atua Nui e Maru Ae i Te Rai, of Puna'auia's marae, Tahiti-Puna'auia. During this era both these kin-Titles were probably assigned: the former perhaps to a certain Maheanu'u (Henry 1928:83), and the latter quite possibly to Puna'auia's high chief, the genial giant, Pohuetea. However, there is no record that these individuals, or anyone else, ever asserted the right to wear a *maro ura* during this era, nor can I discover evidence that either of these legendary *maro ura* actually existed at the time. I shall try in due course to account for this circumstance, but with the stage thus peopled and provided with its most important props, I am now in a position to reconstruct and perhaps better illuminate the drama itself.

CHAPTER 26 *THE EMERGENCE OF THE POMARES*

THE PAPARA DEBACLE

While H.M.S. *Dolphin* (fig. 26–1) was anchored in Matavai Bay in June and July 1767 its personnel were totally unaware of the drama that was unfolding at Papara, 40 kilometers along the coast to the south. This drama reached a climax in December 1768, and by the time H.M.S. *Endeavour* arrived four months later, this particular act had ended, and the principals were contemplating, and perhaps even then preparing for, the denouement.[1]

The first recorded notice of these events appears in Bank's journal, on the date of 29 June 1769, during his and Cook's tour around the island. At Papara the visitors were much impressed both with the size of marae Mahaiatea and with the apparent decline of "Queen" Purea's fortunes, from the high point reported of them by Wallis two years previously. (See fig. 26–2)

The greatest pride of an inhabitant of Otahite is to have a grand *Marai*, in this particular our freinds far exceed any one in the Island, and in the Dolphins time the first of them exceeded every one else in riches and respect as much. The reason of the difference of her present apearance from that I found by an accident which I now relate: in going too and coming home from the *Marai* our road lay by the sea side, and every where under our feet were numberless human bones cheifly ribbs and vertebrae. So singular a sight suprized me much; I enquird the reason and was told that in the month calld by them *Owiráhëw* last, which answers to our December 1768, the people of Tiarreboo made a descent here and killd a large number of people whose bones we now saw; that upon this Occasion Oborea and Oamo were obligd to fly for shelter to the mountains, that the Conquerors burnt all the houses which were very large and took away all the hoggs &c., that the turkey and goose which we had seen with Mathiabo were part of the spoils, as were the jaw bones which we saw hung up in his house; they had been carried away as trophies and are usd by the Indians here in exactly the same manner as the North Americans do scalps. (Beaglehole 1962:I, 304–305)

So much for the first recorded "facts" concerning this first major political upheaval of the European era. Subsequently recorded "facts" about this episode will agree with the bare statements set forth in Banks' report but add enough others to produce some wholly different versions of "what actually happened."

FIGURE 26–1. "A representation of the attack of Captain Wallis in the *Dolphin* by the natives of Otaheite." In Hawkesworth 1773, vol. 1.

FIGURE 26–2. "A representation of the surrender of the island of Otaheite to Captain Wallis by the supposed Queen Oberea." In Hawkesworth 1773, vol. 1.

The most detailed account is provided by Adams.[2] The whole debacle, this version implies, came about as the result of Amo's and Purea's — but mainly the latter's — obstinate desire to elevate even further their son, Teri'irere's, very high-ranking status (and derivatively, his political influence) over all Tahiti and Mo'orea. To accomplish this they undertook, according to Adams, ". . . what no other great chief had ever attempted":

> They not only imposed a general *Rahui* for the child's benefit . . . but they also began a new Marae for Teriirere, in which he was to wear the Maro, and they set their people to work on the enormous task of piling up the pyramid at Mahaiatea which was an exhibition of pride without a parallel in Polynesia. (1901:42)

The immediate consequence of these acts was a series of challenges. I reproduce the full account of this episode, however dubious or clearly inaccurate parts of it may be, because of its exemplification of what appears to have been a very characteristic tactic of social competition.

This was more than Purea's female relations could bear, and it set society in a ferment. The island custom provided more than one way of dealing with pride. Though Purea and Teriirere were admitted to be political superiors, they were socially no better than their cousins, and custom required that if during a *Rahui* any relative or guest of equal rank should come to visit the chief who had imposed it, the *Rahui* was broken, and the guest received by courtesy all that the *Rahui* had produced. Such an attempt to break the *Rahui* was of course an act which could not be ventured by any ordinary chief within the direct control of Papara; but Tefana i Ahurai was independent, and if Purea's own family chose to set up such a claim, Purea would resist it at her peril. Not even she could afford such a quarrel.

The first person who undertook to break the *Rahui* was probably Purea's sister-in-law, no doubt the wife or widow of Teihotu, on behalf of her son, Terii vaetua. [3] She set out from Faaa in her double-canoe, with the house or tent, called *fare-oa*, in the prow, which only headchiefs could use; and a crew of fifty men or more paddled this barge of state, with all the show of a royal ceremony, along the coast to Papara, some twenty miles away, until, opposite to the Point of Mahaiatea, they turned in to an opening in the reef which had on some pretext become sacred, and was known as the sacred pass, through which only sacred chiefs might go. Purea was then living on the Point, and probably was superintending the work on her great Marae. She came out on the beach, and as the double canoe, with its royal tent, passed through the opening and drew towards the land she hailed it:

"Who dares venture through the sacred pass? Know they not that the Tevas are under the sacred Rahui for Teriirere i Tooarai? Not even the cocks may crow or the ocean storm."

"It is Terii vaetua, Arii of Ahurai."

"How many more royal heads can there be? I know none but Teriirere i Tooarai. Down with your tent!"

The Ahurai chiefess wept and cut her head with the shark's tooth till blood flowed down her face, which was the custom of women in sign of great emotion, and meant in this instance revenge as well as grief; but Purea was inexorable, and Terii vaetua was obliged to turn round and go home like any ordinary stranger.

The quarrel, once begun, was extended by another of the Ahurai family, a woman who proved to be more than Purea's equal in most forms of energy. She was Purea's niece, the daughter of Teihotu and sister of the insulted Terii vaetua. Her name was Tetuanui rea i te Raiatea, and she was or became the wife of Tunuieaiteatua i Tarahoi, Cook's friend Otoo, and the missionaries' friend Pomare. A very famous woman in Tahitian history, much talked about by Captain Bligh in 1788 and by the missionaries as Iddeah, Tetuanui i Nuurua was not even mentioned by Wallis or Cook, although the latter, in 1774, frequently mentions "Tarevatoo, the king's younger brother," whom I take to be Terii vaetua, the king's brother-in-law, who had begun the attempt to break the Rahui.[4] Indeed, Cook never saw even Pomare until August, 1773, when Pomare was already thirty years old.

After the repulse of Terii vaetua, this sister undertook to pursue the quarrel. The matter had become uncommonly serious, for a feud between Papara and Ahurai might upset the whole island. Nothing more would then be needed to overthrow the Papara supremacy than the alliance of Ahurai and the Purionuu with Vehiatua, whose fortunes had been made a hundred years before by a similar combination to break a similar *Rahui*. Tradition has preserved the precise words used by the family to avert the peril into which Purea's pride and temper were pushing them.

Tetuanui in her turn made her appearance in the state canoe off the point of Mahaiatea, and as she approached the beach was received by Purea with the same order, "Down with your tent!" Tetuanui came ashore and sat on the beach and cut her head with the shark's tooth till the blood flowed down into a hole she dug to receive it. This was her protest in form; and appeal to blood. Unless it were wiped away it must be atoned by blood.

Then the high-priest Manea interposed. Manea was Amo's younger brother, from whom we are directly descended in the fourth generation, and probably we owe our existence in a double sense to him, for his act wiped out the blood-feud as far as his own descendants were concerned.

"Hush, Purea! Whence is the saying, 'The pahus (drums) of Mataiea call Tetunai for a Maro-ura for Teriirere i Tooarai. Where wilt thou wear the Maro-ura? In Nuura and Ahurai. One end of the Maro holds the Purionuu; the other end the Tevas; the whole holds the Oropaa.' "[5]

Manea quoted the maxim of family statecraft in vain. Purea replied only that she was going to allow no rivalry to her son. "I recognize no head here but that of Teriirere." Then Manea dried the blood of Tetuanui with a cloth, wiping away the feud as far as he was concerned; and so long are these things remembered that forty years afterwards, when the Purionuu savagely raided Papara, Manea's great-grandchildren were supposed to have been spared in memory of Manea's act. (1901:42–46)

Continuing the Adams version, the parents of Teri'irere persisted in their undertaking and assembled a large gathering to witness his investiture in the *maro* (which *maro* is not directly specified) and to partake of the feast that followed. Those invited to the occasion (Adams wrote "summoned") included Pohuetea of Puna'auia; Tepau "A" of Ahurai; Pomare I of Pare-Arue, designated "Terii maro ura" (the *maro*-wearing *ari'i*) of Tarahoi (Pare-Arue's principal marae); along with "the Island of Eimeo" (probably Mahine); Puni, chief of Porapora; Ra'a, chief of Maupiti and Tupai; and Teae of Ra'iatea. This version does not indicate which ones of these notables attended or whether the investiture actually took place, but proceeds to explain that the whole occasion was interrupted and brought to a bloody conclusion by means of an armed attack of Seaward Tevans who (as Banks reported) killed a large number of people, burned houses, collected all moveable loot, and forced Amo, Purea, and Teri'irere to flee (Adams 1901:71; Beaglehole 1962:I, 305).

According to Adams' version, then, the immediate cause of this upheaval was Purea's overweening pride; but in the background certain other factors were involved — one of the weightiest having been the acts of Tutaha, great-uncle of Pomare I and tribal chieftain of Pare-Arue. (Tutaha himself was evidently content to wield the secular authority of the Pare-Arue chieftainship, leaving to his grandnephew the ceremonial honors attending high rank-status, to which indeed Tutaha himself was not even eligible.) Tutaha's part in the Papara affair was aimed immediately at elevating his grandnephew's rank-status even further, which could be done only by diminishing that of the latter's principal rank-status rival, Teri'irere. It is not stated what part Tutaha and his forces played in the actual fighting, if any, but his share of the spoils were described as follows:

While the Taiarapu people carried off the heads and the property of the victims, Tutaha and the northwestern districts carried away the symbol of supremacy, the standard and feathered girdle, from the Marae of Tooarai and Mahaiatea, and placed it in the Marae of Maraetaata in the district of Paea in the Oropaa, or, as it was usually called by the English, Attahuru. Amo and Purea were forced to make what terms they could with Tutaha, and to recognize Otoo, as having a right to the dignity of the Maro-ura at Maraetata. (Adams 1901:74)

(As I noted earlier, I believe that these "symbols of supremacy" were taken not to Maraeta'ata but to Pa'ea's other principal marae, 'Utu'aimahurau; but that need not immediately concern us here.)

It is not clear from this version just what Tutaha's long-range goals were in this affair. An historian accustomed only to Western man's motives would probably conclude that Tutaha sought additional power and influence for himself; but Tutaha was a Maohi, and this version alone does not throw enough light on the man's deeds to permit such a straightforward ascription.

According to the Adams version another major factor involved in the Papara affair was active enmity between Papara and Taiarapu. Some of this marked a continuation of the general, long-time antagonism between the respective leaders of the two tribal complexes.[6] A more specific reason for this active enmity was the long-standing rivalry between the Aromaiterai and Tuiterai branches of Papara's leading family. This came about, it may be recalled, when Aromaiterai, the elder son of the Paparan chief, was passed over in the succession in favor of his younger brother, Tuiterai, and then sent into exile. Thus, when Purahi, the eldest grandchild of Aromaiterai, married Vehiatua I, the Taiarapuan chief, she was thereby provided with the means for striking against Tuiterai's successor, his grandson and lineal successor, Teri'irere.

It is not clear from this version whether the Aromaiterais (in the person mainly of Purahi) had for a long time been eagerly awaiting a favorable opportunity for revenge, or whether Purahi was moved to reopen the rivalry as a result of Purea's pretensions. Nor is it clear whether she hoped to recapture Teri'irere's kin-Titles for her son, or merely to humble somewhat the Tuiterais. In any case, whatever her motives and expectations may have been, she was given full credit (or blame, depending upon the point of view) for the devastation wreaked upon the Paparans by her husband's forces.[7] And although the Tuiterais were duly humbled by these measures, their losses, in terms of rank-status and political influence, accrued as gains not to the Aromaiterais in particular (or to the Taiarapuans) but to Tutaha and Pomare I.

A second version of the Papara affair, which was quoted by Adams but not wholly integrated into the "Adams' version" of the affair, was supplied by Tupaia.[8] The latter is reported as having roused the enmity of Tutaha, as the result of his association with Purea, whom Tutaha wished to supercede as "regent."

> The better to effect it [this purpose] he [Tutaha] began to create divisions between the inhabitants of Otahitee-eta (Taiarapu) [Lesser Tahiti] and of Otahitee-nua [Greater Tahiti], which finally produced hostilities between them. At that time Tobia [Tupaia], who had great sagacity and judgment, having discovered Tutahaw's designs, advised the queen to procure his death privately, as the only expedient to restore peace and preserve her authority; but she, thinking his advice too cruel, refused, for the first time, to comply with it; and he, foreseeing the consequences, retired to the mountains, alleging that this retreat was necessary for the preservation of his life. Soon after, the inhabitants of Lesser Otahitee making frequent incursions into the greater division, and their numerous depredations having thrown the inhabitants of the latter into confusion, which Tutahaw artfully improving to his advantage, they at length offered him the regency, thinking their affairs too much embarrassed for the administration of a female; an agreement was therefore made between Oberea and Tutahaw, in which it was conditioned that she should preserve the title and state of queen, with a certain number of attendants, &c., and that the regency should devolve to Tutahaw; who, respecting Tobia's understanding and sacerdotal character, afterward permitted him to return from the mountains in safety; but he was so much displeased with this revolution that he embraced the opportunity of our departure to leave the island. (pp. 72–73)

The most interesting aspect of this version is its singling out of Tutaha as the prime, indeed the only noteworthy, mover in the affair. As for this account's reference to "the regency," it presumably applies to regency for Teri'irere, although no other version that I know of includes this as one of Tutaha's own objectives, or as one of his spoils of war.

Certain other accounts of the Paparan debacle are simply rehashes of some or all parts of the ones just reproduced,[9] but there are two that cast different lights over the whole affair. The first of these is the version recorded

by the missionary Robert Thomson several decades after the events but based on information from Tahitians who were alive at the time or who had learned about the events from the participants. According to Thomson, the incident that initiated this chain of events was the introduction in Tahiti of the cult of 'Oro — specifically the establishment in Papara of an 'Oro image from Ra'iatea circa 1760. According to this unique reconstruction, which was quoted in chapter 25, after 'Oro's adoption as the god of all Tahiti the decision was reached to build a new marae to house his image, at Mahaiatea: "all the districts engaged to unite in forwarding this national work" (Thomson, History, pp. 26–27). Then, Thomson continued, after the marae was finished about eight years later, and after the god had begun to receive there the homage of all Tahiti, the chief of Papara developed pretensions of his own:

Amo feeling that his district had acquired a new and paramount importance in the island, began to think of dominion, and to devise the means by which he might accomplish this end; afraid to attempt it by war he had recourse to an expedient, probably suggested by Tupaea the priest of Oro who had accompanied the god from Raiatea, and who is reported by the people themselves, as well as by Cook to have been one of the cleverest men of the island. Amo suggested that the flag of Oro should be sent round the island, and each chief show his submission to the new god, by allowing the flag to pass in triumph through his district. The flag used on the occasion was not the one which Wallis had hoisted at Point Venus, but a flag or rather pendant made of some material and woven in the manner in which mats were made, and fringed with red feathers, this pendant was called a *vane*. It was accordingly sent round the island and each chief met it at his marae and allowed it a free passage thru his district. It passed thru all the districts on Tahiti without interruption, till it came to the territory of the haughty chief of Taiarabu, who when he saw it exclaimed, "who are the *'feia inro'* degraded people here who will allow this flag to pass thru the district," and seizing it, he tore it in pieces, and sent it back to Amo; who, much mortified at the failure of his scheme, resolved to avenge it, and declared war against Taiarabu.

His active enemy more prompt at war exploits than himself, did not leave him long time for preparation, he mustered his warriors, sent the portion of his fleet which was on that side of the isthmus to attack Papara, while he and most of his warriors marched by land. Amo in the meantime prepared to meet him, so sudden was the attack that he had not time to obtain the assistance of many allies; when the intelligence reached Teoropa and Purionuu, the chiefs with a few of their people immediately joined Amo, but not until the battle was begun. The conflict was not of long duration but was obstinate and bloody, many hundred were slain on both sides. Amo and his allies were defeated, but brought away with them the priest of Oro, who had charge of the sacred and royal girdle, and various other relics brought with the idol from Raiatea. These were safely deposited in the marae at Atehuru. Amo accompanied Teu to Pare and resided there with him for some time, until he could return in peace to his district. In giving an account of this sanquinary battle the old people say that the beach for a long extent, from the sea side up to the base of the hills was covered with the slain. Numbers too were killed in the canoes which met and fought inside the reef, the whole coast in that neighbourhood

was afterwards strewed with the bones and skulls of the killed, and numbers of
the latter which were lying in the sea were taken possession of by the fishes, especially
by the cuttle fish which lodged in the skull, projecting their long feelers thru the
eyes and other holes in the skulls. And from this circumstance the engagement has
derived the name of "The battle of *mata toroa*". Mai, the brother of Amo fell
in this battle, and Vehiatua had the body cooked in an oven, but whether it was
afterwards eaten, or not, never was known. After desolating the country, the Taiarabu
warriors returned home, And Amo and his friends were soon after taken back to
Papara by his allies.

The chiefs of the northern and western districts having assisted Amo great offense
was taken by Vehiatua, who preparing to attack them, when another circumstance
diverted their attention, and suspended hostilities for a time. This was the arrival
of another foreign ship. (pp. 38–40)

Not a word was written about Teri'irere in this version; and the ambitions which led to the debacle are represented as having been Amo's, not
Purea's. Also, far from joining to defeat Amo (as in the Adams and other
versions), the Porionu'u (i.e., Tutaha) and the Oropa'a are shown in this
version to have been his tardy but loyal allies.

The version put forward by Moerenhout, writing a few years earlier
than Thomson, and like Adams heavily dependent upon Paparan sources
for his information, began with the assumption that Amo was "King" of
the whole island. Translated very freely, Moerenhout's reconstruction is as
follows:

Soon after the departures of Wallis and Bougainville, Amo, who until then had
been king of the whole island, perceived that his influence had diminished relative
to that of the chiefs who lived nearer the Europeans' anchorages. The latter had
been the principal recipients of valuable gifts from European officers and had had
their reputations enhanced and their causes supported through friendship pacts with
Europeans. In addition, these chiefs were the ultimate recipients of the countless
objects collected by their subjects from Europeans. In contrast, Amo and Purea
profited from the European visits only to the extent of a few personal gifts, which
went mainly to Purea; and their subjects gained nothing at all. Thus, as a result
of the European visits, Amo fell behind other chiefs, in affluence and in prestige,
to whom he had previously been superior. Then, on top of this, Amo's power and
influence were further diminished as the result of his disastrous defeat at the hands
of Vehiatua I.

Moerenhout's version of this final act in the Paparan downfall contains some
novel points:

Bougainville became particularly attached to the family that resided near his vessels'
anchorage, which resulted in the enhancement of its social position, thereby threatening the position of the family that had been supreme for so long [i.e., Amo's].
Thus, upon the departure of Bougainville, Amo, fearing opposition from other chiefs,
but wishing to have his son recognized as *ari'i rahi* or king, sent his standard around
the island to receive the sign of submission from other *ari'i* and from the nobility
(*la haute aristocratie*). On the prompting of Tutaha (Bougainville's friend and protégé) Taiarapu's chief, Vehiatua, not only refused to honor the standard but went

so far as to tear it up, an insult which could only be wiped out by war. Going even further, Vehiatua had the audacity to attack Amo near Papara itself, despite the fact that the people of Mo'orea fought on Amo's side. The resulting battle was a terrible one, lasting many hours. It is said that so many people were slain that Vehiatua was able to build a whole marae on Taiarapu entirely out of their skulls and named accordingly Tiahupo'o — certainly one of the most extraordinary temples ever raised to a god. (1837:II, 407–408) [10]

Several points in this reconstruction deserve comment. First of all, it should by now be clear that neither Amo nor any other chief was at that time *the* king of all Tahiti. Second, the prominence accorded Bougainville in this account looks suspiciously like an example of Moerenhout's Francophilia. Tutaha did visit Hitia'a briefly while Bougainville was there, but if Bougainville became "particularly attached" to anyone during his nine-day stay it was to the local chief, Reti; and it is difficult to see how this brief encounter could have shaken established hierarchies as violently as Moerenhout implied. Again, this view that Tutaha was largely responsible for Vehiatua's attack on Papara is incomplete, to say the least. While there is evidence from other sources attesting to bad blood between Taiarapu and at least some Mo'oreans, Moerenhout's is the only account that I know of which identifies Mo'orea as an ally — and indeed the only ally — of Papara in this particular conflict.

To the extent that these different versions were credibly delivered Maohi accounts, and not just Europeans' constructions, they are all revelatory of the mainsprings of Maohis' political actions. In terms of "history," however, we have no way of knowing which version most closely fits the actual events. Nevertheless, I believe that as a consequence of certain events approximating those just described, intertribal relations on Tahiti entered a different and perhaps entirely unprecedented phase. In the island's hierarchy of rank-statuses, preeminence began thereafter to be ascribed not to two individuals but to one. It required several years for this process to be completed, and many more to accomplish a parallel development in the sphere of coercively sanctioned tribal authority.

CONTEST BETWEEN NORTH AND SOUTH

After Papara had been laid low in the war of 1768, intertribal strife on Tahiti became polarized between north and south — or, more specifically, between the island's two most forceful and contentious tribal chiefs, Tutaha of Pare-Arue and Vehiatua I of Seaward Teva. It is difficult to say what led these two to their confrontations; to evoke some general psychological factor, like ambition for personal monopoly of power, may in fact be true, but cannot be specifically documented.

Cook and his *Endeavour* shipmates remained in the dark about the complex relationship between kin-Title rank-status and tribal authority, but

they were emphatic in characterizing Tutaha as the most powerful and influential chief in northwest Tahiti. The *Endeavour*'s personnel had less opportunity for appraising Vehiatua's position at the time, but it is clear from other
evidence that he was the unchallenged master of Seaward Teva, in terms
both of active, effective leadership and of ascriptive paramountcy — that
is, his incumbency of the region's highest-ranking kin-Title, *Vehiatua*
(which, however, did not include the right to don a feather girdle). In the
latter respect he possessed an advantage over Tutaha, whose kin-Title, if
any, was that of a younger sibling; but perhaps Tutaha's regency over Pomare
I's *maro ura* kin-Title served to lessen somewhat that advantage. Seaward
Tevans seem not to have questioned the superiority of Pomare I's rank-status
over that of their own chief, Vehiatua; this was revealed in their conversation
with the Spaniards at Tautira in December 1772 (Corney 1913:307).

The most widely accepted account of the dual between Tutaha and
Vehiatua I is G. Forster's, written in 1774:

Captain Cook found the government of Taheitee in the hands of Tootahah,
when he arrived in the Endeavour. After his departure Tootahah, being greatly
enriched by the presents he had obtained, persuaded the chiefs of O-Taheitee-nue,
or the Great Peninsula, to go against Aheatua, whom he could not forgive on account
of the insult shewn to his family.[11] They equipped a fleet, and went to Tiarraboo,
where Aheatua was prepared to receive them. He was an old man, desirous to end
his days in peace; and therefore sent to Tootahah, to assure him that he was his
friend, and always intended to continue so; and that he desired him to return to
his country, without attacking those who had an affection for him. Tootahah was
not dissuaded from his purpose, but gave orders to engage. The loss on both sides
was nearly equal, but Tootahah retired, in order to attack his enemy by land. Happai,
with all his family, disapproved of this step, and remained at o-Parre; but Tootahah
took o-Too with him, and marched to the isthmus between the two peninsulas. Here
Aheatua met him, and a pitched battle ensued, which ended in the total dispersion
of Tootahah's army. Tootahah himself was killed. Some told us he had been taken
prisoner, and was put to death afterwards; but others, and among them o-Mai, asserted
that he had been slain in the heat of the engagement. O-Too retired precipitately
to the mountains with a few chosen friends, whilst Aheatua, with his victorious
forces, immediately marched to Matavai and o-Parre. At his arrival Happai retired
to the mountains, but Aheatua sent to assure him that he had no quarrel with him
or his family, and that his wish had always been for peace. Those on the mountain
enquired in their turn concerning the fate of Tootahah and o-Too; they heard that
the former was killed, and that no body knew what was become of the other. Soon
after o-Too arrived through many difficult passes, and over precipices, and coming
down from the highest summits, joined his father, and all who were with him. A
general peace was immediately concluded, after which O-Too assumed the reins
of government himself, and the vast improvements in the country, which we noticed
in eight months time,[12] seem to prove that he is a very intelligent man, who promotes
the general good of his subjects. Aheatua died soon after; and his son of the same
name, whom we found at Aitepeha in August 1773, succeeded him. (1777:II, 94–96)

Some importance attaches to the dates of these alleged events. Forster's wording locates them no more exactly than between Cook's two visits of August 1769 and August 1773, and implies that the war had been won, and Tutaha slain, some months before Vehiatua I himself died. Cook's own brief notice of these events places Tutaha's death about March 1773, a date also accepted by Adams (1901:91). Writing at Tautira in August 1773 Cook reported: "These people informed us that *Toutaha*, King of the greater Kingdom of Otaheite was kill'd in a Battle which happen'd between the two Kingdoms about five months ago" (Beaglehole 1961:202). A difficulty in the way of accepting this dating appears in Boenechea's account of his expedition's visit to Tahiti during November and December 1772. At that time the "cacique" at Tautira, where the frigate anchored, was Ti'itorea, whose spouse at the time ". . . was formerly the arii Taitoa's" [probably Vehiatua I] (Corney 1913:335).[13] In other words, Tutaha's principal antagonist had by this evidence died much earlier, possibly even in 1771. This means, of course, that Vehiatua I had not lived to see his Seaward Tevans defeat Tutaha and his forces. Consequently, if this dating of events is correct, then one must impute to this conflict motives broader than the long-standing personal animosities of two contentious chiefs. A further point, not specified in Forster's version, but attested elsewhere, is the circumstance that Te Pau i Ahurai died along with his ally, Tutaha, in the war's culminating battle (Beaglehole 1961:202).

More important than the precise date of Tutaha's death is the question of the disposal of his corpse, but consideration of that will be postponed until I have reproduced a somewhat different version of this calamitous north-south conflict. This is the account recorded, and doubtless elaborated, by Moerenhout, writing many decades after the events themselves.

The results of this battle [the Papara debacle] changed the political shape of the island. Amo was no longer *ari'i rahi*, and nearly every chief went his own way, each one regarding himself as independent and free in his own district. Only Tutaha held on to his visions for the future. The others continued to recognize the son of Amo and Purea as heir presumptive, but Tutaha dreamt of supplanting the latter with young Tu, who was a member of his own family. In order to accomplish this he set about organizing a campaign against the very individual who had contributed to his own rise [i.e., Vehiatua I]; with considerable shrewdness he even managed secretly to enlist Amo to lead the expedition. After extensive preparations their forces embarked in a fleet of several hundred canoes to attack Vehiatua, their most redoubtable rival. Despite the numerical inferiority of the latter's forces, this venerable chief, who was one of the island's most celebrated orators, managed so to inspire his followers that they defeated those of the allied chiefs in a battle in which Tutaha himself was slain, along with several members of his family, although young Tu managed to escape. After laying waste to part of the island, particularly Amo's own district, which was nearby, Vehiatua acceded to the pleas of friends of the vanquished and made peace with them. This chief, who after this great victory was in a position to rule the whole island, was however very old and preferred tranquility instead. Accordingly, he permitted the [chiefly] families he had conquered to retain their former authorities and privileges — except for the family of Amo, which had lost so much in the recent conflicts that they could no longer be counted members of the high aristocracy. Some time after this Vehiatua died; Tu recovered all his former influence, and remained the sole rival of Amo's son, who although still too young to act for himself nevertheless continued to be regarded by most of the island's chiefs and populace as heir presumptive to the crown. (1837:II, 408–409)

A markedly different version of the same conflict was composed by the missionary Robert Thomson, whose stay on Tahiti overlapped Moeren-hout's but began a few years later:

After the departure of Cook, the hostile feelings which Vehiatua entertained towards the chief and people of Purionuu broke out in an open war. The latter party were assisted by the chiefs and people of the eastern district, the first collision took place at Hidiaa, and is termed the battle of "Vaihee," another engagement soon took place in the same district called the battle of bu wue (?) but with no more definite results — if advantage leaned to either side it would seem to have favoured Purionuu, as Vehiatua immediately afterwards sailed for Raiatea, although the object of his visit is not now known. He enjoined the chiefs of the peninsula to carry on the war, which, after the usual rest of a few months and plenty of feasting, they did more vigorously than ever. It may not be improbable that Vehiatua's sail to Raiatea was a visit to Oro to propitiate his favour, as the image of that god which had been sent to Tahiti was now in the hands of his enemies.

In the course of the year 1770 a severe naval battle was fought a considerable distance from land off the coast of Teaharoa, between these two parties. The Purionuu warriors having recoiled a little when the first shower of stones fell upon their canoes, the circumstance has been recorded to their disadvantage in the name given to the engagement "The battle of *taora atahi*." This, and the following, seem to be among the most furious and savage of their wars. Each party being resolved on victory, and determined not to give way, they agreed to take their fleets a long distance out to sea, that no hope might remain for the disabled and shattered canoes of the conquered party being able to reach the land. Each canoe was secured in its position in the fleet, and when the hostile fleets met at sea, there were men appointed with ropes in their hands all ready to tie the contending fleets firmly together, and on this platform of canoes hand to hand with club and spear the warriors fought with desperation and thousands must have perished in these dreadful conflicts. From the description which the natives give of these two fleets, it is probable that upwards of 10,000 men were engaged in this battle, the greater part of whom perished; as the warriors fought until the shattered fleets would no longer hold together, but broke asunder and drifted away. Both parties had suffered so severely that neither was in a position to chase the other, and each made the best of their way to their respective districts. (pp. 45–46)

(There follows a lengthy passage, including excerpts from Cook's description of the famous naval review of 1774, attesting to the vast scale that characterized some naval engagements.)

From these statements of Cook, it is evident that Tahiti at that period possessed a respectable navy and fully justified the accounts which the natives give of the magnitude of their fleets and the bloody character of their wars. After the great battle recorded above, the combatants rested some months, feasting with their friends, detailing their exploits, and repairing their shattered canoes; but both parties were mortified that they had not conquered, and resolved to continue the war. Several months afterwards or about 1771 the combatants having built several new canoes, renewed the war; many of Amo's people who had now forgotten their former defeat, joined the Taiarabuans; and many from Teoropa assisted Teu and Tutaha the principle chiefs of Purionuu, with whom Teaharoa was still leagued. Having completed all their arrangements for this, the most memorable naval battle recorded in Tahiti history, to enflame their passions, and irritate the minds of their opponents, messengers were sent by both parties, to taunt them with cowardice in the last battle, and dare them to the fight. A day having been fixed, the Taiarabu warrors came down to their enemies coast, and after some of the warriors had exerted all their powers of buffoonery in mockery of their enemies, they stood out two or three miles to sea. The Purionuu and Teaharoa fleet were soon in motion, and numbered two or three hundred sail. After the canoes had formed into divisions, and were secured to each other, the warrior, Paetia of Point Venus and ancestor of Taaiirii, who took the chief command mounted the platform on the front of his canoe which was placed in the center, and haranged the warriors. He recounted the deeds of their ancestors, mentioned in chronological order all the battles in which they had engaged, eulogized the chiefs who had shown the greatest bravery, and concluded with a tirade against the enemy, in which no epithet was spared which might expose them to the contempt of the warriors. Two or three other chiefs spoke in a similar strain, enciting them to deeds of bravery. Having thus stimulated their own courage, and worked up their hatred of their enemies, to the highest point, the fleet put out to sea. And as these two fleets were the largest which the people had ever seen they must have carried many thousands of warriors. They met at Toahiro, and from the place where they fought the engagement is termed *"Te pau i Toahiro,"* the destruction at Toahiro! Having made their arrangements as on former occasions, and firmly secured the contending fleets, the work of destruction began, and was carried on with fearful ferocity on both sides. In the heat of the engagement the canoe of the chief Teu in which was his son Tu, afterwards Pomare I, was cut away from the assigned position in the rear of the fleet, and the Royal party believing discretion to be the better part of valour, set their sail, left the combatants behind, and stood away for the little island of Tetiaroa. Whether the flight of their chief affected the spirits of the Purionuu warriors is uncertain, as it is what they had seen performed before, but they began to waver and fought with less bravery afterwards. Towards evening another circumstance happened to damp their spirits, and cheer and encourage their enemies. Vehiatua's war canoe was recognized returning from Raiatea, but before he could join in the battle, night separated the combatants now thinned by many hundred from the fierce engagement of the day. The fleets retired for a little distance and spent the night on the bosom of the deep. Having eaten a little and rested in the night, they began at daybreak to renew the struggle. The day before they had gone out, a good distance to sea, in hopes of a decisive engagement, and cutting off the retreat of the vanquished. But now their feirce passions were aroused, like the tiger which has tasted blood, they could not be restrained, and attacked each other, in the position where the breeze and the current had carried them, in the harbour of Matavai and not far from the shore. The Purionuu warriors felt that they were fighting on their own coast, in sight of their own friends, and fought with renewed valour. But the Taiarabuans still more encouraged by the presence of their renowned chief fought with equal desperation. In close contact with club and spear, no mercy was asked or shown, and death rapidly thinned the ranks of the assailants. The engagement of the preceding day, and the blood which had been so lavishly spilt had drawn hundreds of sharks to the spot, and now when a shattered canoe drifted away from the fleet, the sharks were seen to join in the dreadful havoc, and drag the wretched natives to the deep, who were clinging to the fragments of their wreck or who, in the violence of the struggle had been driven, from their standing, into the sea. It is in vain we try to estimate the numbers who fell, the best idea perhaps may be formed from the circumstance which has given a name to the battle. The whole neighbouring sea even to the beach was tinged with blood, and the engagement is termed "*Te tamai i te tai uteute*," The battle of the red sea! During this bloody conflict the breeze had borne the fleets down upon the shores of Tetiaroa [?] where many of the warriors leaping on the shore the battle was continued for some time partially on land, but the Taiarabuans had still the best of the battle, and pressed hard on their enemies, who feeling themselves giving way on their own soil soon became dispirited, broke and fled in confusion to the hills. The slain now strewed along the beach, were collected near Taunoa and piled up into a long and high pyramid, as an offering to the gods. This pile soon becoming putrid was taken possession of by thousands of rats, and is to this day spoken of as "*Te fare ione*" the house of rats! This horrible structure was said to be about sixty feet long, and upwards of twenty feet high! In addition to this mighty pile, the sea beach from Point Venus to Papeete was for many days thickly strewn with the dead cast ashore by the sea. Numbers had been devoured by the sharks, and those who fell on the first day at Toahiro perished too far out at sea ever again to be heard of! Such is the fearful account which the natives give of this dreadful battle. After desolating the coast, and sending an invitation to the refugees to return to their lands, Vehiatua and the Taiarabu warriors went home laden with spoil. Some days after the battle Teu and Tu arrived at Moorea, and ascertaining that their people had come down from the mountains, they came across and again established themselves in Pare. Peace was not again broken for about two years, and during this period perhaps the most important event was the death of Vehiatua who died in peace at Tautira, but the remembrance of his cruelty to Mae was not permitted to rest in the same grave, Mae's son hearing the same name had vowed revenge, which was afterwards visited on the head of one of Vehiatua's descendants. Shortly after the death of this great warrior, Tutaha, uncle of Tu, and a more firey spirit than his brother Teu the ruling chief of Purionuu, resolved on avenging the former disastrous defeat. In opposition to the wishes of his brother he collected the Purionuu warriors and placing himself and Tu at their head he marched against the Taiarabuans, his old allies joining him as he passed through their districts. A battle was fought between these parties headed respectively by Tutaha, and Vehiatua son of the former chief of that name. The place where this battle was fought is variously stated some asserting that it was on Taiarabu and others that it occurred at Afaira near Papara. Whether it happened the event was again disastrous to the people of Purionuu, who were again beaten and driven to the mountains. Tutaha was killed in the battle by a man called Tehoaraau, and his body having been brought to the marae at Bunaania it was disemboweled, as an expression of great contempt, and hung upon the branch of a breadfruit tree which still stands, immediately adjoining the French fort. When the warriors returned to Taiarabu they carried the remains of Tutaha with them, to deposit on the marae at Tautira. This event was long remembered by the family and thirty years afterwards was avenged by Pomare II on a Taiarabu chief. So deeply is the feeling of revenge seated in the bosom of the savage. (Thomson, pp. 48–52)

The naval engagements described in this version are mentioned in no other source that I know of, and I am at a loss regarding their credibility. Such episodes as Vehiatua's trip to Ra'iatea and Pomare's defection from battle give the account the ring of authenticity; but its details concerning the scale, tactics, and sanguinary nature of the encounters were probably characteristic narrative modes used to dramatize any such tale. What interests us more than these matters, however, is this account's different version of the immediate cause of the conflict, and of the line-up of its combatant tribes.

According to Thomson, the contest was initiated by Vehiatua I because of his "hostile feelings . . . towards the chief and people of Porionuu" (p. 45). The basis of those hostile feelings is not specified, but in Thomson's version of the Papara debacle the Porionu'u were allied with Amo against Vehiatua. As for the tribal line-up, note should be taken of the report that Papara's Amo was allied with Vehiatua, his recent assailant, against chiefs listed elsewhere by Thomson as having been his loyal friends.

I alluded earlier to the importance of the question concerning how and where Tutaha's corpse was disposed of after he was slain in battle against the Seaward Tevans. The answer to that question should indicate in an unmistakable way not only who Tutaha's allies were, and how he was regarded by his enemies, but should also throw some light upon the remaining mystery about his kin ties outside Pare-Arue.[14]

As just quoted, Thomson's answer to the question was that the Seaward Tevans disemboweled Tutaha's body at the marae at Puna'auia (presumably the famed 'Oro-dedicated Taputapuatea on Puna'auia Point) — "an expression of great contempt" — and then deposited it on the marae at Tautira, evidently as a more permanent offering to 'Oro's presence at this latter marae. In connection with this version it should be noted that, while the Tautira marae was within Seaward Teva, the one at Puna'auia was in the territory of the Oropa'a, whom Thomson listed as allies of Tutaha!

In September 1773, when discussing the events that had transpired at Tahiti since his first voyage, Cook wrote that his old friend, Tutaha, lay "entar'd in the family Marai at Oparre" (Beaglehole 1961:213), that is, at Tarahoi. Four years later however, when Cook visited the "Great Morai at Atehuru," which has recently been identified as 'Utu'aimahurau, in Pa'ea, he wrote as follows:

We were told that the late King Tootaha, Tebourai Tamaida, and a nother Chief who fell with them were brought to this Morai, their bowels cut out by the Priests before the great alter, and the bodies afterwards buried in three different places, which were pointed out to us in the great pile of stones which compose the most conspicuous part of this Morai. And the Common Men who fell also in this battle were all buried in one hole at the foot of the pile. This Omai, who was present, told me was done the day after the Battle, with much Pomp and ceremony, and in the midst of a great Concourse of people, as a thanksgiving offering to the Eatua for the Victory they had obtained, while the vanquished had taken refuge in the Mountains, where they remain'd about a week or ten days till the fury of the Victors was over and a treaty set on foot that concluded with Otoo being invested with the Maro and made King which was done with great ceremony at the same Morai in the presence of all the principal men in the island. (Beaglehole 1967:205)

We cannot of course determine which of these versions is the "correct one" but again — as in the case of the discrepant versions of other "historical" episodes — we may infer something useful, however seemingly contradictory, from each of them.

It is interesting to note that 'Oro was looked upon as generally nonpartisan, evidently content to receive offerings from either side in a conflict. Whether Tutaha was disemboweled at Puna'auia's Taputapuatea or at Pa'ea's 'Utu'aimahurau, both these marae were situated in territory belonging to his allies in the war just concluded — which might indicate either that losers' marae were not sacrosanct, or that 'Oro-dedicated marae were not tribally exclusive, or both (or perhaps even that Tutaha's former allies were not unhappy to have him slain). And finally, it was evidently regarded as appropriate for this famed chief to be buried in his own kin-congregation marae, or alternatively just as appropriate to inter him in the principal marae of his victor.

In any case, whatever may have been the causes of this costly north-south conflict, and whatever may have been the actual battle line-ups or the fate of its casualties, Tahiti's political structure was markedly different at its end, both as a result of the conflict itself and of the natural processes of man's aging and dying.

New Alignments

Seaward Teva held together after Vehiatua I's death, but his young successor, the elder of his two sons, did not seem actively inclined to war or other forms of intertribal politics. Indeed, he appeared to have been heavily dependent upon his mother and her new consort, Ti'itorea, for counsel and initiative.

After Tutaha's death whatever coalitions had been put together either fell apart or became inactive, so that by the time of Cook's visit in 1773 there were on Greater Tahiti several tribes of fairly equal political strength — namely, Hitia'a, Pare-Arue, Fa'a'a, Puna'auia, Pa'ea, and Papara — together with several others of secondary strength that were politically affiliated with their stronger neighbors.

Hitia'a's famed chief Reti sided with Tutaha in the war with Taiarapu, and, although he is reported to have escaped Tutaha's fate, we cannot discover how long he lived thereafter. In any case, Hitia'a played little or no part in the island's political maneuvers during the next three decades, either because of distance from the centers of European influence, or of disinterested leadership, or both.

After their defeat by Vehiatua's forces, Amo and Purea retired from active intertribal politics. Although their distance from Europeans based at Matavai might explain the obscurity surrounding their existence, that alone cannot wholly account for the lack of references to them. Their son, Teri'irere, apparently retained the ceremonial privileges associated with his high-ranking Teva kin-Title, including the *maro* — either *ura* or *tea* — linked with it, but the family's other *maro* — the one I have labeled "*maro* Wallis" — was, along with the so-called Paparan image of 'Oro, evidently removed by Tutaha during the Papara debacle and deposited in the 'Utu'aimahurau marae of Pa'ea.

It is not clear just what part the Oropa'a people played in the Papara or north-south conflicts just described, but whatever it was neither Pa'ea nor Puna'auia appears to have suffered any major losses from those events. Puna'auia's tribal chieftainship remained in the hands of the huge and genial Pohuatea. Pa'ea's most prominent chief, Te To'ofa, had not figured in Wallis' journal or in accounts of the *Endeavour*'s 1769 visit, but on his subsequent voyages Cook came to regard him as the island's most impressive chief. Pohuatea and Te To'ofa were independent rulers of their respective tribes but were usually to be found in close alliance with each other in intertribal affairs.

Upon the death of Fa'a'a's chief, Te Pau "A", in the 1773 battle against Seaward Teva, his son, Te Pau "B", succeeded to his Title; but the most influential individual in Fa'a'a was Pa'ea's chief, Te To'ofa, whose unspecified kinship to Fa'a'a's principal family provided scope for his chiefly talents in this district as well as in Pa'ea.

While Tutaha lived, his grandnephew, Tu (Pomare I), had to rest content with the prerogatives attending his high rank-status, but upon the death of the former Pomare I began to exercise authority as Pare-Arue's tribal chief, de facto as well as de jure. As a tribe Pare-Arue was stronger in manpower than was Fa'a'a during the 1770s and 1780s. But even with the support of its semidependency, Ha'apape, Pare-Arue was inferior to Oropa'a both in numbers of warriors and in qualities of leadership — a circumstance that was undoubtedly well known to the whole populace of the island. Similar comparisons between Pare-Arue and Papara or Seaward Teva would probably reveal the same widely recognized disparities in tribal strength and leadership. In other words, in terms of both the tribe over which he ruled and of his qualities as a tribal ruler, other chiefs appear to have held Pomare I in rather low esteem during this part of the Early European Era. Nevertheless, despite his unimpressive reputation as a tribal leader, after the Papara debacle Pomare

I was universally acknowledged to be higher in rank-status than all other persons of Tahiti and Mo'orea.

First of all, through his maternal connection he was privileged to wear a feather girdle — the so-called Tetupaia *maro ura* — in his family marae of Tarahoi (although it seems quite clear that he could not, or so far as I know did not, wear this particular feather girdle elsewhere in Tahiti-Mo'orea). But in this respect he was no more highly privileged than Teri'irere, who exercised a similar right, with at least the Teva *maro*, in Papara. The titular prerogative which made Pomare I preeminent in Tahiti-Mo'orea derived from another rank-associated object, namely, the so-called Wallis *maro ura*, removed by Tutaha from Papara during the upheaval there and deposited in a Pa'ea marae, probably 'Utu'aimahurau. Why this *maro ura* was deposited in Pa'ea and not in Pare-Arue is difficult to explain. To begin with, although Tutaha probably had kin connections in Pa'ea his closest kin connections, and those of his grandnephew-protégé Pomare I, were with Pare-Arue's marae Tarahoi. One possible explanation is that the Oropa'a chiefs overruled Tarahoi as a depository, the price of their efforts in overcoming (or salvaging?) Amo.[15] Another possibility is that Tutaha deliberately preferred a Pa'ea depository, intending thereby to provide his grandnephew with a new base, in this stronghold of potential opposition, for exercising the extraordinary rights associated with this *maro*. Or finally, it may be that 'Utu'aimahurau's *established* position as a center of 'Oro worship (the most important one outside of Seaward Teva) was the decisive factor in depositing the *maro* there. (To the best of my knowledge there was at that time no image of 'Oro at Tarahoi.) The rationale for this last possibility requires some additional comments.

At the beginning of their respective careers as objects of social significance, feather *maro* and 'Oro images are implied to have been associated, if at all, in only indirect ways. For example, in traditions about the Farepua or Teva *maro* no mention whatsoever is made of 'Oro. And, more "historically," in statements concerning the *maro ura* brought by Tetupaia from Ra'iatea to Pare in the mid-eighteenth century, nothing is said of any 'Oro image or even of the god himself.

Conversely, traditions relating to the diffusion of 'Oro worship from Ra'iatea to Tautira, and then on to 'Utu'aimahurau, and so forth, specify 'Oro images but not *maro*. In fact, the only reported instance I know of wherein a *maro ura* and an 'Oro image diffused together from Ra'iatea prior to the European era, was that in which Manea and Maua introduced these objects into Papara, accompanied by Tupaia, the famed 'Oro priest. Since this occurred as recently as about 1760, and since previous diffusions of feather *maro* and 'Oro images seem to have been separate events, I am inclined to believe that the close connection which these two kinds of objects came to have in Tahiti-Mo'orea during the Early European Era derived from fairly recent developments, which I reconstruct as follows.

It is safe to assume that any person's investiture with a kin-Title required the "presence" of the congregation's principal tutelar; and if an image of the tutelar were on hand — a typical but perhaps not unexceptionable circumstance — that image constituted an important element in the ritual of investiture. In the case of feather-girdle kin-Titles such investitures also required the actual use of the *maro* itself, along with the "presence" of the tutelar. This much about kin-Title investiture seems reasonably certain.

Turning now to Opoan kin-Titles, and especially to feather-girdled ones associated with (or derived from) that congregation, although earlier investitures may have been sanctioned by the god Ta'aroa, by late indigenous times the god 'Oro had been assigned that role. Now, as noted above, no actual image of 'Oro seems to have been involved when Pomare I was invested in the feather-girdled Opoan kin-Title passed on to him through his mother, Tetupaia. On the other hand, his subsequent investiture with the so-called Wallis *maro* (and its associated kin-Title) evidently required the actual presence of the Paparan image (which had been taken to Papara along with what was probably the original section of the Wallis *maro*).

In other words, what previously seems to have been a general connection between all Opoan feather-girdled kin-Titles and the god 'Oro (in whichever of his manifestations locally prevailed) came to be superceded in social importance on Tahiti-Mo'orea by a specific connection between one such kin-Title (the Wallis *maro*) and one particular 'Oro image (the Papara *to'o*).

Newbury's statement that an 'Oro image ". . . was ceremonially essential for the investiture of Titles of Ra'iatean origin . . ." (1961:xxxvi) would seem to apply, by implication, to all prominent Opoan Titles; this may have been so, but the only specifically reported examples that I know of were investitures involving the Wallis *maro* and the Papara *to'o*. Indeed, it is possible that the requirement may have been "invented" on Tahiti — done, say, by Amo, Purea, and Tupaia in order to intensify respect for the wearer of the *maro*.

Having departed thus far from documentable generalizations, I am tempted to push my speculations a step or two further, this time concerning the reasons for the connections between feather girdles and 'Oro. These reasons, I suggest, are to be sought in 'Oro's attribute as principal god of war and in his congruous preference for human offerings. My theory is correspondingly twofold.

First of all, a god of war is a singularly appropriate tutelar for a tribe (in contrast, say, to a kin-congregation), and especially for a tribe that is held together by coercive force and is reduced or enlarged through armed conflict. If there is any truth in the conjecture put forward earlier, concerning the increasing role of warfare in the evolution of territorial units, then it is reasonable to assume a corresponding increase of attentiveness to the deities of war. In some instances the sequence may have been the reverse, with intertribal conflict incited by adoption of 'Oro worship; in fact, once started the two processes probably intensified each other — reinforced by 'Oro's reported desire for human offerings.

In my earlier discussions of human sacrifice I pointed out that 'Oro may not have been the only deity with this kind of preference, but during this era he was certainly the most demanding and insatiable one. Quite apart from any functional affinity between 'Oro's attributes as war god and as recipient of human offerings, for which a case could be made, I suggest that command over this explicitly ritual activity — in terms of when to sacrifice and whom — would have reinforced any chief's secular authority to a highly effective degree. (Since we do not know how a Maohi would have rated his own death by sacrifice as compared with other kinds of sanctions, I cannot of course characterize this sanction as the *ultimate* one in Maohi terms; but my hunch is that it was considered to be so.) Although many tribal chiefs probably had the power to execute fractious subjects from time to time, there were usually some implicit and fairly narrow restraints on the exercise of that power. How many fewer restraints there would have been, therefore, upon a chief who had not only the ideologically supported *right* to kill his own subjects, but the solemn *duty* to do so. Again, any tribal chief could and probably did on occasion rationalize an execution in these very terms, but all those phrased as offerings to 'Oro — that is, the majority of human offerings made during this era — required the ritual presidence of an individual invested in a *maro* consecrated by 'Oro. Moreover, the individual so invested was ipso facto a prime vicar to the god, a kind of ritual *and* secular double (as contrasted with an oracle [*taura*] or a cleric [*tahu'a*]). As I indicated above, I am not entirely certain which ones of the *maro* and 'Oro images in Tahiti-Mo'orea bore the ritual human-offering function just described, but as time passed the Papara image (and in the beginning, its associated Wallis *maro*) came to be the only ones so endowed. This, then, may help to explain why Tutaha was at pains to obtain control over these "symbols of supremacy" during the Papara debacle, and why the image played such an important part in subsequent events.

CHAPTER 27 *TAHITI AND MO'OREA*

From the position of Pare-Arue, Fa'a'a, Puna'auia, or Pa'ea (that is, Tahiti's west coast), Mo'orea is closer, more accessible, and a great deal more palpable than, say, Seaward Teva. The two islands had been for centuries closely linked through numerous kinship ties, with their usual train of alliances and feuds. It was inevitable then that the smaller island would have become embroiled in the political contests taking place on the larger one during this era, and especially those of the latter's western shores.

At the beginning of this era two kinship links between the islands turned out to be most significant, politically: the wife of Mo'orea's principal chief, Mahine, was sister of Papara's chief, Amo; and Teihotu, the husband of Mahine's sister Vavea, was brother of Fa'a'a's chief, Te Pau "A".

Another factor influencing political relations between the two islands was a long-standing state of hostility between Seaward Teva's chiefs and some, at least, of the chieftains of Mo'orea. Evidence of the latter is provided in a number of passages. For example, when Don Domingo Boenechea visited Pare in 1772 on his circuit of the island he met there a chief of Mo'orea, who with

. . . an eager assertion, backed by gestures of the most vehement and animated kind, [claimed] that . . . Titorea [a Taiarapu chief] and all his pack were thieves and robbers who went over to raid his island, and that on that account a state of war existed between them. The *arii* Tomegeui [Tomaheui, a local Pare chief] bore out what the Morean Chief had said, protesting that he had right on his side. (Corney 1913:320)

Some women decked in quantities of native cloth presented themselves before the Chiefs in order to strip themselves and make an offering of the cloth to the said Chiefs, being left with only a *maro* on to cover their nakedness. They call this festival a *taurua*, and after it they prepare for a *paraparau*, which is like a *tertulia* or well ordered conversazione of which the main topic is the wars these natives engage in against those of *Morea*. The Chiefs called to me to know whether perchance I would assist them against the *Morea* people, if occasion should arise; and when I replied that I could not do so without superior orders, they seemed surprised. (Corney 1919:43–44)

There was a consultation between the three principal councillors [of Vehiatua II] . . . as to what should be done with the vessel sent over by the *arii* of *Orayetea*

[Ra'iatea], and it was decided she should remain here [at Tautira] to do battle against the people of the neighboring Island of *Morea*. (Corney 1919:189)

> A person arrived from the island of *Morea* with orders from his *arii* to pick a quarrel, but he got no response whatever from the natives here [in Tautira]. (Corney 1919:155)

On the other hand, the hostility does not appear to have been entirely general, or continuous. For example:

> Some people of the Island of Morea who were on a jaunt came [to Tautira], and some glass beads were given to them. (Corney 1919:116)

> The liegemen of this *arii* set out for *Guayotihi*, an islet apart, to offer up prayers to *Eatua*, their God. They told us that the *arii* of the neighbouring island of *Morea* had caused certain persons to be killed who had treacherously murdered a native of this island of *Otahiti*, when it was not war time, and that he had sent the bodies over to Otu, in satisfaction, that he might offer them up in his principal *marae*. Let the truth bide its time. (Corney 1919:195–196)

Two versions exist concerning the immediate state of enmity between Mo'orea and Taiarapu. One is found in Thomson's *History*, and concerns a raid allegedly carried out by Vehiatua I sometime between 1761 and 1766. I reproduced this account in chapter 12, because of the light it casts upon Maohi warfare in general; its present relevance is the information it provides concerning the enmity between Taiarapuans and some Mo'oreans in particular, and concerning the character of Vehiatua I. With respect to the end of this account it should be noted that only part of Mo'orea was involved in this conflict, and further that Vehiatua had his enemies on Tahiti as well.

The second version concerning the immediate cause of the quarrel between Seaward Teva and Mo'orea was given by King, writing in 1777:

> . . . the ground of the present quarrel between the two Islands is this; that some years back the brother of Wa'heeatooa [Vehiatua III] named Tei-a'ree-tetooa a onnona, having some lands at Morea came to settle here, or as some say was sent as a chief in opposition to Maheine, which brought on a battle, where he, many chiefs of Otaheite & relations of his were kill'd. The Otaheitians enrag'd at this, set up Teree tapooe nooe [Teri'itapunui] against Maheine, although his own sisters son by one of the Eiree de hoi's [*ari'i rahi*; probably Pomare I] family. . . . (Beaglehole 1967:1382)

Cook's own, less detailed summary of what was probably the same informant's explanation is as follows:

> On our enquiring into the cause of the War, we were told that some years ago a Brother of Waheatua of Tierraboo, (a boy), was sent to Eimeo at the request of Maheine, a popular Cheif of that island, to be their King, but he had not been there a week before Maheine caused him to be killed and set up for himself, in opposition to Tieratabunue [Teri'itapunui] his sisters Son who became the lawfull heir or else was set up by Otaheite upon the death of the other. (Beaglehole 1967:198)

Parts of this account appear also in other journals:

When they [the Seaward Teva] see a mist rising over against an island near-by, named *Morea*, they believe it means that Teatua [te atua, i.e., 'Oro] wishes them to go and make war on the people of it: they are their greatest enemies, through having killed an *arii* who had gone across to take possession of some lands in that island, that he had inherited. . . . (Written in 1775, by Don Blas de Barreda in a letter to the Duchess of Medina Sidonia. Corney 1915:472)

The sons [of Vehiatua I and Purahi] were Whaeeahtua [Vehiatua II], Tettua-ooaowna [Tetua uaona?] and Warrooary [Varuari?]. The first died [in 1775], the 2nd was killed in Battle with Morea, and the 3rd became Erreerahigh and was no longer called Warrooary but Whaeeahtua [Vehiatua III] and is the present reigning King. (Bligh 1789:II, 63)[1]

Despite these specific references, Seaward Teva's involvement in Tahiti-Mo'orea conflict has been subordinated to western Tahiti's in most accounts of it. One reason for this was of course the Europeans' closer connections with the western districts of the island, from their vantage point in Matavai. Another was Fa'a'a's (and later, Pare's) direct entanglement in Mo'orea's succession controversy.

THE MO'OREAN SUCCESSION WAR

At the beginning of this era, Mahine, the principal tribal chief of northern Mo'orea, seems to have been the island's most powerful and influential individual — but one without any offspring of his own to succeed him. Mahine was also an Arioi, but whether this was the main reason for his childlessness is not known. Mahine evidently sought to keep control of his offices by fostering a boy, Tairihamoetua (?), and naming him successor. (I cannot discover what, if any, were this boy's kinship connections with Mahine.) But for unspecified though transparent reasons some of Mahine's kinfolk wished to name one of his sister's sons to succeed him. A glance at the Mo'orean genealogy (fig. 25–7, p. 1205) will reveal how seriously political this issue was likely to be.

As noted above, Mahine's sister, Vavea, was married to Teihotu, who was a brother of Fa'a'a's ruling chief (and subsequently uncle to the latter's successor). Thus the son of Vavea and Teihotu, Teri'itapunui, better known as Mahau, would have had strong claims, backed by strong supporters, to succeed his mother's childless brother. In addition, Mahau's elder sister, 'Itia, was married to Pare's Pomare I, and his younger sister, Pateamai, to Seaward Teva's Vehiatua III.[2]

The earliest record we have of any large-scale hostilities connected with this war of succession appears in Cook's journal for April and May 1774. I reproduce his comments in full, as they touch on many aspects of Tahiti's politics during this period.

In the Morning I set out for Oparre accompaned by the two Mr Forsters and some
of the officers to pay Otoo a formal Viset by appointment; as we approached Oparre
we observed a number of large Canoes in Motion; but we were surprised when
we got there to see upwards of three-hundred of them all rainged in good order
for some distance along the Shore all Compleatly equip'd and Man'd, and a vast
Crowd of Men on the Shore; So unexpected an Armament collected together in
our Neighbourhood in the space of one night gave rise to various conjectures: we
landed however and were received by a Vast Multitude some under Arms and some
not, the cry of the latter was Tiyo no Otoo and the former Tiyo no Towha, this
Cheif as we soon after learnt was General or Admiral of the fleet. I was met by
him presently after we landed, he received me with great Courtsey and then took
hold of my right hand. A Cheif whose name was Tee, Uncle to the King and
one of his Prime Ministers, had hold of my left, thus I was draged along as it
were between two parties, both declaring themselves our friends, the one wanted
me to stay by the fleet and the other to go to the King, at last coming to the general
place of Audience a Mat was spread on the ground for me to sit down upon and
Tee went to bring the King, Towha was unwilling I should sit down but partly
insisted on my going to the fleet but as I knew nothing of this Chief I did not
comply; presently Tee return'd and wanted to conduct me to the King and took
me by the hand for that purpose, this Towha opposed so that between the one party
and the other I was like to have been torn to pieces and was obliged to disire Tee
to desist, and to go with the Admiral and his party to the fleet. As soon as we
came before the Admirals Vessel two lines of Arm'd Men were drawen up on the
shore before her to keep of the Crowd and clear the way for me to go in, but
as I was determined not to go (unless forced) I made the Water which was between
me and the Canoe an excuse, this did not answer for a Man immediatly squated
himself down at my feet and offered to carry me in and then I declar'd I would
not go and that very moment Towha quited me without my seeing which way he
went nor would any' one inform me; I therefore turn'd back and inquired for the
King, Tee who I beleive never lost sight of me, came and told me he was gone
into the Country Mataou and advised me to go to my boat which we according
did as soon as we got all together for Mr Edgcumb was the only gentleman that
could keep with me, the others were jostled about in the crowd in the same Manner
as we were. When we had got into our boat we took our time to view this fleet,
the Vessels of War consisted of 160 large double Canoes, very well equip'd, Man'd
and Arm'd, altho' I am not sure that they had on board either their full compliment
of Fighting men or rowers, I rather think not. The Cheifs ie all those on the Fighting
Stages were drist in their War habits, that is in a vast quantity of Cloth Turbands,
breast Plates and Helmmets, some of the latter are of such a length as to greatly
incumber the wearer, indeed their whole dress seem'd ill calculated for the day of
Battle and seems to be design'd more for shew than use, be this as it may they
certainly added grandure to the Propsect, as they were complesant enough to Shew
themselves to the best advantage, their Vessels were decorated with Flags, Streamers
&ca so that the whole made a grand and Noble appeerence such as was never seen
before in this Sea, their implements of war were Clubs, pikes and Stones. These
Canoes were rainged close along side each other with their heads a Shore and Sterns
to the Sea, the Admirals Vesel was, as near as I could guess, in the center. Besides
these Vesels of War there were 170 Sail of Smaller double Canoes, all with a little
house upon them and rigg'd with Masts and sails which the others had not; These
Canoes must be design'd for Transporte or Victulars or both and to receive the

wounded Men &ca; in the War Canoes were no sort of Provisions whatever. In these 330 Canoes I judged there were no less than 7760 Men a number which appears incredible, especially as we were told that they all belonged to the districts of Attahourou and Ahopatea. (Beaglehole 1961:383–386.) [See frontispiece vol. 1, this work.]

When we got on board the Ship, we were told that this fleet was a part of the armament intended to go against Eimeo whose Chief had revolted from Otou his Lawfull Sovereign. (p. 387)

The King seem'd not only to pay the Admiral much respect himself but was desireous I should do the same, he was nevertheless certainly jelous of him, but on what account we knew not for it was but the day before he frankly told us the Admiral was not his friend. Both these Chiefs when on board to day Solicited me to assist them against the people of Tiarabou altho at this time the two Kin[g]doms are at peace and we were told go with their joint force against Eimeo. To this request of theirs I made an evasive answer which I believe they understood was not favourable to their request. (p. 388)

We had no sooner dispatched our friends than we saw a Number of War Canoes coming round the point of Oparre. . . . This fleet consisted of Forty sail, were equiped in the same manner as those we had seen before and belonged to the little district of Tettaha and were come to Oparre to be reviewed before Otou as those we had seen before had done. . . . (pp. 400–401)

When I was last here I conceived but an inddifferent Opinion of *Otou*'s Talents as a King, but the improvements he has sence made in the isles has convince'd me of my Mistake and that he must be a Man of good parts, he has indeed some judicious, sensible men about him who I beleive have a great share in the Government. I was sorry to see a jealousy subsisting between him and other great Men, he publickly told us one day that neither Towha the Admiral nor Poatatou, two leading Chiefs, were not his friends, this Shews that there are Divisions amongst the great people in this state as well as in Most others, probably this jealousy arose from their great power for Otou on all occasions seem'd to pay them much respect and so far as we knew they raised by far the greatest Number of Boats and Men to go against Eimeo and were two of the Commanders on the expedition which we were told was to take place five days after we sail'd. Oheatoua of Tiarrabou was also to send a Fleet to join those of Otous to assist him in reducing to Obedience the Chief of Eimeo. One would think so small an Island would hardly attempt to make head against the United force of the two Kingdoms but endeavour to settle Matters by Negotiation, but we heard of no such thing, on the Contrary every one spoke of nothing but fighting. Towha told us more than once that he should die there which in some Measure shew'd what he thought of it. Odiddy told me the Battle would be fought at Sea, in which case they must have a Fleet nearly if not quite equal to the one going against them and as this is not probable it is more likely they will remain on shore upon the defensive as we have been told they once did when attack'd by the People of Tiarrabou whom they repulce'd. Five general officers were to command in this expedition of which number Otou was one and if they named them according to the Post they held he was only the 3rd in Command, this seems probable enough as being but a young man could not have the experience necessary to command such an Expedition where the greatest Skill and judgement is required. (pp. 404–405)

Cook's view of this whole episode was warped by two assumptions, both of them false and both probably deliberately implanted by Pomare I's partisans. One was the notion that the expedition was intended to put down Mahine's "rebellion" against Pomare I, "his Lawfull Sovereign." The other was the idea that navies of the several tribes had come to Pare to be "reviewed" by their "King" preparatory to battle. No additional remarks are needed to establish the fallacy of the first of these assumptions; as for the second, the main purpose behind the assembly seems to have been to rendezvous, at what was the most convenient port of disembarkation, and possibly also to use this show of strength in an effort to persuade the reluctant Pomare I to add his contingent to the expedition.

Fa'a'a's commitment to this cause is easy to account for: namely, its support for Mahau, whose father was a member of the district's principal family (see fig. 25–5, p. 1187). This same connection also probably explains Te To'ofa's part in the affair — another instance of the influence of ties of kinship upon intertribal relations — for I know of no other reason for Pa'ea's hostility toward Mahine. As for Pohuetea's commitment of Puna'auia's forces to the expedition, again I know of no direct reason for his enmity with Mahine, and am left to conclude that it was based on his friendship with Te To'ofa and Te Pau, reinforced perhaps by his eagerness for a good fight and the possibility of spoils. I am similarly perplexed about the reasons for Ha'apape's (or, at least, Matavai's) participation in the preparations, and can offer no specific explanation.

By ordinary Maohi standards, Pomare I had a very good reason for taking part in the assault against Mahine — that is, he was either betrothed to, or actually married to, Mahau's sister, 'Itia. (He *may* also have had the additional reason of his sister Auo's betrothal or marriage to Mahau; but we cannot be certain when this connection was actually established.) Yet, there are grounds for concluding that Pomare I played little part in the campaign. Cook, it is true, stated that Pomare I would be "the 3rd in Command" of the forthcoming expedition, but no mention is made of any Pare forces. In fact, Adams went so far as to assert that Pomare I played no part at all in the expedition (1901:94), but this opinion may have been just another expression of Adams' systematic detraction of the Pomares.

Two explanations may be offered for Pomare I's conduct thus far outlined and for his role in events still to be described. One was the man's well-attested cowardice in the face of physical danger; even his greatest champions described him as "timerous" (Beaglehole 1961:206), "of fearful disposition" (G. Forster 1777:I, 327), et cetera — all confirmed by subsequent accounts of his reactions to threats and of his outright craven behavior in battle. The other explanation for Pomare I's conduct in this affair may have been his desire, based on his equally well-attested political canniness, to avoid a situation in which he would inevitably have been dominated by the powerful figure of Te To'ofa, in terms both of his own tribe's indifferent military strength (despite its larger population!) and of his own personal shortcomings as a military leader. Attention should be drawn to the statement that "Oheatoua [Vehiatua II] of Tiarrabou was also to send a Fleet to join those of Otous to assist him in reducing to Obedience the Chief of Eimeo" (Beaglehole 1961:405). No specific mention is made of a Taiarapuan [Seaward Tevan] contingent in the naval "review" just described, and I can discover no *direct* evidence one way or another that such a contingent actually took part in the subsequent attack on Mahine; on the other hand, the Seaward Tevans in general, and their chief in particular, had ample grounds for joining in the campaign. However, it should be noted that the intended participation of Vehiatua II in the cause against Mahine evidently did not induce Pomare I or Te To'ofa to embrace the Seaward Tevans as friends.

The only contemporary report that I know of on the outcome of the Tahitians' descent upon Mahine came from Cook and his companions, writing in August 1777, after nearly three years' absence from the islands:

The difference which subsisted between the two islands in 1774 as mentioned in my last Voyage has partly subsisted ever sence; the Armoment I saw at that time actually went against the Malecontents of Eimeo but returned without effecting much. (Beaglehole 1967:197)

We can only speculate about what went on between Mahine and his Tahitian adversaries during Cook's absence from the islands — at least, an uneasy truce seems to have prevailed; but when Cook reappeared on the scene the conflict became heated again. Shortly after the English arrived in Matavai in August 1777,

. . . some messengers arrived from Eimeo with an acco^t that the people in that island were in arms and that Otoos friends had been obliged to fly to the Mountains. . . . On the arrival of these messengers all the Chiefs that were at Matavai assembled at Otoo's house where I happened to be at the time. One of the messengers opened the assembly in a long and set speach, but little of which I understood any further than the general purport, he explained the situation of affairs in Eimeo and endevoured to excite the assembly to arm on this occasion. After this there was great debates on both sides which were carried on with great order, no more than one man speaking at a time but at last they became very noisy and I expected it would have ended like a Polish Diet, but I found they cooled as fast as they heated and soon returned to order, at length it was resolved to send a strong force to assist their friends at Eimeo: but this resolution was not obtained without some opposition. Otoo was silent all the time except now and then speaking a word or two to the speakers. Those who were for procecuting the War asked for my assistance and all of them wanted to know what part I would take. Omai was sent for to be my interpreter, but as he was not to be found I was obliged to speak for my self and told them as well as I could that as I was not throughly acquainted with the dispute and the people of Eimeo having never offended me I could take no part in it, with this declaration they either were or seemed satisfied. After this the assembly broke up, but before I left them Otoo desired I would come to him in the afternoon and bring Omai with me. Accordingly a party of us went, he carried us to his Father when the dispute with Eimeo was renewed. I wanted to have found out some method to have made up this breach and sounded the old gentleman on that head, but we found him deaf to any thing of that kind and fully determined to procecute the war and wanted very much to prevail on me to give them my assitance. (Beaglehole 1967:197–198)

T'towha [Te To'ofa] one of the Chiefs of Attahourou and a man of much weight in the island happened not to be at Matavai at this time consequently not present at any of these consultation, it however appeared that he was no stranger to what had happened and entered with more spirit into the affair than any other chief, for early in the Morning of the Ist of Sepr he sent to acquaint Otoo that he had killed a Man to be sacrificed to the Eatua, to implore the assistance of the God against Eimeo. This was to be done at the great Morai at Attahourou, where on this occasion Otoo's presence was absolutely necessary. (Beaglehole 1967:198–199)[3]

The line-up appears to have been much the same as in 1774, with Te To'ofa and Pohuetea spoiling for a fight, and Pomare I no more eager to involve himself or his Pare force than before (even though by this time his wife 'Itia probably added her forceful voice to the others' on behalf of intervention). Pomare I did lend his essential presence to a human-sacrificial service to 'Oro, imploring the god's help against Mahine, but he appeared less than eager to join in the atttack. In fact, as Cook perceived, sentiment was anything but unanimously in favor of war: ". . . I found there was three parties in the Island, one extremely Violent, one perfectly indifferent about the Matter and the third openly declaring themselves friends to Maheine and his party" (Beaglehole 1967:205–206).

Anderson's account provides a more connected summary of these events, including the differences of sentiment just noted:

We had enquird at Tiaraboo about the success of that expedition and were told that it prov'd fruitless, in so far that the inhabitants of Morea had retir'd to the mountains on the approach of the Ta'heiteans and the last return'd without effecting what they intended. Since that time we were told they had been at peace, but to day some people arriv'd with an account of a disturbance that had happened there wherein some partizans of Otoo had been worsted and fled to the hills for security. Upon this several of the principal people met and consulted what should be done but did not seem unanimous, as the debates were carried on with some warmth, though it would seem they at last concluded on going over to fight them as they were urgent with Captn Cook to grant them some assistance or go there with the ships.

This news however seem'd only to affect the few chiefs whose business it was to prepare for war; for the populace paid so little attention to it that their usual mirth was not in the least interrupted. The women, who it might be suppos'd would feel most on the occasion, were if any thing less concern'd than the men; for in the evening a great many of them having collected together stood upon the side of a small river near the middle of the Bay and exhibited a sort of dance that rather bespoke an excess of joy and licentiousness, though perhaps it might be their usual custom. (Beaglehole 1967:977–978)

The element of "indifference" extended to other domains of social relations, as Cook noted in a retrospective comment written while at Kauai (Hawaii):

There is something in the Police [civil polity] of these People wholly unintelligible to us — by their manner of talking I should suppose that Tu'mutta'ah'ra and Ta'ma'ha'no could not well meet without proceeding in some measure to hostilities, as they are doubtlessly now at open War with each other, but here I was mistaken. A circumstance of somewhat a similar Nature occur'd during our stay at Matavai: whilst Otu and many of the Arees of that part of Otaheite were at war with Imaio (as recorded in the Account of those times) many of the Imaio People would come to us and trade, the Otaheiteans would observe sometimes that they were ē'no (that is bad) but never offer'd to molest them in their business — though at Imaio old To'haw the Otaheitean Admiral with his Fleet were making all the devastation they possibly could. (Beaglehole 1967:579) [4]

These fragments bring into focus an aspect of Maohi society that receives little or no illumination in most of the sources. As I pointed out earlier, and as must be clearly evident to the reader by now, the Europeans who first recorded their observations about the islands concerned themselves almost wholly with the doings of "the Principal People," "the Better Sort." And for the most part this concern is true of the Maohis' own myths that survived long enough to be recorded: stories about gods, demigods, chiefs, heroes, and the like — and very little about the rest of the population. All this restricts us to a one-sided view of Maohi society, a shallow perspective, of course, but less shallow perhaps than would be the case of some society structured along less hierarchic, aristocratic lines. For, here in these islands the doings of "the Principal People" affected to a very decisive degree the fate of the populace at large. While recognizing this we should not, however, lose sight of that other part of the population, whose members provided the principal people with the resources for their political contests but who were most of the time individually unconcerned with their leaders' motives and social maneuvers.

Returning to the narrative, the supplicatory offering to 'Oro was carried out at 'Utu'aimahurau at the beginning of September. After that Pomare I returned to Pare, where discussions continued concerning the advisability of an expedition against Mahine. While these were still going on "T'towha, Potattow and another Chief were already gone with the Fleet of Attahourou, for a messenger arrived in the evening with an account of their arrival and that their had been some skrimishing without either loss or advantage on either side" (Beaglehole 1967:210). After this, wrote Cook, Pomare, ". . . who never entered heartily into the spirit of this war . . . receiv'd daily messages from Towha importunating him to hasten to his assistance, who we were told was surrounded by Maheines fleet, but neither the one nor the other durst hazard an engagement'' (Beaglehole 1967:211–212).

But instead of joining his allies at Mo'orea, Pomare I led his forces in an impressive and colorful naval review at Pare. As one Englishman noted: ''We have much parading with the war Canoes, and the Admiral (Toohaw) [Te To'ofa] is gone to Emio with 30 Sail of War Canoes, but Otoo does not seem disposed to fight nor does any of his brothers. — & many of the Chiefs say he is a Coward'' (J. T. Bayly, p. 13, quoted in Beaglehole 1967:211n).

The ''Paradings'' were interrupted on September 22 by news from Mo'orea that Te To'ofa and his companions had concluded a peace with Mahine and had returned home: ''Soon after we got their [to Pare] a Messenger arrived from Eimeo and related the terms of the Peace or rather a Truce for it was for a limited time. The terms were disadvantagious and all the blame fell upon Otoo for not going to assist Towha in time'' (Beaglehole 1967:214).

No record remains of the actual fighting in Mo'orea, but from subsequent observations it appears that the Tahitians had moored their vessels off Opunohu for several days and had destroyed some of the nearby settlements, without, however, engaging Mahine's forces in a decisive battle of any kind. Later, when Cook himself visited this part of Mo'orea, and inflicted similar damages in a punitive effort, one of his men referred to the destruction as ''. . . these Losses together with those they suffered by Admiral Tohaw, are very heavy . . .'' (Beaglehole 1967:232n).

A passage from King's journal records the immediate reaction to the news of the Mo'orea truce:

. . . upon this intelligence all warlike preparations [at Pare] ceas'd & the Canoes went away to the Etward. We however proceeded to Oparre, & found Otoo & the Royal family in Violent agitation on the late news; Otoo's Sister & Mother told Capt that Towha was so inrag'd at his conduct that he & the Tyarra'boo people [5] were determin'd to wage war against him, & they appeard much to dread this event, imploring our assistance. Otoo's father on the other side was as violent against the rash proceedings of Towha, foreseeing the advantages that woud have happen'd in their expeditions going seemingly under our protection; in the midst of these heats a Messenger came from Towha & laid a plantan branch at Otoo's feet, & repeat'd his message; which we understood was requiring Otoo to go & perform some ceremony at Attahooroo, at the Royal Marea, they call'd it Heeva E'ree . . . (Beaglehole 1967:1377)

It is impossible to say whether Te To'ofa's irritation with Pomare I was due to the latter's nonfulfillment of a prior agreement or refusal of an emergency plea for aid, but it must have been a chief-size dudgeon! ''The old Admiral [Te To'ofa] was Irritated to a Degree of Madness, he Abused him [Pomare I] Every where and was very glad to get any of us to Listen to him He would Curse Ottou for an Hour to gether and Foam At the Mouth with rage'' (Home, Ottihiti, quoted in Beaglehole 1967:211–212n).

The terms of the truce were regarded as unfavorable to the Tahitian principals' interests, but there is no specific record of what those terms actually were.[6] From subsequent events, however, and from the nature of the quarrel itself, we may conclude that Mahine permitted Mahau to continue his rule over Mo'orea's Varari district, while retaining authority over most of the rest of the island for himself and his protégé, Tairihamoetua (?). Later, when Cook arrived at Mo'orea and expressed the wish to see Mahine, ''. . . it was not till after much invit'ing that he quitd his Canoe & ventur'd on board, & then with evident mark's of fear; & mentioned immediately to the Captn that Otoo was his Chief to whom he would submit'' (King, in Beaglehole 1967:1382). Like most other Maohis, Mahine probably acknowledged Pomare I's ceremonial preeminence, but his talk of ''submitting'' to Pomare I as ''his Chief'' was undoubtedly based on his fear of Cook's guns and knowledge of the latter's championing of Pomare I. In his subsequent conduct toward Pomare I, this independent-minded chief expressed anything but submission to the Pare *ari'i*.

The ceremony held at 'Utu'aimahurau to formalize the truce with Mahine was attended by Te To'ofa, Pohuetea, an unnamed Seaward Teva chief, a representative of Mahine (reputedly his brother), and Pomare I. Despite the contempt and bitterness the other Tahitian principals may have had for Pomare I, his presence at the ceremony was indispensable, inasmuch as validation of the truce, by 'Oro, required a human offering, over which only Pomare I, as wearer of the distinctive Wallis *maro*, could officiate. (It was for this specific purpose, I believe, that Te To'ofa, at the crest of his rage, sent a plantain leaf to Pomare I, and not as a sign of general reconciliation.) The ceremony itself was witnessed by King, in Cook's stead; in view of the fact that it included most of the principals of the war under consideration, and that it is one of the few records left us of a specific, as opposed to a generalized account of such a ceremony, I reproduce Lieutenant King's description in detail.

It was Sunset when we embarked in a Canoe and left Oparre, about 9 oclock we landed at Tettaha at that extremety which joins to Attahourou; before we landed the people called to us from the shore, probably to tell us that Towha was there. The meeting of Otoo and this Chief I expected to be curious and worth seeing; Otoo and his attendants went and seated themselves on the Sand close to the Canoe in which Towha was. On the Servants of this cheif wakening their master and mentioning Otoo's name, immediately a plantain tree and a Dog were laid at Otoo's feet, and many of Towha's people came and talked with him, as I conceived about their expedition to Eimeo. After I had remained for some time. seated close to Otoo, and not perceiving Towha to stir from his Canoe, nor hold any conversation with

us, I went to him. He asked me if Tooti was angry with him, I told him no, that
he was his Taio and that he ordered me to go to Attahourou to tell him so. Omai
had a long conversation with this Chief, but I could gather no information of any
kind from him. On my returning to Otoo, he seemed pressing that I should go
to eat and then to sleep. Accordingly Omai and I left him. On questioning Omai,
he said the reason of Towha's not stiring from his Canoe was his being lame, that
presently Otoo and he would converse together in private, this seemed true, for
in a little time those we left with Otoo came to us, and about ten minutes after
Otoo himself came and we all went to sleep in his Canoe. The next morning the
yava was in great plenty. One man drank so much that he lost his sences, I should
have supposed him in a fit from the convulsions he was in; two men held him
and kept plucking off his hair by the roots. I left this spectacle to see a nother
more affecting, this was the meeting of Towha and his Wife and a young girl that
I understood to be his Daughter; after the ceremony of cuting their heads and discharg-
ing a tolerable quantity of blood and teers, they washed, embraced the Chief and
seemed unconcerned. But the young Maids punishment was not yet to an end, Terry
Derry came and she went with great composure to perform the same ceremony to
him she had to her Father. Towha had brought a large War Canoe from Eimeo,
I enquired if he had killed the people belonging to her, and was told there was
no men in her. We left Tettaha about ten or eleven and landed close to the Morai
at Attahourou a little after noon. There were three Canoes hauled up opposite the
Morai with three hogs exposed in each; the sheds had something under them which
I could not discern. We expected the Ceremony to be performed the same afternoon
but as neither Towha or Potattow came nothing was done.

A Chief from Eimeo came with a small pig and a Plantain tree and placed
them at Otoo's feet, they talked some time together and the Eimeo chief often mentioning the words *Warry warry* ('false') I supposed that Otoo was relating to him
what he had heard and that the other denied it. The next day (Wednesday) Towha
Potatow and about eight large Canoes came and landed near the Morai, many plantain
trees were brought on the part of different Chiefs to Otoo. Towha did not stir from
his Canoe. The Ceremony began by the first Priest bringing out the Maro wrapt
up, and a bundle shaped like a large fidd; these were placed at the head of what
I understood to be a grave, then three Priests came and sat down opposite and at
the other end of the grave, bringing with them a Plantain tree the branch of some
other tree and the Sheath of the flower of the Cocoanut tree.

The Priests, with these things in their hands seperrately repeated some thing,
and at times two and sometimes all three sung a Melancholy ditty little attended to
by the people. This praying and Singing continued for an hour; then, after a short
prayer, the high priest exposed the Maro and Otoo got up and wrapt it about him and
held in his hand a Cap or Bonnet made of the red feathers of the Tail of the Tropic
bird and other dark feathers. He stood in the Middle space facing the three Priests
who continued their prayers for about ten minutes; when a man started from the
Crowd, said something which ended with the word *Heiva* and was answered by the
Crowd *Earee* three times, and this as I was told before, was the principal part of the
ceremony. The Company now went to the opposite side of the great pile of stones,
where is what they call the Kings Morai, which is not unlike a large grave. Here the
same ceremony was performed over again and ended in three cheers, the Maro was
now wrapt up and increased in richness by a small piece of red feathers which
one of the priest(s) gave Otoo while he had it on and which he stuck into it. From
this place the people went to a large hut close by the Morai, where they sat themselves
down in much greater order than is usual among them. A Tierrabou man then made

an Oration of about ten Minutes, he was followed by an Attahourou man, afterward Potattow spoke with much greater fluency and grace than any of them, for in general they spoke in short broken sentences with rather an awkward motion of the hand; Tuteo Otoo's orator spoke next and after him a Man from Eimeo. Two or three more speaches were made but not much attended to. Omai said that the Speaches declared that they should not fight but be all friends. As many were warm it might possibly be some recriminations and protestations of their good intentions. In the Middle of their speaking an Attahourou man got up with a Sling fastened to his waist and a large stone held on his shoulders, with this he marched in the open space repeating something in a singing tone. After parading near a quarter of an hour he threw the stone down. This Stone and a Plantain tree that lay at Otoo's feet were, after the debates ended, carried to the Morai and one of the priests and Otoo with him said something on the occasion. On our return to Oparre the Sea breeze set in which Obliged us to land and we had a pleasant walk through almost the whole extend of Tettaha to Opare, a tree with two bundles of dried leaves suspended from it was the boundary of the two districts. The Man who had performed the Ceremony of the stone and sling came with us, with him Otoo's Father had a long conversation, he seemed very angry, I understood he was enraged at the part Towha had taken in the Eimeo business.

From what I can judge of this ceremony it had not been wholy a thanksgiving as Omai at first told us, but rather a solemn confirmation of the Treaty or Truce, or perhaps both. (Beaglehole 1967:215–218)

Thus ended the Mo'orean Succession War — for the moment, at least. For, as King reported in his description of the battle's aftermath, Te To'ofa and his allies rankled at Pomare I's dereliction and vowed publicly to punish him. Cook's version of this threat, and of his reaction to it, are worth reproducing; his own warning proved to be a potent factor in political events of the next few years:

The terms [of the truce] were disadvantagious and all the blame fell upon Otoo for not going to assist Towha in time. The current report was now, that Towha assisted by the forces of Waheatua would, as soon as I was gone, come and fall upon Otoo; this called upon me to support my friend by threatening to retaliate it upon all who came against him when I returned again to the island, if there was any truth in the report at first this had the desired effect, for we heard no more of it. (Beaglehole 1967:214)

Thus was formulated a more or less "official" English policy which was to have a very material influence upon the political developments of the next four decades. For, just as Wallis had made a "Queen" of Purea, and Cook a "King" of Tutaha, with the latter now dead the principal personage in the vicinity of Matavai, namely Pomare I, was duly given that label, and was courted with official courtesies and innumerable valuable gifts. In the person of Tutaha the visitors had a man of unmistakable coercive authority and wide political influence — a real "king" in the civil, temporal sense of the word. In the person of Pomare I they at first recognized his shortcomings and limitations in civil affairs, but acknowledged, as did most Maohis, the preeminence of his rank-status. But Cook, through his warning, had managed to increase Pomare I's authority in civil affairs far beyond the point warranted by the latter's own resources. We cannot tell the extent to which Cook's promise of support, along with the other English attentions, served to enlarge Pomare's own ambitions, but these factors undoubtedly improved the chances of their ultimate realization. Some historians appear to imply that this "official" policy adopted by the English visitors came about unwittingly, almost wholly the result of the use of Matavai and Pare anchorages. This may indeed have been so in the beginning, but a case could be made that later voyagers (and even some of the earlier ones) fostered this policy deliberately and with eyes wide open.

To the ritual-minded Maohis the numerous courtesies extended to Pomare I by the English — including the daily associations, the meals on board, the royal salutes, et cetera — must have added some luster to his already preeminent rank-status. The large quantities of English gifts that passed through or ended up in Pomare I's hands, provided him with unmatchable resources for rewarding supporters and for courting the loyalty, or at least the neutrality, of other chiefs. And, with Cook's promise of armed support, Pomare I was provided with the means of complementing his rank-status and gift-bribed cooperation with coercion-sanctioned *authority*.

Needless to say, the peers of Pomare I were unhappy about these goods in the hands of an individual whose personal qualities some of them held in contempt; but they were compelled by Cook's unequivocal warning to bide their time.

Cook's party left Matavai shortly after the truce ceremony just described and made their way to Mo'orea. There they met Mahine, as earlier described, and experienced anew the frustrations of trying to recover stolen property — in this case some goats. Cook himself became so deeply involved in this matter, and his temper so enflamed, that he had his men destroy numerous houses and canoes in an area already damaged during Te To'ofa's campaign. Eventually Mahine was prudent enough to see that the stolen property be returned, and he even voiced his intention to continue "submission" to Cook's protégé, Pomare I; but he too was simply biding his time.

TE TO'OFA'S REVENGE

Cook, of course, never returned to Tahiti. In fact no European vessel put in there for about eleven years,[7] at which time Bligh, Christian, and the others of that famous crew turned up on H.M.S. *Bounty*, intent on collecting a cargo of breadfruit plants for Jamaica, where it was hoped they would answer the planters' need for a cheap staple for their slave labor. H.M.S. *Bounty* remained at Matavai from October 26, 1788 to April 4, 1789; during this time Bligh faithfully kept a journal whose usefulness is enhanced by virtue of his prior experience on the island, gained in 1777 as master aboard Cook's *Resolution*.

The visitors found Pomare I in a sorry state. The *ari'i* was described as "... a Man only nominally possessed of power, or otherwise he has not abilities to govern, which may be the Case, as the Cheifs revile him upon all occasions" (Bligh 1789:I, 375). As for his formerly populous and prosperous district, Bligh reported:

The extensive Houses that we have seen before are no where to be found, and every habitation seems to have no more pains taken with it than to make it answer its use. They are nothing but small light sheds, the largest of which taken by the four corner supporters, might be taken away by four Men. Their large Cannoes also are gone except two or three, so that I imagine the injury these People have sustained is very great. (1789:I, 379)

What had happened was reported to Bligh by Pomare himself:

He said that after five Years and three Months, from the time of our sailing, counting 63 Months, the Imeo People joined with Tettowah, (the noted old Admiral called by Captain Cook Towah) and made a descent at Oparre . . . that after some resistance by which many Men were killed, he and all his People fled to the Mountains. The People of Imeo and those of Atta-hooroo under Tettowah now being masters of all their property, destroyed every thing they could get hold of, among which were the Cattle, Sheep, Ducks, Geese, Turkeys and Peacocks left by Captain Cook in 1777. (p. 378)

Evidently Cook's warning had had its effect — for five years at least. Then Te To'ofa, probably concluding that Pomare I's friends would not return, descended upon Pare as he had threatened to do. Taiarapu seems also to have joined in the attack, and although Fa'a'a and the northeastern districts are not specified as having participated in the actual fighting — indeed, their forces would have been superfluous — they certainly did not offer any comfort to Pomare I. (Bligh pp. 396–397)

We cannot be certain that Mahine's forces actually joined with Te To'ofa's in attacking Pomare I, but they played a major part in the latter's rout. Each of the chiefs had his own grievances against Pomare I, but it may seem surprising to see them as allies, in view of Te To'ofa's previous espousal of Mahau's claims against Mahine, and of his own earlier attack upon Mo'orea. Nevertheless, it appears that these two chiefs' shared antagonism against Pomare I overrode their differences regarding the Mo'orean succession. Te To'ofa's grievance is well documented: a general resolve to deflate Pomare I's unwarranted political pretensions, and a particular desire to punish the latter for his conduct during the earlier Mo'orean campaign. Through inaccurate but comprehensible reasoning Mahine probably blamed Pomare I for the destruction meted out by Cook on Mo'orea, in the episode of the stolen goats (Bligh 1789:I, 378). But in addition, Pomare I was doubly identified with Mahine's rival, Mahau, by virtue of Pomare I's marriage to the latter's sister, 'Itia, and of Mahau's own marriage to Pomare I's sister, Auo — for both of these unions were evidently established by 1782, the approximate time of the attack upon Pare.

Although Mahine's (and Te To'ofa's) forces lay waste to Pare and forced Pomare and his family to flee, the Mo'orean chief himself was slain, reportedly by Pomare I's younger brother, Vaetua (who as a consequence was "esteemed as a great Warrior") (Bligh p. 411).[8]

Mahine was succeeded in his tribal chieftainship by his adopted son, Tairihamoetua (?); Mahau retained his office as chief of Varari, in northwest Mo'orea, and an uneasy peace prevailed between the two. Meanwhile, Pomare I's relationship with Tairihamoetua (?) was hostile but fairly quiet; when Bligh asked the former about this he was told that they were still at variance and that ". . . if an Otaheite Man went to Imeo he would be killed, and the same would be done at Otaheite [read, Pare] by a Man from Imeo" (1789:I, 378–379). As an indication of this relationship, Bligh attended a *heiva* performed at Pomare I's direction as "publick mark(s) of honor as a reward for publick or meritorious Services" in honor of a Pare warrior who had happened to be "ill used" while on a visit to Mo'orea (1789:II, 61).

Te To'ofa, Pomare I's other principal antagonist, evidently died shortly before Bligh's arrival, but his son and successor appears to have sustained the father's hostility toward the Pare *ari'i*.

According to Bligh, "The inhabitants also of Tiarraboo had made some attack on this devoted place [i.e., Pare] . . ." (1789:I, 397); and from what Bligh could learn at Matavai their hostility had not abated — a somewhat surprising state of affairs inasmuch as 'Itia's (and Mahau's) sister, Pateamai,[9] was probably by then married to Seaward Teva's *ari'i*, Vehiatua III.

Pohuetea, whom Bligh also characterized as one of the island's "great Personages," invited the English to visit Puna'auia but would not travel to Matavai, "such is the Mutual jealousy of these People" (1789:II, 77). Indeed, about the only influential chief on Tahiti not hostile to Pomare I at this period was Te Pau"B", of F'a'a'a, and even this relationship appeared threatened:

Tynah [Pomare I] was uneasy on account of Teppahoo being ill at Tettahah, who he esteems above all other of his friends. He tells me that when Teppahoo dies the district will then join with Attahooroo and fight against him, as the Erree then will be a Brother of Teppahoos, (he having no Children) who is a great enemy to him. (Bligh 1789:II, 48–49).[10]

During the five-months' visit of H.M.S. *Bounty*, Pomare I's many enemies carried out no overt attack against him (perhaps because of the ship's presence at Matavai), and Pomare I did his best — or rather, Bligh's best — to conciliate them:

As I make it my study to do every thing for the good of our Friends here [i.e., Pomare I and his family], I have therefore to establish peace around them as I consider it their greatest blessing, given Tynah the power of making Friends if possible by presents. In consequence all his late powerful enemies have received presents, Saws, Shirts and many other things, this however I fear will but whet their inclinations for War as soon as I am gone; he is nevertheless apparently anxious to conciliate their regard, in which I am happy to assist. (Bligh 1789:II, 38)

There is no better way of summarizing Pomare I's political predicament than by quoting another statement of Bligh's, which, in addition, shows how faithfully the conscientious lieutenant continued to carry out the policy of "king making" so clearly enunciated by his former captain, James Cook:

There is a great deal due from England to this Man and his Family; by our connections with him and them we have brought him numberless Enemies. Their elligble situation for our Ships has brought us intimately connected with them, and by this perhaps we have not only sown the seeds of discord but of revolution. On one side he has Attahooroo disposed to attack him, and on the other Tiaraboo ready for a total extirpation of his Authority, while he has an Enemy equal to the other two in Imeo (or Morea) who will venture anything buoyed up by their former Successes. All those I am confident will on my leaving this Place make a joint Attack on this part of the Island, and these poor people will have no resource but to fly to the Mountains and defend themselves there. It will certainly be against them, my not taking vengeance on the Attahooroo and Morea people for taking the Cattle and destroying part of them, and was it not for the particular trust that is reposed in me to complete the Undertaking I am sent on, I would certainly adopt such means as to oblige those people to repent of their incursions.

I hope however, and have given Tynah and all the principal People reason to think, that they will never be forgot by us, because it will at any period or case be justifiable in England to support the Otow family, and they have shown that faith and Affection to the Erree no Pretanee, as their expression is, ·as demands all our Assistance and utmost efforts to defend them. If therefore these good and friendly people are to be destroyed from our intercourse with them, unless they have timely assistance, I think it is the business of any of his Majestys Ships that may come here to punish any such attempt. (1789:II, 28)

When H.M.S. *Bounty* arrived at Tahiti, Pomare I exercised secular authority over Pare-Arue, and at least western Ha'apape; but the label of *ari'i rahi*, and the prerogatives and duties associated with *maro ura* rank — presumably with both the Tetupaia and Wallis *maro* [11] — had already been transferred to his eldest son and successor, whom I shall call Pomare II.[12]

According to Bligh's account, 'Itia had borne five offspring to Pomare I. The first, a female, was slain at birth, Pomare I having been an active Arioi at the time (1789:II, 56; I, 387, 389). The second, a male born about 1783, was, as had been his father, generally called Tu (Pomare I having relinquished this name and become Tina). The third, a female born about 1784, was named Teri'i na Vaho Roa. The fourth, a male born about 1786, was named Teri'i Tapanoai (?), and the fifth, a female born about 1787, was named "Tahamydooah" (Tahamitua?). During Bligh's *Bounty* sojourn these "royal" progeny dwelt with their attendants in a set of households apart:

I do not often speak of Otoo [O Tu, Pomare II], for his being a Child and kept out of our way we have of course no intercourse with him. I however see him perhaps once a Week and the other Children, but we never come nearer each other than 30 or 50 yards. At those times I carry them some little presents and by this Means they are always rejoiced to see me. The River separates their dwelling from the part we are at, and it would be considered as a great violation were we to cross it near their dwelling. There are two Brothers and two Sisters but they do not eat or sleep under the same Roof. On that account the Girls have a House about ¼ of a Mile from their Brothers. Each of them are situated on the side of a pretty River which has its source out of a Rock on the side of the Hill near Otoo's House. The Parents sleep every night at the Girls House, but are mostly absent from them in the day. (1789:II, 56)

With these children also lived the two offspring of Pomare I's sister, Auo, and the latter's husband, Mahau; and, according to Bligh, these latter ". . . have similar marks of Attention & respect paid to them" (p. 56).

Turning now to other members of what Bligh was pleased to call "the royal family," old Teu (Hapai) and his wife Tetupaia ("Oberreeroah") were still alive, but evidently wholly retired from engagement in political affairs. Of their three surviving daughters, the eldest, Te Ari'i na Vaho Roa (also called Tetua Nihura'i) still presents something of a mystery; I am fairly well convinced that she had married Teri'irere, *ari'i rahi* of Papara (now become Temari'i), but she evidently bore him no children and seems to have dropped out of sight by 1788, probably through death. The next eldest daughter, Ari'ipaea Vahine, resided in Ra'iatea and was not in evidence during Bligh's stay. The youngest daughter, Auo, who was married to Mahau of Mo'orea, seems to have divided her time between her husband's Varari district in Mo'orea, and Pare, where, as just noted, her children lived.

Of the four sons of Teu and Tetupaia, the condition of the eldest, Pomare I, is well documented. During Bligh's visit to Matavai, Pomare I's next younger brother, Ari'ipaea (Te Ari'i Fa'atou), was residing with his wife nearby; concerning the relations of these two brothers Bligh was informed that

. . . Tynah and his Brother Oreepyah were on bad terms and that they would quarrel and fight as soon as I sailed. I have observed some coolness between them and knew they did not heartily like one the other, on every opportunity therefore I had endeavored to make them friends, but it has had no effect. This dislike has arisen from the disagreement of the Two Wives. (1789:I, 407)

That the two wives in question had disagreements should occasion no surprise — both having been strong-minded, ambitious personalities, from familes of divergent political interests.

Pomare I's next younger brother Vaetua (Te Tupai e te Ra'i, Maiore, Paiti), resided in Ha'apaino'o, but spent much time at Pare, where he seems to have distinguished himself to Bligh mainly through his steady consumption of kava. The youngest son, Te Pau "C", eventually succeeded to tribal chieftainship of Fa'a'a, but during *Bounty*'s sojourn he remained little noticed by the English.

The newest person of note to appear on the Matavai scene during Bligh's visit was Ha'amanemane, also known as Tuteha. The first reference to this man, who was to play a very important role in Tahitian politics, appears in Bligh's journal under date of November 4, 1788: "A Cheif of much consequence and related to Tynah [i.e., Pomare I] has been here these two days from Ulietea [Ra'iatea]. He is called Toota-ah" (1789:I, 385). Ha'amanemane was also known as Mauri. About four months later Bligh described "Toota-ah" as being ". . . generally with Tynah, he is a Priest and considered to have great Knowledge" (1789:II, 45). Ha'amanemane was a brother of Pomare I's mother, Tetupaia, and was evidently forced to flee from Ra'iatea during that island's wars with Porapora. As we shall see he came to have a weighty influence over Tahitian affairs.

CHAPTER 28 *WARS OF THE*
BOUNTY MUTINEERS

What happened to Lieutenant Bligh and H.M.S. *Bounty* after leaving Tahiti is of course widely known, but, as Adams put it:

What Bligh said to Christian, and what Christian said to Bligh, and what Peter Heywood said to both, and how Thursday October Christian made his dramatic appearance at Pitcairn Island, and a thousand other details of the picturesque story, have been told a hundred times, and always to interested audiences; but no one has taken the trouble to tell how great an influence Bligh and his mutineers exercised over the destinies of Tahiti, and especially of its old chiefs. (1901:98)

After setting Bligh and his closest supporters adrift in the ship's launch off Tonga, on April 28, 1789, the mutineers returned for a brief visit to Tahiti in June, to collect livestock and some Maohi companions, and then sailed for Tubuai where they hoped to settle.

The next European vessel to call at Tahiti was the Swedish brig *Mercury* (Captain Cox commanding), which remained at Matavai from August 12 to September 2, 1789. One of the *Mercury*'s officers, Lieutenant George Mortimer, compiled an account which, while recording no change in the island's political situation, does supply some useful confirmatory details. He wrote, concerning Pomare I and some members of his family:

We remarked that his [Pomare I's] subjects paid him very little respect, and seemed under no kind of restraint in his presence, every dirty fellow entering freely into conversation with him; indeed, were it not for the distinction of being fed, and that the women sometimes uncover their shoulders in his presence, it would be difficult to tell him from any of his people. (1791:30)

Otoo [Tu, Pomare I] happening to see a pair of scissars, with a long chain suspended to them, given by our second mate to his [Pomare I's] wife, had a great desire to possess them, and demanded them of her; but she positively refused to give them up: upon which he fell a-crying, and was not to be pacified till he obtained a pair like them. After this, he gave us another proof of the childishness of his disposition, by employing a man for two or three hours in sewing additional buttons down the back and on the flaps of a coat Mr. Cox had given him. His wife Etea is a clever sensible woman, and the only one of her sex permitted to eat in the presence of the men: she makes use of a knife and fork nearly as well as an European; and she is fond of tea. Her Majesty is likewise an excellent shot, and hit our buoy the first time she fired, with a single ball, though it lay at a considerable distance from the ship; she having first taken the musket from Otoo, who was afraid to discharge it. (pp. 31–32)

The men [of Mo'orea] made us a tender of their women, and seemed to think it a necessary proof of our friendship that we should accept their offer. The ladies on their part seemed to have no aversion to comply with the requests of their husbands and relations, not excepting her Majesty. This did not surprise us after what we had heard at Otaheite: for we were there informed that Otoo's wife made no scruple of granting her favours to some of the great chiefs; and that Otoo sometimes solaced himself with his brother Orepia's wife, which she acknowledged, and seemed to think an honour. (p. 44)

. . . we were frequently troubled with the company of a younger brother of the king's named Widouah [Vaetua], a very impudent, dissolute young man. (p. 45)

The principal matter of interest to us in this journal is an account of the officers' three-day excursion to Mo'orea. There they met Varari's chief, Te Ari'i Tapu Nui (i.e., Mahau) and his wife (presumably Auo, the younger sister of Pomare I), along with a boy identified as their son. Mahau himself was described as ". . . a tall, stout, good-looking man, speaks but little, and seemed to be of a timid disposition" (p. 38). Then, on the return trip they stopped at Opunohu Bay, where they witnessed a brief skirmish between some of Mahau's partisans and what I assume was a small force of Tairihamoetua's people. The whole incident attests to resumption, or continuation, on Mo'orea of the long-seated war of succession.

Later in September 1789, the *Bounty* mutineers returned to Tahiti after having met with a hostile reception at Tubuai, and then the ship sailed almost immediately again for what turned out to be Pitcairn Island; this time, however, sixteen of their number elected to remain at Tahiti. Until March 1791, when the survivors of those who remained on Tahiti were sent back to England on H.M.S. *Pandora*, the ship sent out to capture them, they played important, probably decisive roles in Tahiti's political affairs. Of great good fortune for the historian and student of Maohi society, one of the mutineers who survived was James Morrison,[1] who compiled an account of his stay on the island, along with a most valuable description of many other aspects of Maohi culture, from which earlier chapters in the present work have abundantly drawn.

The sixteen mutineers met with a very hospitable reception in Matavai and Pare, and at the beginning most of them elected to settle there. Soon, however, two of them responded to a general invitation from Vehiatua III and went to live in Taiarapu, and another moved to Papara at the invitation of Temari'i (the then current name of Teri'irere). Of those remaining in Matavai-Pare some embarked upon the difficult undertaking of building a schooner in which they hoped to reach Batavia, and thence find passage to England.

Throughout their stay the mutineers saw much of Brown, the seaman left ashore by the *Matilda*, but most of them remained wary of him. Brown, however, proved far less troublesome to his compatriots, and to the Maohis, than did Churchill, the *Bounty*'s master-at-arms, who, in fits of temper, killed or wounded several Maohis and who managed to become a "chief" for a brief period before he himself was murdered.

It is not possible to discover the whole range of relationships obtaining between this wide assortment of aliens and their Maohi hosts. Each of the former seems to have had close, *taio*-like, relations with one or more Maohis (usually with upper-class ones), and many of them also had Maohi mistresses. The fact that they were in general so hospitably and deferentially treated, despite their obvious weakness in numbers and armaments, is undoubtedly due to a number of reasons. Great value was evidently attached to their presumed knowledge and technical skills, particularly with respect to warfare. Moreover, the well-founded expectation that other European vessels would in time appear and revenge mistreatment of them probably exercised some constraint, but there seems also to have been other, less tangible factors at work. I have already pointed out how generally hospitable the Maohis were toward aliens who happened to land on their shores. Exceptions of course occurred, but by and large a stranger cast ashore on one of these islands stood a better chance to be fed and left unharmed than would have been the case in many other South Sea archipelagoes. And finally, in addition to the numerous instances of sincere friendships formed between individual Maohis and Europeans during this first quarter century of contacts, there seems to have developed a respect for certain Europeans, which in the case of James Cook reached the dimensions of cult veneration.[2] Whatever the reasons behind individual cases, some Maohi chiefs competed to secure the friendship and services of the European castaways — and well they should have, in view of subsequent events.

The first of these events took place in early March 1790, when Mahau set out from Mo'orea with canoe loads of hogs and tapa for the youthful Pomare II. When rumors circulated that a force of Oropa'a was planning to waylay the expedition, Morrison and some of his compatriots were sent for to frustrate the attack. Their appearance under arms had the desired effect and the attack never materialized (Morrison 1935:89); and thus it was that part of the mutineers became actively identified with Pare, and the ambitions of the Pomares.[3] Others of the *Bounty* people, however, became associated with the Pomares' rivals in Seaward Teva.

Early in their stay, two of the mutineers, Churchill and Thompson, moved to Seaward Teva, where the former became *taio* and principal aide to Vehiatua III. In fact, the relationship was so close that when Vehiatua III died shortly thereafter, in mid-March 1790, and without issue, his supporters elected Churchill to succeed him; but this troublesome man did not live long to enjoy his position. Within a month he had quarrelled so violently with Thompson that the latter killed him — and was himself killed by Churchill's supporters to avenge the death of their new "chief." After this unsuccessful experiment the Seaward Tevans reverted to their usual practice and named a nephew of Vehiatua III to succeed him (the exact nature of the kinship tie is not reported). As the successor was only about four years old at the time, his father was appointed regent for him.

Meanwhile, it is interesting and somewhat surprising to learn that during all these proceedings, and for some months previously, Pomare I was living on the peninsula, in the district of Afa'ahiti (Morrison 1935:76, 96). According to the latter's reports to Morrison he was treated "very uncivil" by the people of Seaward Teva, but evidently not to the extent of making his life intolerable. The land on which he resided, described as "some possessions given to himself," is not further specified, but may well have been some estate inherited from his father's mother, Tetuahuri, who was the daughter of an earlier Vehiatua. Pomare I's major object in remaining in this uncongenial situation was, as he expressed it, his ". . . hopes of gaining a party in his Sons favour" (p. 96). In view of Vehiatua III's lack of issue, and of Pomare I's descent from the Vehiatuan Tetuahuri, his own son was undoubtedly eligible for consideration as a successor to Vehiatua III. The Taiarapuans' general hostility toward Pare's principal family was probably responsible for their passing over Pomare II, but the reason they gave was that, in their belief, Pomare II was a bastard, having been sired by his mother's commoner paramour, and not by Pomare himself.

The next episode of political significance involving the mutineers occurred during the early part of April 1790:

In the Mean (time) the Morea People haiving rebell'd against Mottooarro, Chief of that Island & Brother-in-law to Matte, he sent to us to know if He should send his arms over to quell them, to which We agreed, but told Him to send His own people to use them; and Heete-heete being present was appointed to the Command. The Arms being brought to us we Cleand them and put them in order when they set off and Arriving at Moria soon brought them to subjection, Heete-heete having himself killd the Inspired Priest of the Rebels and their Chief, (the adopted Son of the late Maheine) Tayreehamoedooa, forced to fly to Attahooroo, leaving the Island in posession of Mottooarro whose right it was, but from which he had been kept by Maheine his Uncle and His party, till the Bounty had Saild in April 89, when he having formed a strong party was Calld Home from Taheite where he then resided and having strengthend his party from Taheite was admitted as Joint Chief with Tayreehamoedooa who now became Jealous of His power, and had taken up arms to drive him out again, but the fire arms gave Mottooarro such strength that He was forced to relinquish all Claim & fly to Taheite for refuge. From Attahooroo he went to Papaara where Tommaree gave him land and where he now resides private with His Mother & Aunt (Wa Vaheine) who was the Wife of Maheine deceased. (Morrison 1935:92–93)

Thus in one brief action the seventeen-year-long Mo'orean Succession War was brought to a conclusion favorable to Mahau, and hence to the Pomares.

The mutineers' firearms were probably decisive factors in the conflict, but the hero of the action was Hitihiti, the well-known man who had accompanied Captain Cook on his southern swing in 1773 and 1774, and had since become principal aide to Pomare I. Hitihiti was also Pomare I's uncle-by-marriage, but whether this relationship preceded or followed his occupational attachment to Pomare I is not recorded. The skills and knowledge Hitihiti acquired during his seven-months' service with Cook probably account for his prominent position in Pomare I's entourage, because he does not appear to have been otherwise gifted.[4]

Tairihamoetua's (?) right to refuge in Papara evidently derived from his "aunt," Mahine's widow, who was the sister of Papara's Amo. From these circumstances it would seem likely that the principal people of Papara were maintaining their posture of hostility — or at least coolness — toward the Pomares, but such apparently was not the case. For example, under the date of March 1790, Morrison recorded that two of the mutineers had gone to Papara to live, and that Pomare I raised no objections to the arrangement, inasmuch as he was "in alliance" with Temari'i (Teri'irere), the Chief of Papara (p. 91). Elsewhere, Morrison recorded that Pomare I's brother, Ari'ipaea, was visiting Papara. This introduces a set of events not specifically reported by any contemporary, on-the-spot observer, but presented in Adams' history as reliable oral traditions of Papara's chiefly family.

The gist of Adams' account, abstracted from intricacies too confused, ill founded, and irrelevant to concern us here,[5] is that the young Papara chief, Teri'irere-Tamari'i, became more sympathetic to the aspirations of the Pomares than his parents had been — more specifically, to those of the young Pomare II. Adams proposed that this change in sentiment was affected mainly by Pomare I's brother, Ari'ipaea, whose wife was Amo's niece.[6] Ari'ipaea was undoubtedly friendly with Teri'irere-Temari'i, and may have contributed to the improved relations, but one will also recall that the latter's first wife was Pomare I's eldest sister, and his mother was 'Itia's father's sister. While ties of kinship were no warranty of amicable relationships, as must by now be clear, they cannot be dismissed as irrelevant.

However it came about, relations between Pare and Papara were such in mid-1790 that the warriors of these two districts fought more or less simultaneously to defeat a common enemy, even if they did not join together to fight as close allies. The next set of events in Tahiti's political history commenced in September 1790:

> September 12th. this Day a Messenger arrived from the Young King desiring our Immediate Assistance to quell the People of the District of Tettahah who had rebelld, and made an inroad into Oparre, burning all before them; the Messenger also informd us that the Oparre people had repuls'd them forcing them to leave two of their Dead behind them which were brought to the Young Kings Morai, and that they were preparing for another attack, being set on by the People of

Attahooroo. — he told us also that areepaeea-Waheine the Young Kings Aunt who had been at Ryeatea for some years, was arrived at Oparre with a Numerous Fleet which were all ready for War. (Morrison 1935:100)

The Ari'ipaea Vahine referred to in this passage was none other than Pomare I's elder sister. (Morrison elsewhere described her as Teu's and Tetupaia's eldest offspring.) I cannot discover what induced her to return to Tahiti — perhaps only to pay a visit to her family — but the presence of her entourage could not have been better timed.

More inexplicable is the fact of Tetaha's (Fa'a'a's) ''rebellion'' against Pare. To begin with, this small district on Pare's southern border could not have ''rebelled'' against the Pomares because it had not been under their domain. On the other hand, since the death of Te To'ofa some years earlier, Fa'a'a's relations with the Pare chiefs appear to have been more friendly than otherwise. The matter is complicated by the question of the identity of Fa'a'a's chief (or chiefs) at the time of this ''rebellion.'' In March 1789, it will be recalled, Pomare I revealed to Bligh his uneasiness over the ill health of Fa'a'a's chief, and Pomare I's friend, Te Pau ''B'', stating that if the latter died he would be succeeded by his (Te Pau ''B's'') brother, who was an enemy of Pomare I. When Bligh returned, some three years later, he found Te Pau ''B'' to have died, and the chieftainship of Fa'a'a held by Pomare I's youngest brother, Te Pau ''C'' (1792:135). Another limiting date was provided by Morrison, who in a passage yet to be reproduced, reported that upon the defeat of the Fa'a'a ''rebels,'' in September 1790, the Oropa'a victors appointed Mahau, then chief of Mo'orea, to the Fa'a'a chieftainship. In other words, unless Te Pau ''B'' had turned against his friend Pomare I, between March 1789 and September 1790, for which there is no evidence whatsoever, it appears likely that Te Pau ''B'' had died prior to the ''rebellion,'' and that his place had been taken by someone hostile to the Pomares — probably the unnamed brother whose enmity Pomare I had earlier reported to Bligh.

Morrison's account of the next chapter in this conflict continued:

As we did not know that ever we should be able to effect our purpose, tho evry thing was getting forward, we found it necessary for our own sakes, to assist them, and therefore returnd for Answer that we should be at Oparre Next morning — and Armd Accordingly. On the 13th, leaving one to take Care of the Schooner, We marchd to Oparre, where Areepaeea-Waheine received us, and a Dressd Hog was presented to us. — Byrn & Ellison being at Tetooroa and Musprat on a Visit to Papaara with his Friend Areepaeea, we were now only Eight in number, but were here Joind by Brown, who informd us that the Attahooroo people had made war on Tommaree; which was further Confirmd by a Letter from Burkett desiring our assistance. Having made our breakfast we proceeded to Tettahah Surrounded by a Multitude (with Poeno & Pyeteea two Chiefs at their head) from Maatavye.

Before that we had proceeded half a Mile We found the Marro Eatooa or Signal for War (which is several Fathoms of Cloth in one piece passd round several Trees, crossing the path several times) and a Hog tied to each tree which the Marro passes round; this is generally Put up with some Ceremony, and the Enemy are defied to take it down.

On seeing this our party ran instantly and seized on the Marro & hogs, when the Enemy who lay conceald till now, made their appearance, and a Fray instantly commenced and Several heavy blows exchanged before We were observed by them — on our approach they Fled, but this Confused Method of engageing prevented us from knowing our own people, who were so scattered that we were not able at a Distance to tell them from the Enemy and we were therefore of No use but to look on while the Enemy retreated to the Mountains & our party returned with a deal of Plunder, & several Canoes which they had not been able to remove. We Now informd the Chiefs that they must alter their mode of Fighting, and bring their people under some Command, in Case they should have occasion to go to war again which they promised to do; and having Demanded Matts to make sails for the Schooner, we took our leave of Fatowwa, or Areepaeea Waheine, and returned to Maatavye. (1935:100–101)

About a week later the conflict started up again:

Mean while the Tettahah & Attahooroo people had united their forces & were began to Commit Hostilitys both on Papaara & Oparre, and on the 20th we were demanded to assist again, which for our Credit we could not refuse, nor was the Sails any excuse, as we were wanted on Shore, and the Enemy looking on our peaceable inclination as the effects of Fear, sent us word that they would Come to Maatavye & burn the Schooner and a Challenge sent to each Separately by their Warriors, who bid us defiance, telling us that each would have his man to Carry to the Morai, and much more such language. — they had also entered Oparre again burning and destroying all before them.

On the 21st early in the Morning, we got into our Canoes and paddled to the Lower end of Oparre. Here we were Met by Poeno, Tew, & Fatowwa, and almost all the Men of Maatavye with Pyeteea, & Mattaheyapo at their head who were both principal men & their head Warriors. We were now but Eight in Number, and having given the Chiefs such directions as we thought necessary, they promised to observe them, and being willing to take the Cool of the Morning, we set forward in Good order, surrounded by Multitudes of all ages from both Districts, but the Maatavye men kept Close to us, claiming the preeminence, and keeping the others in the rear. — on our approach the Enemy retreated to a high steep eminence in the Mountains, which Commanded a narrow pass, which was the only one by which they could be approachd, and as this place had resisted all Former attacks, they had got all their property to the place in readiness, & had formd an encampment of Huts ready to dispute the Pass; however we determined to proceed, as we could not hope for Peace without driving them from their strong hold: but it being some miles up in the Mountains, it was Noon before we got near enough to see the pass & the situation of the enemy, who we found well posted. The heat became so intense that we should have been in a bad plight had not our friends brought with them plenty of Cocoa Nuts which we found very refreshing and tho we had Marchd at a slow pace, we now stood in great need of — having halted a few minutes we proceeded to the Pass, which was along a Narrow ridge where two men could scarcely pass in safety. — the Taheiteans made a full stop when they came to the place but seeing us proceed they followed, and Pyeteea & Mattaheyapo came in the Van to be our guides over. — in crossing the pass we found ourselves open to their Stones with which they plyed us briskly from the Eminence above our heads, where our Musquets would not reach to do execution — tho we were forced to walk over at an easy rate for one Hundred yards or more, none of us except Coleman was hurt, and he only received a blow of a Stone in the leg which did not disable him — however his Taheite friend received a blow between the Mouth & Nose that brought him down, & having English Cloaths on was Mistaken for one of Us and they gave us a loud Shout & redoubled their Vollies of Stones, by which upwards of twenty more we(re) wounded before we could.fire a Shot. However we got over and with a warm fire advanced up the Hill; when they soon gave way. As soon as this was observed by our Party they rushd in, & three of the Enemies Head warriors having fallen by our shot they fled; and our party persued them down the other side of the Mountains. Mean time the Plunder of their Camp was seized by the Oparre Men, the Maatavye people being more intent on driving their Enemies; the Chief part of their Houses being burnt, and distroyd, we returned in the evening to Maatavye. The Number of Hogs taken here were incredible; several of the largest died with the fatigue of coming down, their own weight & fat being more then they Could support. (pp. 102–103)

I cannot identify the exact location of this battle, but infer from later events that it was in Fa'a'a, and that the defenders were largely Fa'a'a men. Also, it is reasonable to conclude that the Pare-Matavai forces would not have won the engagement without the firepower and leadership of the eight Englishmen. It remained to dispose of the larger forces of Puna'auia and Pa'ea:

. . . the Party in Attahooroo, being Yet in arms, the Young King was desirous that we should assist him to quell them, and force them to restore the Marro-Oora, or Royal sash, together with the Morai Tabbootaboatea, being the Movable place of sacrafice; — the Pehharaa or Sacred Chest wherin their Images are kept with the Valuables belonging to the Deitys; the Farre 'Atooa, or house of God, with several other things which belongd to them, which the Father of the Present T'towha Chief of Attahooroo had taken in war from oToo or Matte and which had been kept in Attahooroo ever since, but we found it so fatigueing that we Got the Sails ready in Order to Shorten our marches. — We had by this time between 6 and 7 hundred weight of fine Pork Salted, & got it on board, and having bent the sails and Got our Amunition on board, on the 26th we saild for Oparre leaving the Houses in charge of the Natives with what things We did not want and leaving only Skinner in Maatavye who was bad with sore eyes which made our Number still but Eight. At Oparre we found Heete-heete who had come from Papaara where he had been with Burkett & Sumner Who with the Assistance of Muspratt, Brown & Himself had repulsed the Attahooroo & Tettahah people with a great slaughter but as they would not submit to Tommaree, they Had Sent him to us to desire that We would keep them in play and appoint a day to let the Armies of Papaara & Tippirreonoo meet in the Center of Attahooroo. We kept Heete-heete and armd him with one of Matte's Musquets. — we found at Oparre a large Fleet assembled under the Chiefs of Tippirreonoo, who inform'd us that they waited our Orders. the Canoes with provisions being arrived from the different districts and the Morning of the 27th being Calm the Canoes drew up in a line and took the Schooner in tow. The line consisted of 40 Canoes paddling 50, or 60 hands; they had pieces of Painted Cloth

hoisted on the Sterns of each, & Drums beating & flutes playing made a very war
like show the Warriors Cutting a Number of Capers on their Stages, being dressd
with Featherd headdresses & all in their best Apparal, the smaller Canoes being
kept at a Distance on each side the line began to move forwards within the reef
towards Attahooroo. Mean time Multitudes Went a head by land, and the beach
appeard Covered all the Way as we passd. As we entered the enemys Country,
they fled to the Mountains, and our party on shore persued them, Burning the Houses,
and destroying the Country where ever they Came by rooting up the Plantains &
Tarro, and notching the bark round the Breadfruit Trees to stop their Growth, and
laying all in ashes before them. About Noon we anchord at Taboona, part of
Attahooroo, under Pohooataya, the Same known to Captain Cook by the Name
of Potatow. The Canoes were here hauld up, and an encampment made with the
roofs of the Houses, which had escaped the fire, or that had been spared for that
purpose. We were now informd, that the Enemy had posted themselves in a Strong
hold in the Mountains, and Could observe them with the glass going up in large
bodys to the place where they intended to stand a Siege. — A Council of War
was now held, and finding it would be difficult to approach them, it was agreed
to send out several partys to burn the reeds on the Sides of the Hills to prevent
them from approaching unseen, or laying in ambush for any Stragling party. Heete-
heete was appointed to this business, and in the mean time Ambasodors were sent
to demand a Surrender, and a White Flag was hung out on board the Schooner
and an(other) sent to be stuck up at about 2 miles distant. During the time the
Hills were burning several Skirmishes took place between our party & theirs; but
Heete-heete having the Musquet with him always repulsed them, and they were
forced to retire to their Strong hold, as we did not approve of their destroying the
Trees the partys were Calld in and placed to look out and Heete-heete always caused
one or More of His party to Cry out 'alls Well' in the best Manner they Could
pronounce it every half Hour on Notice being given on board the Schooner, for
which purpose, we fixed one of the Hoops of the Ships Anchor stock to serve as
a Bell, striking it with a hammer, and this was repeated by all who happened to
be awake in the Camp, which together with Continual fires which were kept burning
all night, served to shew the Enemy that we were always prepared for them.

   In the Afternoon of the 29th we observed a White Flag coming down the Hill,
and orders was given not to Molest any who came with it, and before Sunset the
Chief Pohooataya with his Wife, attended by a Priest bearing the Flag, came to
the Camp. A Council was now held of the Chiefs & Principal Men; when it was
determined that peace should be made, on Condition that evry thing should be restored
to the Young King; and that the Chiefs of Attahooroo should acknowledge him as
their Sovereign. To all which Pohooataya agreed, & with His Wife Came on board
the Schooner as hostages for the performance of his part. — but as several of the
things were in posession of the other Chief T'towha, messengers were sent to Him
to demand them, with orders to tell him if they were not produced in 24 Hours
that He might expect no quarter. In the Night Came Burkett from Papaara, and
told us what dispositions were made there, and We informd him how we intended
to proceed if Tetowha was obstinate and having appointed the time for storming
him on both sides Burkett return'd to Papaara. He inform'd us that Te'towha had,
in their attack, been forced into the Mountains & had several killd & wounded.

31*st*. This Morning we were informd that Te'towha had pass'd by in the Night,
and was gone to Oparre with the Royal Marro which he intended to present to
the Young King in person, and hoped to get Peace by it alone without surrendering

the Morai &c. — as soon as we knew this, a Double Canoe was got ready, and Millward was sent to bring Him to the Schooner, which he did in the evening. — the same Day passd by Areepaeea and Muspratt, from Papaara, they Calld on board, and Areepaeea made each a present of a Hog & a piece of Cloth, and set forward to Oparre to get ready for us. When T'towha came on board, he seemd apprehensive that we intended to kill him, and made his fears known to Pohooataya, who Cheerd him up, telling him that he knew the English better, and that for Captain Cooks sake they would not suffer either of them to be killd. When we knew his fears we told him He should not be Hurted, telling him that Englishmen never used those ill who the Chance of War made their Prisoners; at which he seem'd easy, and promissed that evry thing in his posession should be restored, and that He would submit to evry thing we demanded in favour of the Young King. — T'towha's friends soon Came after him to the Schooner, and he gave them Orders to go and Bring evry thing that belongd to the Morai; which they Obeyd. (pp. 103–106)

Thus it was that the proud and fierce Oropa'a fell before the combined forces of the Porionu'u and the Paparans, and their English supporters. On the basis of Morrison's description of the battles, the only one we possess, I am bound to conclude that they would have ended either in stalemate or in a victory for the Oropa'a had the English not been engaged. In view of the nature of Maohi politics the verbal promises of submission exacted from the Oropa'a chiefs would probably have been no more durable than the length of the Englishmen's stay on the island, but their obligation to transfer the Wallis *maro* and the Papara 'Oro image and associated objects from 'Utu'aimahurau to Pare constituted decisively tangible evidence of a shift in political strength. Thenceforth, the young Pomare II would have in his immediate possession two of Tahiti-Mo'orea's three most potent emblems of preeminent rank-status — the Tetupaia and Wallis *maro*, along with the principal receptacle of the god 'Oro, whose avatar was essential for validating the wearing of the Wallis *maro* and for transmitting the human offerings required to gain that god's fullest support. (In other words, whereas Pomare II had previously been required to travel to 'Utu'aimahurau to exercise his exclusive right, and duty, to officiate at offerings of human victims to 'Oro, he now was able to do so at Tarahoi.[7] The transfer was carried out in short order, as were some other political dispositions resulting from the war:

On the 1st of October the Canoe bearing the Morai, Ark &c. — was brought and deliverd into charge of the Priests of Maatavye and Oparre; who proceeded with her directly to Oparre, and Orders were now given for the Fleet and Army to return home, when they accompanied the Sacred Canoe escorting it Carefully to Oparre, and in the afternoon a breeze springing up we Weighd, having Poeno & the Two Attahooroo Chiefs, and run up to Tettahah where we anchord for the Night, and weighd at 9 Next Morning the 2nd. here we were Joind by Burkett and Oammo [8] who came to assist at the Peace and Worked up to Toa Roa harbour where we anchord in the afternoon where we landed the Chiefs and Went with them to the Morai, where the Peace was Concluded, and by our advice they were continued in posession of their Land; and Paa, and Old Chief who was out of Commission, was put into the District of Tettahah as a Substitute for Mottooarro to whom it was voted, the Attahooroo Chiefs promised on their parts that they would always honor the Young King as their Sovereign, and by way of strengthning the Peace each of them took one of us as his Friend. Great feasting now took place a Volly of Small arms was fired on the occasion and all the Chiefs of Taheite Nooe or Substitutes for them attended. Much feasting now took place, & on the 4th we weighd and workd up to Maatavye, where we arrived by Noon. (Morrison 1935:106)

We learn from a later passage that a new temple was built adjacent to those already constituting the Tarahoi marae complex at Pare, for accommodating the 'Oro image, and so forth, brought from 'Utu'aimahurau (p. 116).[9]

The fact that the Oropa's chiefs, Te To'ofa "B" and Pohuetea, received such leniency, with respect to their lives and their lands, may have been due to the mutineers' counsel to the victors, but I suspect that it was also in tacit recognition of the likelihood that Pare and Papara would not have prevailed without the mutineers' assistance. Now and then in Maohi wars noblesse oblige may have served to temper a victor's treatment of his helpless adversary, but such niceties were not ordinarily observed when the stakes were as high as in the conflicts now under consideration. The likelihood of Pare and Papara maintaining their advantage over the Pa'ea part of the Oropa'a was improved shortly thereafter by the death of Te To'ofa "B"; as noted earlier, having no heirs of his own this young chief was succeeded by the four-year-old son of his sister, who was made regent for him (Morrison 1935:107).

Another item of considerable interest in the passage just reproduced is the one regarding the chieftainship of Fa'a'a — that is, the victors replaced the incumbent, whoever he was, with Mahau, now the unchallenged chief of most of Mo'orea, and named a "retired" minor chief, Pa'a, as Mahau's locum tenens. Mahau's appointment to this office was, of course, the result of his close ties of affinity and political alliance with the Pomares; his claims to the office derived from his consanguineal ties with Fa'a'a's chiefly family — his father having been a younger brother of Te Pau "A" and he himself thus first cousin to Te Pau "B", who had evidently succumbed by this time.

It should be noted that in the campaign just concluded, the victors had depended upon their handful of English friends not only for firepower but for tactics and combat leadership as well.

Now that the trappings of highest rank-status and the principal avatar of supernatural efficacy were concentrated at Pare, it remained to use them to consolidate and perhaps even extend the newly won political authority and influence. An opportunity for doing so was provided by the formal inaugural rites still to be held for the young Pomare II. As a preliminary to the main ceremony, the standard (*vane*) of the young *ari'i* was carried around the island, in order that each tribe's chief pay ritual obeisance to it, thereby expressing recognition of the young *ari'i*'s supremacy. As I indicated earlier, I am not certain whether this type of formal recognition referred only to the *vane* owner's rank-status or to his political paramountcy as well. In the present instance it probably was intended to refer to both. Morrison was visiting in Papara when the flag reached there.

> While I was here the Young Kings Flag arrived, and was received by Tommaree and Conducted to His Morai, but they kept by the Beach close down in the Surf till those who Carried it were abreast of the Morai, when they turnd short round and proceeded to the Morai — as the Flag passd, the Inhabitants hid themselves, and all Fires were put out — we attended them to the Morai, where Tommarees priests having set the Flag up, made the Usual peace Offering of a Hog and a Plantain tree, the Priests repeated it and several young Pigs & Plantain Trees were Offered with long Harrangues and Tommaree made a long speech declaring Toonooeaiteatooa to be his Chief, and ordered a feast to be provided for those who bore the Flag — this Flag was the Union Jack which they had got from Captain Cox, and was Slung a Cross the Staff with a stick in the tabeling as we sling a Pendant, it was decorated with Feathers Breast Plates Tassels &c. — as the Chief People of the District were present, we honord the Ceremony by firing our Musquets, — which was received as an honor, and some of those who were present interpreted this into a declaration on our part to support it in Circumventing the Island, as it was Composed of English Collours, and they made no scruple to say that War would be instantly made on those who should attempt to stop it.
>
> It was kept one Night in the Morai, during which time prayers were Constantly saying by one or other of the Priests which attended it; and when it proceeded they returnd to the Water Side, where they had before been, & proceeded along by the edge of the Surf towards Tyarrabboo. (1935:114–115)

The Captain Cox here referred to was skipper of the brig *Mercury*, which had called at Matavai some sixteen months previously. I do not know whether the Union Jack in question had been incorporated into young Pomare II's *vane* with the deliberate intent of symbolizing English support for the Pomares' pretensions, but it evidently was so interpreted.

From Papara Morrison went on to Taiarapu, where he visited Pomare I (now going under the name of Mate) at the latter's residence in Afa'ahiti:

> He [Mate] now informd us that the people of Tyarrabboo had used him very uncivil, altho the Flag had been received, and passd with all the Ceremonies; which he said was only for fear of us and not their regard to His son. He told us that we had yet a right to Chastise them for Killing Thompson, and said that if we once made our appearance in Arms in Tyarrabboo they would never make any resistance and he would be at the Expence of the Amunition, that his Son might be Sole King, he also told us that he had conversed with Tommaree who was ready to furnish Men & Canoes when ever we thought proper to take it in hand.
>
> Having told him that we would Consider of the Matter we signified our intention to go homeward. (p. 115)

Back at Pare Morrison found large numbers of people assembled to attend the approaching ceremony, including Mahau (of Mo'orea) and, in Morrison's words, "all the principal Men of the Island." The rites took place on February 13, 1791. (I reproduced this passage earlier but do so again because of its direct relevance to the events now under discussion.)

> This day the Ceremony of Investing the Young King with the Marro Oora or Royal Sash took place; the Sash is of fine Network on which Red and Yellow Feathers are made fast, so as to cover the netting; the sash is about three yards long, and each end is devided into six tassels of Red Black & Yellow feathers, for each of which they have a name of some Spirit or Guardian Angel, that watches over the Young Chief while the Marro is in his Posession and is never worn but one day by any one King; it is then put into the Sacred Box and with a Hat or Shade for the Eyes Made of Wicker & Covered with feathe(r)s of the same kind and never used but on the Same occasion it is delivered to the priests, who put it Carefully by in the Sacred House on the Morai, where no person must toutch it. (p. 116)

This was evidently the *maro* whose original section, at least, was introduced into the Pomare family by Pomare I's Ra'iatean mother, Tetupaia. I cannot vouch for Morrison's interpretation of the significance of the tassels; nor is there any direct evidence that I know of to support Gunson's suggestion that each tassel stood for each district over which Pomare II exercised "spiritual hegemony" (1964:57). But, to return to the ceremony itself:

> This Ceremony was performed at Oparre on the New Morai which was built for the reception of the Movable Morai &c. which we had brought from Attahooroo and where these things were now kept. The Chiefs (or their Substitutes) of Tipperroonoo and Morea attended, and Toonooeaiteatooa the Young King being placed on the Morai, a Priest making a long Prayer put the Sash round his Waist and the Hat or Bonnet on his head & haild him King of Taheite. Mottooarro then began by His Orator making a long Speech and acknowledging him his King, when three Human Victims were brought in and offered for Morea, the Priest of Mottooarro placing them with their head towards the Young King and with a long speech over each, he offered 3 Young Plantain trees. He then took an Eye out of each, with a Piece of split bamboo, and placing them on a leaf took a Young Plantain tree in one Hand, and the Eyes in the Other Made a long speech holding them up to the Young King, who sat above him with his mouth open: after he had ended his Speech & laid the Plantain trees before the Young King the Bodys were removed & buryed by his priests in the Morai, and the Eyes put up with the Plantain trees on the Altar — the rest of the Chiefs then brought in their Sacrafices in the Same Manner, going through the like Ceremony, some bringing one Victim & Some two according to the bigness or extent of their districts, after which large Droves of Hogs and an immense quantity of other Provisions such as bread, Yams, Tarro, Plantains, Cocoa nuts &ca. were brought and presented to the Young King. Several large Canoes were also hauld up near the Morai on the sacred ground; these were dressd with several hundred fathoms of Cloth, Red Feathers, Breast plates &c. — all which were secured by the priests & Young Kings attendants — the Marro being now removed and taken Care of by the Priests, they all repair to feasts prepared

for them, which lasted some weeks, the Number of Hogs destroyd on this occasion were beyond all conception, besides Turtle, Fish &c. &c. —

I enquired the Cause of the Eye being offered, and was thus informed. The King is the Head of the People for which reason the Head is sacred; the Eye being the most valuable part is the fittest to be offered, and the reason that the King sits with his Mouth open, is to let the Soul of the Sacrafice enter into his Soul, that he may be strengthend thereby, or that He may receive more strength of disernment from it, and they think that His Tutelar Deity or Guardian Angel presides to receive the Soul of the Sacrafice.

Several Large Hogs were placed upon the Altar and the Human sacrifices offered this day were 30, some of which had been Killd near a Month.

These were the First that had been offered since our coming to the Island. (pp. 116–117)

The question of attendance at the ceremony is important, but it is not one that can be conclusively answered. In one place Morrison recorded that "all the principal Men of the Island" were assembled, but a few passages later he reported that "None of the Chiefs of Tyarrabboo had assisted at the Ceremony of investing the Young King with the Royal Sash" (p. 117). In his description of the ceremony itself he mentioned as having attended only "The Chiefs (or their Substitutes) of Tipperroonoo [Te Porionu'u] and Morea." In other words, no specific mention is made one way or the other of representatives of Pa'ea, Puna'auia, Papara, Hitia'a, and so on, whose presence one would expect but cannot confirm.

In any case, the all too evident absence of representatives of Seaward Teva was received as additional grounds for waging war against that tribe, and plans were formulated accordingly, with the English now clearly taking the initiative in the whole affair:

Feb. 20, 1791: Arrived Millward and McIntosh who having settled the Matter relative to the War, we determined to put it into execution, as None of the Chiefs of Tyarrabboo had assisted at the Ceremony of investing the Young King with the Royal sash. Tommaree had proposed to Make a Grand Feast, under Cover of which he Could have his Men and Canoes collected before he told them what he wanted them for, and by that means would prevent it from being blazed about — the English were to be there as partakers of the Feast, and when we were ready to attack them we could be in their Country before they knew what we were at, and by this means make an easy conquest. This appearing to us a very good plan, we agreed to prepare for it as fast as possible, and began to get things in order for Launching the Schooner; but from the Number of Visitors which daily came to see us, owing to the Number collected together in the two districts, we were not able to make any Progress, and it was the 1st of March before we Got her Launched. We filld the Water for Ballast and Stowd the Casks with Stones and Wood, we also got the Pork on board, masted and rigg'd the Vessel, but still kept our intentions a secret. (Morrison 1935:117–118)

But this ambitious undertaking, which would probably have removed all effective opposition to the Pomares for a while, never took place. The day after most of the Englishmen arrived in Papara to put the plan into operation, a messenger appeared and announced the arrival in Matavai of H.M.S. *Pandora*, which had been sent to capture the mutineers and return them to England for trial.

Pandora remained at Tahiti until May 8, and then sailed homeward with the fourteen surviving mutineers, and Brown. Records of the stay are contained in reports of her commander, Captain Edward Edwards, and in a journal kept by the ship's surgeon, George Hamilton. The former account is terse and matter-of-fact; the latter is more detailed and entertaining,[10] although much of it deserving of little credibility.

The passages from Edwards' reports most relevant to our present interests have to do with relations between Teri'irere-Temari'i and the Pomares. In Morrison's journal these relations were seen to be friendly and mutually supportive, with Teri'irere-Temari'i actually acknowledging Pomare II's supremacy, as exemplified in his reception of the latter's *vane*. But note Edwards' view of their relationship:

> The next morning Lt. Hayward was sent with a party in the pinnace to join the party in the launch at Papara. I found the Otoo ready to furnish me with guides and to give me any other assistance in his power, but he had very little authority or influence in that part of the island where the pirates had taken refuge, and even his right to the sovereignty of the eastern part of the island had been recently disputed by Tamarie, one of the royal family. Under these circumstances I conceived the taking of the Otoo and the other chiefs attached to his interest into custody would alarm the faithful part of his subjects and operate to our disadvantage. I therefore satisfied myself with the assitance he offered and had in his power to give me, and I found means at different times to send presents to Tamarie (and invited him to come on board, which he promised to do, but never fulfilled his promise), and convinced him I had it in my power to lay his country in waste, which I imagined would be sufficient at least to make him withhold that support he hitherto, through policy, had occasionally given to the pirates in order to draw them to his interest and to strengthen his own party against the Otoo. (Edwards and Hamilton 1915:32)

Edwards' grasp of the political geography and structure of the island was superficial, to say the least, but there must have been some evidence for his view that Teri'irere-Temari'i was not in Pomare II's pocket at the time. Also, his suggestion that the hospitality of the former to the mutineers was based in part on a desire to separate them from Pomare II is characteristic enough of Maohi political tactics to be quite credible. Some Paparan partisanship seems also to have rubbed off onto surgeon Hamilton, who described Teri'irere-Temari'i as "the proper king of Otaheitee, the present family of Otoo being usurpers" (p. 102). Hamilton also picked up from some source a report that Teri'irere-Temari'i was with the help of the mutineers planning to attack the Pomares, when *Pandora* arrived and so brought an end to the enterprise. Many high-ranking Paparans of that era probably did indeed consider the Pomares to be "usurpers" (as Paparans continued to do for

several generations thereafter); and the proposed attack against Seaward Teva
may indeed have included some hidden objectives designed to strengthen
Teri'irere-Temari'i's cause vis-à-vis that of Pomare II. But these considerations do not require me to revise my earlier estimate of the Pomares' political
position in early 1791 — that is, they were *primi inter pares* of Mo'orea
and of Tahiti's larger peninsula, the only serious challenge to their
paramountcy having come from Seaward Teva.

CHAPTER 29 *RANK VERSUS POWER*

AGGRANDIZEMENT BY KINSHIP

The next few years were to see an increase in the Pomares' political *potential*, mainly through the forming of new ties of kinship and the wider deployment of old ones. (I italicize *potential* since some of the individual, *interpersonal* relationships in question remained to be tested in terms of actual *intertribal* alignments.) During this period several European vessels visited Tahiti. H.M.S. *Discovery* and H.M.S. *Chatham* (Captain George Vancouver commanding) anchored at Matavai from the end of December 1791 to January 24, 1792. Vancouver himself had accompanied Cook during the latter's second and third voyages, and had some familiarity with the local scene; he devoted many pages in his journal to Tahiti and his stay there.[1]

During February 1792, a small British whaler, the *Matilda* (Captain Weatherhead commanding), called briefly at Matavai for refreshments; then, after the vessel was wrecked on a Tuamotuan reef, Weatherhead and his crew managed to make it back to Tahiti, where they were plundered of their possessions but otherwise hospitably received. As far as I know none of the *Matilda*'s company left a written account of their adventures on Tahiti.

During March 1792 two other small vessels, *Prince William Henry* and *Jenny* spent a few days at the island and took off some of *Matilda's* men — others choosing to remain. Again, no records of the visit are known to have been preserved.[2]

The next vessels to call at Tahiti were *Providence* and *Assistant*, under the command of Bligh, whose mission it was to obtain a new load of breadfruit as replacement for the one lost with H.M.S. *Bounty*. This expedition remained at the island from April 7 to mid-July 1792 (figs. 29–1 through 29–5) and left with the remaining members of *Matilda*'s company, except six who chose to remain. Bligh's account of this stay is rendered more useful due to the knowledge he had gained on previous visits, but he persisted in viewing the island's politics with a "king" Pomare bias.[3]

Finally, in February 1793, the British storeship *Daedalus* (Captain New commanding) paid a short visit; she took off one of the *Matilda* survivors upon departure, but left behind a crew member, "Peter the Swede," who

FIGURE 29–1. "On Matavai River, Island of Otahytey, 1792." Watercolor by G. Tobin. Mitchell Library, Sydney.

FIGURE 29–2. "The observatory . . . Point Venus, Otahytey, 1792." Watercolor by G. Tobin. Mitchell Library, Sydney.

FIGURE 29–3. "Tanna Heads in Matavai bay . . . Island of Otahytey, 1792." Watercolor by
G. Tobin. Mitchell Library, Sydney.

FIGURE 29–4. "Matavai Bay, Island of Otahytey . . . Sunset, 1792." *Admiral* and *Providence*
shown in background. Watercolor by G. Tobin. Mitchell Library, Sydney.

FIGURE 29–5. "Point Venus . . . Island of Otahytey, 1792." Watercolor by G. Tobin. Mitchell Library, Sydney.

became a lifetime fixture of mixed influence on the island. No other European vessel was to arrive until March 1797, when the ship *Duff* put in with its company of hopeful but sadly misinformed missionaries — but that begins a new chapter in this era, and a new section of this history of it.

Up to the time of Bligh's departure, in July 1792, the most lasting instance of consolidation of the Pomares' influence outside Pare was their connections with Mo'orea. Although Pomare I had been disastrously dilatory about supporting Mahau against Mahine in terms of military action, the mutineers' arms and Hitihiti's leadership ultimately defeated Mahine's successor;[4] and Mahau remained attached to Pomare I by double affinal bonds. Moreover, Pomare I and his two wives, along with his father and mother, spent more time on Mo'orea than on Tahiti. Finally, the interests of the two familial domains — Parean and Mo'orean[5] — became merged, literally, upon the death of Mahau, which occurred in January 1792 during Vancouver's visit.[6] Thereupon, the succession to tribal chieftainship passed to Mahau's four-year-old son, Tetuanui, whose mother was Pomare I's sister Auo. In addition, at about this time the young Pomare II became betrothed to Tetuanui's younger sister, who was thus his own first cousin Tarovahine.[7]

When the *Pandora* arrived in Tahiti on March 23, 1791 to capture the *Bounty* mutineers, she interrupted preparations for an attack against Seaward Teva designed to overcome that tribe's opposition to Pomare II. A few months later, in January 1792, Vancouver wrote the following about

Pomare II's younger brother, Teri'itapunui (who was about four years old at the time): "The youth . . . had taken the name of *Whyeadooa* [Vehiatua], in consequence of his being the acknowledged sovereign of *Tiarabou*, under his brother *Otoo* [Pomare II]" (1801:273). Elsewhere, Vancouver added:

At this time [i.e., the successful overthrow of the Mahine regime in Mo'orea] *Whyeadooa* the king of Tiarabou died, leaving only a very distant relation to assume his name and government; who was by *Pomurrey* and his adherents obliged to relinquish all pretensions to such honours, and with the people of Tiarabou to acknowledge *Pomurrey's* youngest son as their chief, under the supreme authority of his eldest son *Otoo* [Pomare II]; which on their assenting to, the youth assumed the name of *Whyeadooa* as a necessary appendage to the government. . . .

Urripiah [Ari'ipaea], the next brother to *Pomurrey*, having acquired the reputation of a great warrior, has taken up his residence on the borders of Tiarabou, to watch the conduct of those people in their allegiance to his nephew *Whyeadooa*; and on the least appearance of disaffection or revolt, to be at hand for pursuing such measures as may be required to bring them back to their obedience. (pp. 324–325)

It should be noted that during Vancouver's visit the newest Vehiatua — the four-year-old Teri'itapunui — resided at Pare with his older brother, Pomare II, and their nurse-attendants.

Aside from his failure to mention Churchill's brief reign as successor to Vehiatua III, Vancouver's reference to the succession having gone to a "distant relation" agrees with Morrison's report. Bligh, writing on May 8, 1792, added some corroborative details, but neither his nor any other account that I know of describes how Pomare I's supporters persuaded the Taiarapuans to acknowledge young Pomare II's legitimacy, and hence his fairly weighty claims upon the office:

In my last Voyage I have given a particular account of the Principal Families of this Island . . . From a connection in the female line, the present Otows Grandmother being Sister to the then King of Tiarraboo, his grand child is now become Erree of that place, the Heirs of Whaeeahtuah in the male line being extinct. — The late Whaeeahtuah whose Wife Tynah is now connected with, died without any Children, and on his death (since my last Voyage) Terreetapanooai Tynahs second Son was sent to Tiarraboo to be elected, or more properly, acknowledged Erree of that part of the Island.

The Tiarraboo People always insisted that Whaeeahtuah was Errerahigh of that Country, & Otoo Ereerahigh of the Western part of the Island, but all the Otoo family & connections, say there is only one Erreerahigh — their power however has not marked any superiority over the Tiarraboo People since our time, and the present Terreetapanooai, has taken the Name of Whaeeahtuah. — We may date the birth of this Boy in the Year 1787 and his being acknowledged as Erree in 1790. (1792:144)

With reference to Bligh's assertion that the Taiarapuans had acknowledged Teri'itapunui to be their *ari'i* in 1790, it will be recalled that the principal people of the district had indeed "received" Pomare II's *vane* during January

1791, when it made its circuit of the island, but that they had subsequently failed to "assist" at the investiture ceremony that followed, thereby providing the Pomares' supporters with a cause (or at least a pretext) for preparing an attack upon them.

Summarizing this phase of the Pomare expansion one can say, then, that sometime between March and December 1791, some of the leaders of Seaward Teva were persuaded to recognize the Pare family's claims to the Vehiatua kin-Title and its tribal perquisites. That this recognition was not universal, or wholehearted, is indicated by the circumstance that a constant watch had to be maintained, by Ari'ipaea, against too disruptive dissent.

Another direction in which the Pomare family appears to have extended its influence, and perhaps even coercive authority, was the large northern district of Ha'apaino'o. Like other tribal districts of northeastern Tahiti, Ha'apaino'o seems to have been linked with Pare-Arue by ties of alliance over a long period of time. But a passage in Vancouver indicates that something more solid than alliance now joined the two tribes; Vancouver referred to Ha'apaino'o as ". . . one of the districts belonging to Whytooa [Vaetua]" (1801:305), who was Pomare I's second brother — after Ari'ipaea, and before Te Pau. This attribution was later confirmed, in connection with Pomare I's efforts to recover the goods taken from the *Matilda* crew. No clue, however, is provided as to how Vaetua came to occupy the office of chief of this tribe — a largely absentee official, it should be noted, since Vaetua appears to have resided mostly in Pare, where he was charged with safeguarding the interests of his young nephew, Pomare II — Pomare I meanwhile having retired to Mo'orea.

But the Pomare pretensions did not stop at the boundaries of Tahiti and Mo'orea. While Vancouver was at Matavai, he was informed that young Pomare II was "supreme sovereign" of Huahine, and that he would eventually succeed to such offices in Ra'iatea and Taha'a as well. These pretensions involved two men who were at Pare at the time, the one visiting and the other evidently there to stay; the former was called by Vancouver "Matuarro," the latter "Mowree."

The appearance in the sources of another Matuaro (i.e., Vancouver's "Matuarro") constitutes one of those situations capable of reducing the ethnohistorian to utter despair. Vancouver distinguished between "Matooara Mahow," the Mo'orean chief whose funeral he witnessed, and "Matuarro," whom he described as *ari'i rahi* of Huahine:

In consequence of *Pomurrey's* [Pomare I] connexion with *Mahow's* family [i.e., Pomare I's wife 'Itia having been sister of this Mahau], his son *Otoo* [Pomare II] in right of his mother [i.e., 'Itia] was acknowledged as the supreme sovereign of Huaheine; and *Matuarro* the king of that island, had consented to the superiority of *Otoo* [Pomare II] over him, as 'Aree Maro Eoora' [*ari'i maro ura*]; but that he *Matuarro* was 'Aree de Hoi' [*ar'i rahi*]. (1801:326)

I take this passage to mean that Pomare II was acknowledged in some quarters (notably by Huahine's tribal chief, Matuaro) as "supreme sovereign" of Huahine, but I am uncertain as to what Vancouver meant by the rest of the sentence, or what he meant by "sovereign." If Vancouver intended to convey that Pomare II's alleged "sovereignty" over Huahine came to him through his mother's connections there, then I must confess that I can find no specific genealogical evidence for such a connection. If on the other hand the writer was referring to Pomare I's mother (and Pomare II's grandmother), Tetupaia, then some such connection can of course be traced — for example, Tetupaia was second cousin to Mato, a former chief of Huahine; but even so I fail to see why this would have qualified Pomare II for "supreme sovereignty" over Huahine. Indeed, I suspect that this was another example of a European's confusion between rank-status and tribal chieftainship, and of the Pomares' efforts to trade on such confusion — or even to convert the former into the latter. As for the visiting Matuaro, described by Vancouver as an Arioi, and *ari'i rahi* of Huahine (p. 258), I suppose that his alleged acknowledgment of Pomare II's "supremacy" referred mainly if not solely to the latter's rank-status as a twice-over *maro-ura*-wearing kin-Titleholder.[8]

Vancouver's "Mowree" [Mauri] was probably none other than Ha'amanemane, whom we have met with before. About him Vancouver wrote:

Excepting the daughter of *Opoone* [Puni], who reigned over Bolabola, and its two neighbouring isles, we had now the presence of all the sovereigns of this group of islands. *Opoone* had formerly conquered and annexed the islands of Ulietea and Otaha to the government of Bolabola; but, on his death, the sovereignty of these islands had, in right of natural, or original succession, fallen to a chief whose name was *Mowree*. He was a shrewd sensible fellow, affected to be well acquainted with the English language, and certainly had acquired some words which be pronounced so as to be understood. He was a brother of *Pomurrey's* mother, was on a visit to the royal family here, and was by them treated with much respect and attention. (1801: 278)

In Henry's reproduction of Mare's genealogy of the Pomares' Ra'iatean antecedents (1928:247ff.), the offspring of Tamatoa III are listed as follows:

by his first wife, Mai-he'a
1. Te-tu-paia (f), who married Teu and mothered Pomare I
2. Teri'i-na-vaho-roa (m)
3. Teri'i-tari'a (m)
4. Hapai-taha'a (f)
by his second wife, Te-hani
1. Te-moe-ha'a (m)

2. Ara-po (m)
3. Te-ha'ame'ame'a (f)
4. Vetea-ra'i Uuru (m)

Elsewhere in the sources both Terano (wife of Te Pau "B") and Te Pau (wife of Hitihiti), have also been identified as siblings of Tetupaia; whether these are the same as or additional to either of the above females, I cannot say, and I am in a similar quandary respecting Mauri-Ha'amanemane. My guess is that the latter was the Teri'i na Vaho Roa in the Mare genealogy, as he is described by Vancouver as having succeeded to his office by right of "natural or original succession," and as Teri'i na Vaho Roa was the eldest of Tamatoa III's sons.

Otoo, in right of his grandmother by his father's side, on the death of *Mowree* will claim the sovereignty of Ulietea and Otaha. *Mowree*, who is brother to *Pomurrey*'s mother, is an Ereeoe of an advanced age. He seemed extremely fond of *Otoo*, and proud of his succeeding him in the government of those islands; saying, that, at present, there were two sovereigns, that "*Maw ta Tarta*," but when he should die then there would be but one, meaning *Otoo*. This expression, in its literal signification, means "*to eat the Man*;" the idea, however, which in this sense it is intended to convey, is to point out those, whose rank and authority entitle them to preside at human sacrifices; a power which at present is possessed only by *Mowree* and *Otoo*. (Vancouver 1801:327)

Evidently, having been "an Ereeoe of an advanced age," Ha'amanemane had had no offspring of his own, so was in a position to foster or otherwise designate someone to succeed him in his office; in this instance that person appears to have been Pomare II. As for the nature of that office, Vancouver went on to say that ". . . it does not appear that even *Mowree* himself has much influence in those islands [Ra'iatea and Taha'a], notwithstanding that he is their acknowledged sovereign" (p. 328). In other words, Ha'amanemane's preeminence, which he shared with Pomare II, consisted mainly of "presiding at human sacrifices," — a function associated with the holding of an 'Oro-sanctioned, feather-girdled kin-Title, and being only indirectly related to tribal authority.

As I recorded earlier Ha'amanemane had arrived in Tahiti in 1788, during the *Bounty*'s stay at Matavai, and Bligh remarked upon his social eminence, calling him Tutaha, which name he evidently went by at the time. By 1792 Tutaha (Ha'amanemane, Mauri) had made an important place for himself in Pare:

Tomorrow Morning I am to have a sight of it [the tabernacle of an 'Oro image], and to hear prayers performed by Tootaha the Priest — This Man is a great Orator among them, and highly respected for his abilities, as well as being a Chief of consequence — he has always been the Prime Minister of Tynah [Pomare I], is their Oracle, and Historian of this Country, and possesses a great fund of humour

— he is now called Hammenemanné, but was spoken of in my last Voyage by the Name of Tootaha — He is remarkable for speaking English, and could he write is capable of forming a vocabulary of near a thousand English Words. (Bligh 1792:135)

Ha'amanemane was also a distinguished Arioi, but his relevance to our present concern has to do with his alleged introduction of yet another set of insignia of 'Oro-sanctioned rank. According to Mare, Ha'amanemane brought with him to Tahiti the following: the *maro ura* named Teraipu Tata, the sunbonnet (*taumata*) named Te Ata o Tu, the fan (*tairu*) named Hotu, and some priests of 'Oro (Newbury 1967a:14). Later, in the proceedings that were conducted by French officials with the evident hope of establishing Pomare, and hence French, claims to the Leeward Islands, witnesses implied that Ha'amanemane bequeathed these items (which constituted his Ra'iatean inheritance) to the young Pomare II, who was probably his grand-nephew and whom he also "adopted."

I do not know what to make of this statement. For example, was this *maro ura* in addition to the one already introduced by Tetupaia decades earlier and, if so, what ritual use was made of it thereafter? And, if Ha'amanemane did in fact introduce another 'Oro tabernacle (and 'Oro image), what was its relation to the Papara image removed to Tarahoi after the mutineers' war against Atehuru, in September 1790?

In any case, even though I cannot confirm from eyewitness accounts the introduction of these ritually important items, Ha'amanemane himself was indisputably there at the time, and through him the Pomares' social ambitions toward the Leeward Islands were undoubtedly nourished. In fact, through their combination of preeminent rank-status, other distinguished kinship connections, death of rivals, mutineer-achieved military successes, and English advocacy, the Pomares' political ambitions reached what in Maohi thinking was probably an entirely new scale, as witnessed in the following passage from Vancouver:

In consequence of the extensive dominion that has devolved upon this young monarch, he is not now distinguished by the title of *Aree de Hoi*, but by one which is considerably more eminent and comprehensive; since they say there may be many *Arees de Hoi*, but there can be but one *Aree Maro Eoora*; which means the chief of the red feathered *Maro*; and under which title, *Otoo*'s authority is acknowledged in Otaheite, Morea, Mattea, Tetero, Tupea-mannoo, and Huaheine. But the people of Ulietea and Otaha, seem much averse to this submission; and it does not appear, that even *Mowree* himself has much influence in those islands, notwithstanding that he is their acknowledged sovereign. Since the death of *Opoony*, the government of the islands under his late authority appears to have been ill administered; the inhabitants having been very turbulent and much disposed to anarchy: and in consequence of the disinclination which the people of these islands have manifestd to subscribe to the supreme authority of *Otoo*, an expedition was in contemplation from Otaheite, to enforce the power of the *Aree Maro Eoora* over them, and little doubt was entertained of its success. Another favorite object was the annexing to *Otoo*'s present dominions by conquest, (for no right was set up) the islands of Bolabola, Mowrooa, and Tapi, which, since the death of *Opoony*, had been governed by his daughter, and were said, in a great measure, to have lost their former high reputation as a martial and warlike nation.

Pomurrey and his brothers having procured from the vessels which had lately visited Otaheite, several muskets and pistols, they considered themselves invincible; and the acquiring of new possessions for *Otoo*, now seemed to occupy the whole of their study and attention. They were extremely solicitous that I should contribute to their success by augmenting their number of firearms, and adding to their stock of ammunition. Of the latter I gave *Pomurrey* a small quantity; but of the former I had none to dispose of, even if I had seen no impropriety in complying with his request. Finding there was no prospect of increasing their armory, they requested that I would have the goodness to conquer the territories on which they meditated a descent, and having so done, to deliver them up to *Otoo*; and as an excuse for their subjugation, insisted that it was highly essential to the comfort and happiness of the people at large, that over the whole group of these islands there should be only one sovereign. On satisfying them that the islands in question were quite out of my route, and that I had no leisure for such an enterprize, *Pomurrey*, in the most earnest manner requested, that on my return to England I would, in his name, solicit his Majesty to order a ship with proper force to be immediately sent out, with directions, that if all those islands were not subjected to his power before her arrival, she was to conquer them for *Otoo*; who, he observed, I well knew would ever be a steady friend to King George and the English. This request was frequently repeated, and he did not fail to urge it in the most pressing manner at our parting. (1801:327–330)

An opportunity to learn how the facts of everyday political life corresponded to those grandiose political pretensions is presented by the *Matilda* incident.

THE *Matilda* INCIDENT

In February 1792, the crew of the English whaler *Matilda* made it back to Tahiti after their ship was wrecked in the Tuamotus. The captain and part of the ship's company left Tahiti in March aboard the *Jenny* and *Prince William Henry*, but the rest of the survivors were still on the island when Bligh arrived on April 7. Bligh described the incident:

[After their wreck] They proceeded fortunately [in their boat] to Maitea [Me'etia], & after a Nights rest and kind treatment, they Sailed for Otaheite on the 5 March. — On the next Night, by bad Weather, the Boats were separated, two arrived at Matavai, one at Oaitepeah, and the other round by Attahooroo. The People of Oaitepeah were too hostile to induce the Boat to remain with them, she therefore proceeded to Matavai and joined the Party that had got there before them. — Afterwards, in the course of eight Days, the Men who had landed at Attahooroo also came to join their Companions. — It however appeared so much the opinion of the Captain that they should not all remain at one place, that some resided at Matavai, some at Oparré, and some at Attahooroo. — They were all dispossessed of their Cloaths & Articles they had with them; but the greatest prize fell in the hands of the Matavai People, under the command of Poeeno the Chief, and one Tabyroo a Person of some power. — The circumstances no sooner became

known than Otoo demanded the Articles taken at Matavai, consisting of Money
& Arms, in behalf (as he asserts) of his Friends the English; but no restitution
was made. — some deliberation immediately took place, result of which was, that
on the 19th March, War was proclaimed, and the Oparré People came to Matavai
destroying Houses, & all the provision kind they could lay their Hands on. — The
Matavians made very considerable resistance; still retain their Booty, and at this
instant the Parties are violently at War with each other.

Notwithstanding our Countrymen were robbed of their Cloaths, they were treated
afterwards with much kindness & attention, it would however have been better,
if the whole had gone to Oparré under the protection of Otoo, and as there were
three, at this time absent with the Matavians; the first step I took was to order
them to join their Ship Mates.

The War was interrupted by the arrival of a Schooner called the Jenny from
Bristol burthen 90 Tons. — This Vessel remained here untill the 31st March, when
she Sailed for the NW Coast of America and by this opportunity Capt. Weatherhead
with Two Boys and One Man, had the means of returning home. — He had one
passenger more than he expected, a Seaman secretted himself on board & sailed
with them as it is supposed, for he has not been heard of since.

While the Jenny remained here the Second Mate, — Campbell undertook to
go away in one of the Whale Boats for Port Jackson. — It was fitted up in a miserable
manner with Mat Sails, and himself with two Men, Phillip Christall & Jn. Basster
sailed the same day.

The Number of Men now remaining on the Island are 21 including the Convict
who has absented himself. — Among them is the Chief Mate, Surgeon, Boatswain
& Carpenter. — The whole of them I directed to stay at Oparré where they are
well taken care of. (1792: 125–125b)

The next episode in this war between Matavai and the Pomares' supporters from Pare took place on April 11:

In our return to the Ship I saw a miltitude of Men on the low land of Matavai
all Armed, preparing for an Attack on the Matavians who they had already driven
from the Spot, and burnt all their Houses. The Afternoon produced the result of
their determination. — The Oparré people drove the others to the Mountains, killed
one Man, & returned victorious. — I have been sollicited very much to join Otoo's
Army, but I only promised to interfere should the Matavians attempt to go near
Oparre, in which case I assured them I would land a Party of Men & drive them
back, which gave great pleasure to our Oparré Friends. — I also sent the Surgeon
of the Matilda to Poeeno and Tabyroo, to order them to return the Captains effects,
if they ever wished to be on good terms with us, & he brought me back Word
from them, that everything would be returned. — The Surgeon informed me that
he was conducted through an immense number of Men armed with Spears, Clubs
& Slings, who appeared extremely anxious to know the Message he had brought,
& if I intended to act against them. — They behaved with much decorum and some
attention to the Chief who went with him; for the front of each army was so near
to each other as to use their Slings, — hostilities ceased during the parley. — There
Men when heaped together in such numbers armed with Spears 12 or 14 feet long
or more, have a tremenduous appearance, they nevertheless do very little mischief
to each other, for I believe they seldom come to a serious charge, but content themselves with the execution they are able to effect by Slinging Stones, by which means
some Men are Maimed and sometimes killed. (pp. 126b–127)

In due course the Matavaians were driven into the mountains, and Bligh sent emissaries to their leaders:

At day dawn I sent away Mr. Norris Surgeon of the Matilda with a Message from me to Poeeno & Tabyroo for Mr. Weatherheads Money, & some other articles that were in their possession, particularly the Musquets. — After a troublesome Walk of Six Miles he found Poeeno & Tabyroo at Wapyhanoo. — They received him in a very friendly manner and promised that the Money should be returned as soon as it could be got from Teturoah where they had sent it for security. — They refused to give up the Musquets, unless by mutual consent all those that were on the Island were to be given to me; — in that case they had no objection to comply; but in their present situation they could not think of it, as it was necessary for them to preserve some Means to regain their property, or to establish themselves in another situation. — They would do any thing to serve me, and hoped I would not be angry with them — it was the Mob, they said, had taken away the peoples Cloaths, and hauled the Boats on Shore — they endeavoured to restrain them, but could not. — If I came after them, they said, all that could be done, was for them to fly farther. — They called Matavai my Country, and described that the People of Oparré had destroyed all their Houses, Barked their Trees, destroyed what I had left among them, and done the Country irrepareble injury. (p. 128b)

Soon thereafter Pomare I returned to Pare from Mo'orea, where he was then residing, and attempted to persuade Bligh to intervene more actively against the Matavaians and others:

Poeeno & the Matavai People seem to be objects of great dislike to Tynah and his Father, they requested I would undertake the War with them to destroy those People, as well as the Inhabitants of Paparrah & Oaitepeeah, who had a number of musquets. — they knew it was an object worth their most strenous endeavours to persuade me to, but they had the good sense not to be seriously offended at my refusal, when I told them it would interfere with the busyness I was sent on. — I however still threatened the adverse Party unless they brought in the Arms & Money. (pp. 129b–130)

So much for the Pomares' ''supreme sovereignty'' over Papara and Taiarapu — not to speak of nearby Matavai!

On April 26 Bligh was able to report an end to hostilities, temporarily, at least:

Peace is established — Poeeno and Tynah have had a meeting, and it is agreed that Poeeno shall live again at Matavai. — They have promised to return C. Weatherhead's Money, but I am in doubt about their sincerity — I however dare not involve myself in any trouble with these People to get either one part of his property or the other, altho I will do my utmost to regain it by every fair Means I am capable of. (1792:136)

On May 4, however, the ''peace'' was disrupted again:

An account was brought me to day, that Poeeno and all his adherents had left Matavai and fled to Itteeah, the cause of this was owing to an attempt of Wydooah (the younger Bror. of Tynah) to seize on the Musquets, which Tabyroo had the charge of, and kept at a distance from Matavai. (p. 141b)

Meanwhile, Tapiru and Poeno implemented the return of all the money they and their people still held, but refused to give up the arms — this, in view of their knowledge of the Pomares, one can put down to their realistic desire for self-survival. Further insight is derived from a passage of Bligh's regarding relations between Pare and Papara:

> Oreepyah, with his Nephew Otoo, (the King) & Hammennémanné came to take their leave of me on their going to Paparrah to see their Relation Tomaree the Chief of that place, who lies very Ill and is expected to die; But their principal object is to see what can be done, to take away some Musquets which the People of that District are in possession of from the Seamen of the Matilda's Boat who put in there. Nothing can equal the rage these people have after Arms — there is nothing they would not sacrifice to procure them, but the Parties who have them in possession I believe are too wise to part with them. Could the Otoo Family get Arms I have no doubt but they would govern the whole Country, — a Right which they say is inherent in themselves.
>
> Before they sat out on their expedition it was necessary to consult me. — Tynah therefore came with the party to give his interest for them to be so equipped with presents of different kinds, as would insure them a welcome reception.
>
> I indulged him in the most he asked for, and they left us with light hearts, — dressed in European Clothes, and a large quantity of Iron Work and Trinkets in their bundles. (p. 145b)

Another event connected with the Pare-Matavai war occurred on June 19:

> I was sorry to hear again of a human Sacrifice. — Iddeeah informed me that the Chiefs of Waennah (called Ohaaine in C. Cooks Map) had sent one to Otoo — I found it wrapt up in a platted Cocoa Nutt branch and Slung to a Pole as usual — it stunk very much, and on that account was hung up among the Bushes a part form any dwelling. — The late disturbance and War between Matavai and Oparré People was the cause of this Sacrifice — the People of Waennah took part with Matavai, and the offence was not to be forgiven but by this melancholy claim. — The absence of Otoo prevents any thing being done untill his return, when the Eye will be presented, and the Etuah supplicated to continue the friendship between the two Districts. (Bligh 1792:162) [9]

Bligh sailed on July 18, with Tapiru and Poeno still beyond reach of the Pare forces and with the *Matilda* loot still unreturned. How the affair was finally settled — if it ever was — we shall never learn.

OTHER CHANGES IN MAOHI LIFE

My emphasis in the foregoing chapters of this volume has been on political developments; let us now look at some parallel (and in part interdependent) developments which occurred in other domains of Maohi life. I begin with a trivial but highly indicative example, that of personal attire:

> The quantity of Old Cloaths that has been left among these People is considerable. Any article of Dress they set the highest Value on. — they wear such rags and dirty things as are truly disgusting, and deform themselves in a very great

degree. — It is a rare thing to see a person dressed with a neat piece of Cloath, which formerly they had in abundance and wore with much ellegance. — Their general habiliments are now a dirty Shirt, and Old Coat, Jacket or an Old Waiscoat, so that they are no longer the clean Otaheiteans, but in appearance a set of Raggamuffins with whom it is necessary to have great caution in any intercourse with them. (Bligh 1792:134b)

According to Bligh and Vancouver these substitutions had extended to their basic tools and manufacturing processes:

So important are the various European implements, and other commodities, now become to the happiness and comfort of these islanders, that I cannot avoid reflecting with Captain Cook on the very deplorable condition to which these good people on a certainty must be reduced, should their communication with Europeans be ever at an end. The knowledge they have now acquired of the superiority and the supply with which they have been furnished of the more useful implements, have rendered these, and other European commodities, not only essentially necessary to their common comforts, but have made them regardless of their former tools and manufactures, which are now growing fast out of use, and, I may add, equally out of remembrance. Of this we had convincing proof in the few of their bone, or stone tools, or untensils, that were seen amongst them; those offered for sale were of rude workmanship, and of an inferior kind, solely intended for our market, to be purchased by way of curiosity. I am likewise well convinced, that, by a very small addition to their present stock of European cloth, the culture of their cloth plant, which now seems much neglected, will be intirely disregarded, and they will rely upon the precarious supply which may be obtained from accidental visitors, for this and many others of the most important requisites of social life.

Under these painful considerations, it manifestly appears that Europeans are bound by all the laws of humanity, regularly to furnish those wants which they alone have created; and to afford the inhabitants from time to time supplies of such important useful articles as have been already introduced, and which having excluded their own native manufactures, are, in most respects, become indispensably necessary to their whole œconomy of life: in return for which a valuable consideration would be received in provisions and refreshments, highly beneficial to the traders who may vist the Pacific Ocean.

The various manufactures in iron and in cloth have become so essentially requisite to their common concerns, that instead of these commodities being reduced in their value by the frequent visits of Europeans, or their supplies of food and refreshments being less plentiful in return, we were served with every article in the greatest profusion. Six hogsheads of very fine pork were cured; and had we been better provided with salt, we might have secured ten times that quantity; and sailed with a large supply for present use, which comprehended as many live hogs and vegetables, as we could find room to dispose of; the whole procured at least 200 per cent. cheaper than on any of Captain Cook's visits, notwithstanding the recent departure of the Pandora. (Vancouver 1801:332–334)[10]

I have forgot if I have taken notice of the loss of originality in the use, Among these People in a great measure, of their implements. It is now a rare thing to see them use any other than Iron Tools. In their natural State they used a peice of Bamboo for a Knife, a hard black Stone brought to a blunt edge for an hatchet, and a Splintered peice of the same for a Drill, and their teeth were always sufficient to clear a Cocoa Nutt of its Rind to give them food and drink. But now they will do nothing without a Knife and a Hatchet. It is however very extraordinary altho they see the valuable Use of a Saw that they do not take to the use of them. They prize Needles and Scissars and even Pins they make Hooks of to take small Fish. (Bligh 1789:II, 63–64)

Vancouver, a perceptive visitor, also noted a radical change in military tactics:

> Great alteration has taken place in the military operations of these people. On our first discovery of these islands their wars were principally of a maritime nature; but at present it should seem they were conducted in a very different manner. For although some of our gentlemen extended their excursions to a considerable distance, not a single war canoe was seen belonging to Otaheite. I had much conversation with *Urripiah* on this subject; from whom I learned, that in their late contests they had found them so unmanageable, particularly when the wind blew at all strong, that they had intirely given them up, and now carried on their enterprizes by land, using the larger sort of their common canoes, when their wars were offensive, to convey them to the place of their destination, which was generally effected under cover of the night, or in dark rainy weather. (1801:334–335)

In this connection the radically new tactics that the mutineers introduced, and by which they were able to dislodge the Atehurans from their mountain fortress should be recalled. As for firearms, the consequences of their introduction should by now be crystal clear, as seen, for example, by the military advantage they bestowed upon their fortunate owners, and by the extremes to which individuals would resort in order to obtain them. With his usual attention to detail, Bligh endeavored to compile a list of all the firearms known to be on the island at the time:

> From the most authentick account I can get, I find the Otaheiteans have got from different Ships, Musquets &c as follows. —

	Musquets	Pistols
Belonging to Oparre —	8	5
At Oaitepeha	5	5
At Itteah	1	0
Attahooroo	0	5
Matavai	5	0
Paparrah	8	6
[?] one Swivel	Total 27	21

(1792:131)

Central, of course, was the change in the number of people involved in the political developments under study. As I indicated in chapter 2 the only eyewitness estimate we have relevant to the time span just considered is Morrison's guess, made between 1789 and 1791, of 30,000 (1935:171), which according to my own "calculations" (if so pretentious a label may be given to my method of inference) would represent a diminution of the island's population by about 5,000 from its size in 1767. If credence may be given to Maohi opinion expressed to Bligh, an even greater decline took place as the result of an epidemic introduced, presumably, by Vancouver's expedition in 1791–1792. We cannot identify the disease this visitation is believed to have introduced, but the extent of its fatal consequences evidently left a deep impression even upon these inured people.[11]

Before commencing with the next chronicled chapter in the Pomares' political career, I reproduce a passage from Vancouver characterizing some changes remarked by him in the personality of our principal character:

I cannot take leave of my friend, for to such an epithet from me *Pomurrey*'s conduct justly entitles him, without adverting to the alteration which seemed to have taken place in his character, since my former visits to this country. At that time, he was not only considered as a timid, but a very weak prince; on this occasion, however, he did not appear deficient either in discernment, or intrepidity; although it must be acknowledged his fears were exceedingly awakened at the display of our fire-works, and that he always appeared to regard fire-arms with a considerable degree of terror; which possibly might arise from his knowledge of their destructive powers, whilst at the same time he remained ignorant of the extent to which they were capable of doing execution; but this description of weapons out of the question, we had reason to believe his courage was equal to that of his neighbours, of which he certainly gave an undeniable proof by joining our party alone and unarmed at the encampment; in direct opposition to the counsel and apprehensions of his surrounding countrymen. On former occasions, I had also considered his general character to be haughty, austere, and combined with much low cunning. When he condescended to speak, or converse, which was not frequent, little or no information could be derived; whilst the questions he asked in return, did not tend to the acquisition of useful knolwedge. His conduct and deportment on the present occasion, were extremely different; and, when compared with that of his associates, were marked with an evident superiority, expressive of the exalted situation he filled; and indicated that he possessed a just knowledge of himself, and an open generous, and feeling heart. In conversation, there were few from whom better information could be acquired; nor was he now deficient in directing his observations and enquiries to useful and important objects. For this purpose only, he would remain whole days in our working tents, observing with the strictest attention the different transactions going forward; and frequently interrupting the mechanics, to require explanations of their several operations. The whole tenor of his behaviour towards us was so uniformly correct and meritorious, that, on his taking leave, I could not resist making him, and his wives, such acknowledgments in useful articles, as he conceived they could have no possible claim to; and suspecting I was about to make some addition, he caught my arm, expressed how highly repaid and gratified they were with what they had received, and observed, as I was going to visit many other countries where such things would be equally valuable; I ought to be careful and œconomical. (1801:330–332)

MISSIONARIES ARRIVE

THE POLITICAL SITUATION IN 1797

On March 4, 1797 the British ship *Duff* (Captain James Wilson commanding) arrived at Tahiti intent on landing eighteen Englishmen and the wives of five of them, for the purpose of establishing a Protestant mission. (In addition, the *Duff* carried eleven other missionaries to establish missions in the Marquesas and Tonga islands.) As one can imagine, this event marked a new and wholly different kind of relationship between Maohis and Europeans. These "visitors" were there to stay, and they cherished the hope of revolutionizing almost every aspect of Maohi life. (Figs. 30–1, 30–2.) In fact, so different was this new breed of visitors from their predecessors, and in so many respects, that — as their chroniclers put it — the Tahitians ". . . profess hardly to know what we are, and suspect we are not Englishmen, or like any others they have seen who have ever visited their island" (Wilson 1799:156). In the course of time the Maohis came to discover that some of this new breed did not differ from other, less Calvinistic Europeans in their reactions to nubile and half-naked young women; but the majority of the missionaries abided by their moral code. Cook and some other earlier visitors had declined personal invitations to sample the charms of Tahitian women, but no previous set of visitors had prescribed this and other tenets of Calvinism as official policy.[1]

The full story of the English missionary enterprise on Tahiti deserves a separate volume, which would look beyond the tragi-comedy of this preposterous confrontation and provide a deep and comprehensive analysis of its effects upon Maohi life. But I leave this task to others, and limit myself to indicating, as explicitly as possible, how the missionary presence influenced political developments.[2] Needless to say, years passed before the missionaries began to comprehend those developments; as time went by they acquired, by bitter experience, a much deeper knowledge of Maohi political structure than Cook or Bligh ever achieved, but this did not lead them to

Note: In this chapter, unless otherwise indicated, page number only refers to Wilson 1799 and volume and page number refer to the LMS Transactions.

FIGURE 30-1. "The Cession of the District of Matavai to the Missionaries, 16 March 1797."
Painting by R.A. Smirke. London Missionary Society.

FIGURE 30-2. "Missionary House and Environs in the Island of Otaheite." Sketch by W.
Wilson. In J. Wilson 1799.

revise their belief in the desirablity, the ultimate *rightness*, of a monarchical form of government.

Perhaps the most useful way to open this new chapter in Maohi political history is by summarizing the changes that had taken place since Bligh's last visit in the situations of the island's principal personages.

In 1797 the arrival of the *Duff* found Pomare I, now in his mid-forties, living with Pepiri, "a very stout young woman," the daughter of a Papeuriri subchief. His second connubial partner, Vaiariti, was no longer with him, having "left him through dislike[,] for one of far inferior rank." (p. 73.) Meanwhile, 'Itia had long since ceased to share Pomare I's sleeping mat, and was living openly with one of her lower-class paramours. And while she had her own domestic establishments and was in fact a chiefly person in her own right, she continued to ally herself faithfully and energetically with Pomare I against his many ill-wishers.

Pomare I's next younger brother, Ari'ipaea, died a year or so prior to arrival of the *Duff*; his widow, Vahine Metua, was described as "chief over all Hedeah [Hitia'a]" (p. 190), and she also held sway over a small subdistrict of Ha'apaino'o, called "Whyripoo," said to have been presented to her by Vaetua, her late husband's brother (p. 185).

Vaetua himself continued in active authority over Ha'apaino'o, and resided mainly there. As for Pomare I's youngest brother, Te Pau "C", earlier described as having succeeded to the chieftainship of Fa'a'a, I find no mention of him under any identifiable name in missionary accounts.

Pomare I had two surviving sisters. No mention of Ari'ipaea Vahine, whose timely home visit in 1790 had helped overcome the Oropa'a, appears in the first missionary chronicles, so she may be assumed to have returned to Ra'iatea, or to have died. The other sister, Auo, the widow of Mo'orea's chief, Mahau, was found to be married to Mauroa, a petty chief, characterized as "a man of good sense and great authority" (p. 151). Auo herself was described as "presiding over" Teahono'o, the eastern subdivision of Matavai (Ha'apape?), but she and her husband resided also in Pare (p. 183).

At the time of the *Duff*'s arrival, Pomare II was about sixteen or seventeen years old and living at Pare with his wife, Tetuanui, daughter of Auo and Mahau (and hence his first cousin), of about the same age. Both Pomare II and his young wife traveled on the shoulders of bearers when away from their own estates.[3] Wilson characterized the couple as follows:

> Otoo, the present king, is about seventeen, and very large limbed, promising to be of a size like his father. Though he is absolute, he lives in the greatest familiarity with the lowest of his subjects. He is differently represented: some say he looks solid, and of a thoughtful aspect; whilst others call him stupid, and his countenance vacant. His queen, Tetua, daughter of Wyreede, relict of Motuãro, is about his own age, and rather the larger of the two. Her countenance is pleasing and open, but masculine, and widened by the usual method of pressure, called touroome. (p. 321)

The king and queen were always attended by a number of men, as carriers, domestics, or favourites, who were rãa, or sacred, living without families, and attending only on the royal pair; and a worse set of men the whole island does not afford for thievery, plunder, and impurity. (pp. 321–322)

Although cohabiting, Pomare II and his wife were already seeking some of their sexual partners elsewhere, Pomare II being described as "given up to unnatural affections" (LMS Transactions: I, 122), and Tetuanui as being "a perfect Messalina," living in "a promiscuous intercourse with all her porters" (p. 322).

Though the dwelling of Pomare II in Pare was characterized as "a very humble one," the labels applied to everything about his situation reflected the preeminence of his rank-status:

The king's title is *Otoo-noo-ey-te-Atooa*; the meaning of which we do not clearly understand, but as the word Atooa is used to express the object of worship, it is doubtless as full of arrogancy and pride as is possible. His house is called *Yow-rye*, (clouds of heaven); his double canoe *Anooanooa*, (the rainbow); his manner of riding on the shoulders of an attendant *Mahowta*, (flying); his torch *Ooweera*, (lightning); and a drum that is frequently beating for his amusement *Pateere*, (thunder). (LMS Transactions:I, 121)

Other aspects of the young chief's behavior will be discussed later on.

Teri'i na Vaho Roa, the younger son of Pomare I and 'Itia, was found by the missionaries to be residing in Seaward Teva, where he was called *ari'i rahi*, bearing the Title Vehiatua ("V"). His wife was Tupu, younger daughter of Auo and Mahau (and hence sister of Pomare II's wife, Tetuanui). Vehiatua V and Tupu resided in "Matowee," or "Mattahwey" (Mata'oae?); how much actual authority — as distinct from rank-status — he exercised over the rest of the Seaward Teva is hard to say. His parents, Pomare I and 'Itia, resided occasionally in nearby Teahupo'o.

Turning now to Temari'i-Teri'irere,[4] chief of Papara, this individual, now approaching forty years of age, was generally conceded by the missionaries to be the island's second most important chief. His wife at this time was "Tayreede" (Tairiti?), daughter of the chief of Papeuriri. When Teri'irere-Temari'i first visited the missionaries he was described as a "chief priest," and either an "*atua*" or "*ta'ata no te atua*" (a god, or a god's human — i.e., a shaman subject to long periods of possession by some god). Some time previously he had "adopted" Pomare II and, as we shall see, was the latter's close friend and ally. (pp. 161–162)

As we thus see, most of the individuals playing important roles in the political developments of this decade had undergone some changes in their situations since Bligh's departure in 1792, but none so much as Ha'amanemane, the *ari'i* priest, who had sought refuge on Tahiti in November 1788, after suffering political reversals on his home island of Ra'iatea. Even during Bligh's last visit this elderly man had become the island's high priest of 'Oro and Pomare I's principal political aide; in addition he is said to have "adopted" Pomare II, and bequeathed to him the various insignia, and so forth, symbolizing his Ra'iatean kin-Titles. Now, some five years later, Ha'amanemane was found to be identified more closely with Pomare II than with the latter's father, and to be embarked on a political career of his own. While he plotted to retrieve his authority in Ra'iatea, he seemed no less intent upon gaining some in Tahiti as well. The missionaries were informed that his influence rested on his effectiveness as priest (and sorcerer?).

His own power seems to depend on his priesthood: the poor natives say, "If we deny him any thing, he will pray to the Eatooa, and we shall die." We often, as far as our knowledge of the language will admit, enter into conversation with him respecting his notions of religion, and find him very bigoted in his opinions, concerning the gods of Otaheite, but from no other authority than, as he says, "my grandfather told my father, and my father told me." (LMS Transactions:I, 12)

Not the least of the old priest's characteristics was his physical vitality:

Nov. 23d. — Mannemanne, who, though nearly blind with age, is as libidinous now, as when thirty years younger; and, in order to gratify his lust, has frequently upwards of a dozen females with him, some of them apparently not above twelve or thirteen years of age; had to-day two of his concubines eloped from him; a great stir was made upon the occasion, and about three in the afternoon, near two hundred men and boys, armed with spears, clubs, and sticks, issued forth into the neighbourhood, to beat the bushes in search of the two women, but without finding them. (I, 88)

Although Ari'ipaea's widow, Vahine Metua, was characterized by Wilson as "chief over all Hedeah [Hitia'a]" (p. 190), the person who seems to have exercised that authority was one Teohu, whose relationship to Vahine Metua (or to anyone else) I have not succeeded in tracing.

From these and other fragments of information it is possible to essay some kind of political geography of Tahiti at the end of the eighteenth century. It will be found to be incomplete and in part less than credible — that is, since most of the information was obtained from the Pomares, or from individuals allied with them, some of it will be biased, if not actually wrong — but worth the effort anyway. We can begin with Seaward Teva, which in the recent past, at least, constituted a fairly unified tribe under the chieftainship of its line of Vehiatuas. In 1797, as we have seen, the individual who bore that Title was Pomare I's youngest son, Teri'i na Vaho Roa, who resided on the peninsula, without reported opposition from any of his "subjects"; but this appraisal might of course reflect lack of information rather than lack of any such opposition. In any case, when Pomare I was engaged in collecting objects for a ceremony to be held at Papara, the missionaries reported having seen "most of the chiefs of Tiaraboo" assembled with their contributions. (pp. 198–199)

In their survey of the peninsula's population, the missionaries listed twenty-one territorial subdivisions (including an uninhabited one) and the "cheif" of each; among the latter are included Pomare I, 'Itia, and Ha'amanemane; but the other names listed resist identification (p. 199).

According to the missionaries, the chief of Vaiari was "Maahehanoo" (Ma'ahehanu?), a girl of about fifteen, whom I cannot otherwise identify. The same account has her "betrothed" to a youth of the same age named "Towha" (Te To'ofa), identified as son of another "Towha," whose identity I am unsure of.[5] This young couple was said to have been under guardianship of a man named "Tootahah" (Tutaha), described as "having descended from the earees," but he was not otherwise identified.[6]

The missionaries named "Tayredhy" (Tairiti?) as current chief of Vaiururi (Papeuriri, Mataiea) and Atimaono, succeeding her father. As she was at the time married to Teri'irere-Temari'i it may be assumed that the long-standing political connections between these districts and Papara were still extant. (The then current state of the similarly long-standing connection between Papara and Vaiari was not specifically reported, but in the absence of contrary evidence one may assume that it also was extant.)

Papara was, of course, under the chieftainship of Teri'irere-Temari'i. As for the Oropa'a, the missionaries stated that "Attahooroo is divided into two or three departments, over which chiefs subordinate to Temarre preside" (p. 207). While it is true that the warlike residents of this large region had been defeated by the mutineers and other forces aligned with Pomare I and Teri'irere-Temari'i, I very much doubt that they had remained "subordinate" to either of the latter in the sense that the missionaries attached to that term. Their lack of leaders such as the former Te To'ofa and Pohuetea undoubtedly served to weaken their independence, but much of the old spirit was still alive. By 1797 the famous "Papara" image of 'Oro, which had been taken to Pare after the mutineers' victory in 1790, was again housed at Pa'ea's marae 'Utu'aimahurau.[7] When and how it came to be returned there from Pare we do not know; the only reference I find to the transfer occurs in the missionary Jefferson's journal under the date of April 20, 1801: "We also hear that the ground of the quarrel between Pomerre &c. and the district of Attahooroo is, because some persons belonging to that district stole some time ago from Oparre the image of their great god O'oro and have secreted it. . ." (Jefferson, Journal, LMS Archives). As we shall see, the efforts by Pomare II to recover this immensely important object were a central element in island politics during the next few years.

At the time of the missionaries' survey in July 1797, Fa'a'a was listed as being under the chieftainship of Pomare I (p. 210). Previous reports had named Pomare I's youngest brother, Te Pau "C", as chief of this unit, but what his role was in 1797 — if indeed he were still alive — is not reported.

Pare-Arue were of course still the headquarters and the principal base of the Pomares, father and son, and many of their nearest kin also resided there. Ha'apape was also under Pomare's overall authority, but had its local subtribal chiefs as well.

Ha'apaiano'o came under the chiefly authority of Pomare I's brother, Vaetua, and while the latter was not openly opposed to his elder brother's interests, neither was he obediently aligned with them at all times.

At this point in history Tiarei and Mahaena were as usual somewhat aloof from political developments elsewhere, probably the result of their inaccessible situations and their thin populations. On those few occasions when they were drawn into the island's larger political conflicts they seem to have followed the lead of their larger neighbor Hitia'a.

The identity of the tribal leadership of Hitia'a is a puzzle. In one context the missionaries attributed the office to Ari'ipaea's widow, Vahine Metua, whose father had previously held authority there. This forceful woman did indeed maintain a residence and a retinue there, but three years later, when a confrontation occurred between Pomare II and Hitia'a, the chief of the latter was a man named Teohu, whose antecedents I am unable to identify.

Turning now to Mo'orea, there is no indication of a change having taken place in the political geography or chieftainship of that Pomare refuge. The unity of the island is suggested by a brief passage in Wilson, describing a visit there by some of the ship's company. Upon arrival at Uponohu they found a *rahui* in effect:

This rahoo is laid on by the chiefs to repair the desolations their inordinate feastings make, and is always religiously observed by the people. It seems that the whole island of Eimeo was at this time under this injunction, but at Otaheite it is only imposed on a few districts at one time, during which none of the residents dare sell a pig, or kill one for their own use. However, they may take hogs from those districts that are free, and use them as they please. (p. 83)

From the fact that Pomare I and 'Itia spent much of their time there, one may assume that its chieftainship was still in the hands of Mahau's (and Auo's) son, and that the latter's uncle, Pomare I, continued to exert a large measure of authority, or at least influence, there. (Ha'amanemane seems also to have used Mo'orea as an occasional residence, but he, of course, was closely identified with both the Pomares at the time [pp. 58–59].)

Finally, any summary of these Islands' political geography in 1797 must mention the existence of its handful of beachcombers. The Swedish Andrew Lind, then about thirty years old and formerly a member of *Matilda*'s crew, had been in Tahiti since 1792. A second Swede, Peter Haggerstein, then about forty years old, had been there since 1793, when he was left by *Daedalus*. A third Swede, "John," also from the *Matilda*, spent some of his time on Mo'orea, and was considered by his compatriots to be insane.

SON AGAINST FATHER

In addition to its other lacunae, the résumé just given leaves unspecified the most fateful element of all in the political geography of Tahiti and Moʻorea — namely, the developing rivalry between Pomare I and his son and successor, Pomare II. It is impossible to discover when that rivalry overtly began. Perhaps it was just one more example of an inevitable, even habitual, consequence of the Maohi mode of kin-Title succession, wherein the trappings of the office devolved upon a Titleholder's successor at an early and fixed time, while the substance of any associated authority was transferred sometime later, and usually in steps that varied in magnitude and in timing according to factors of personality and situation.[8] It may be that most or all such authority transfers involved a type of rivalry, and that the one between the Pomares, father and son, has attracted attention mainly because of the size of the stakes, and of course the illumination cast upon it by the European spectators.

The missionaries were in Tahiti for one year before they began to acknowledge how things stood between Pomare I and his son, but the signs were there all along. In a word, Pomare II's close friendship with Papara's chief, Teriʻirere-Temariʻi, stood in sharp contrast to the latter's avowed hostility toward Pomare I. And although the Raʻiatean Haʻamanemane maintained in public a friendly and more or less respectful relationship with Pomare I, he sought to undermine him in private — in contrast to his identity with the interests of Pomare II. (pp. 61, 206.)

The first time the missionaries saw most of these principal personages together was at Papara, in August 1797, after the *Duff* had departed for England. The occasion for this meeting was a *taurua*, a large-scale assembly held at Papara which included a human offering and presentations of food and other objects by the host to certain of the guests. The missionaries' description of this event is so sketchy that I cannot identify it specifically with any of the distinguishable types of large-scale assemblies characterized in previous chapters. The first reference to the event occurs in the *Duff* officers' account of their meeting with Pomare on Taiarapu during July 1797:

When I asked him [Pomare I] his reasons for not going to Matavai, he answered, that at present he could not possibly go, it being a very busy time with him, having to collect canoes, cloth, hogs, &c. to give away among the different chiefs and arreoies, who would attend him to the great feast at Papparā, which was to take place in a few days, and for which all the island was looking up to him. This excuse I had reason to believe, for public care seemed engraven on his countenance. (p. 198)

A month later some missionaries saw Pomare I just prior to the assembly at Papara, where he was again preparing objects for distribution:

When we arrived at the habitation of Pomere, we found him busily employed in superintending his servants in dying of cloth, it being customary for him to make large presents to the chiefs and Areeoies at the annual feast, which is near at hand, for which he has been making provision some time past. (LMS Transactions:I, 6)

The description of the occasion as an "annual feast" is puzzling, inasmuch as its timing, in mid-August, seems to distinguish it from the great plant-food ceremonies, which usually took place at the beginning and climax of food ripening, in December through January and in April through May. Nor does this occasion correspond to the periodic "intertribal" assemblies at which the flow of goods was from subject to chief. Indeed, Pomare I, the host of this particular occasion, seems to have been the principal donor, and the political-diplomatic emphasis of the event was heightened by another aspect of it: ". . . at this feast it is also customary to offer human sacrifices, and distribute the limbs of the victims to the populace, in the same manner as they do the cloth, the heads being deposited on the Morai, and the eyes presented to the young king [Pomare II]" (I, 6).

Evidently, the affair was sponsored and largely provisioned by Pomare I, to maintain and revalidate the rank-status of his successor, Pomare II. Why it was held at Papara, and not at Pare (Pomare I's own marae) or at 'Utu'aimahurau (where the principal 'Oro image then was) is not explained, but I suggest that it may have been done deliberately as a means of demonstrating Pomare II's ascendancy in this rival center of rank-based preeminence and political influence. One of the passages quoted above seems to imply that all the island's principal chiefs assembled for this occasion, but the only ones specifically named were Pomare, father and son, Teri'i na Vaho Roa (Pomare I's youngest son, the current Vehiatua), Teri'irere-Temari'i, and Ha'amanemane (whose presence was required to help officiate at the human sacrifices).

The two missionaries who attended this occasion (mainly in order to protest the human offerings) did not see the religious ceremony or the distribution of objects, but, more relevant to our interests, they were witness to a clash between Pomare I and Teri'irere-Temari'i, which they described in the following words:

On our arrival [at Teri'irere-Temari'i's residence], we were informed of a very awful and affecting circumstance having taken place: viz, that the servants of Temaree had killed a man; on enquiry, they informed us, that the man was a thief, that they caught him robbing the plantations of Yavva, and stoned him to death. We were desirous of knowing, if they had offered the man as a sacrifice to their Eatooa; the replied, no: that they had buried him, and that thieves should be punished. To this we could make no reply, being unable to inform them (for want of knowing their language) how to proceed in such cases. In the afternoon, several men from Tiaraboo came to Temaree, and seemed much displeased, on account of the man's being killed. In the evening, the natives who came with us from Matavai, being alone with the writer, informed him that it was very bad of Temaree to kill the man, who was no thief, but only came to ask for (or demand) the Yavva, being a principal servant of Pomere, but that they were afraid to say much for fear of the images, or gods, which Temaree had in his house, who would come at night, when they were asleep, and kill them. I endeavoured to convince them their fears were groundless, but to no purpose, they told me, I might ask Peter, or John the Swede, if what they told me was not true. It growing dark we took some refreshment, and the writer engaged in prayer, after which he retired to rest, leaving brother Main in conversation with Temaree. In a short time we were alarmed with the cry of Tamai! Tamai! i.e., War! War! occasioned by a report that the people of Tiaraboo intended to attack Temaree in the night. (LMS Transactions:I, 6–7)

. . . the alarm of war having in some measure abated, the natives were quiet, and turned their attention to the Yavva, the juice of which is an antidote to all their cares and complaints. After breakfast I went to Pomere's house, where I was surrounded by many natives, who, thinking I was a friend to Temaree, looked very sternly at me; having their war weapons in their hands, and their turbans on their heads, their appearance was truly formidable. I remained at the house the whole of the night, but had but little rest, being often disturbed with the cry of war! Pomere slept with a spear by his side, and had a musqueteer to guard him. Having been preserved from danger through the night, the next morning I set off for Matavai, with orders from Pomere to inform the brethren there would be no war. Pomere advised me to go over the Isthmus, to avoid any ill-designing men among the opposite party, and make the best of my way home. (I, 7–8)

On August 22, Brother Main returned to Matavai and reported that the difference between Pomare I and Temari'i had been "amicably settled" — or so it appeared at the time.

At this early stage the missionaries were so preoccupied with their own personal and domestic problems, and so ignorant about the workings of Maohi society, that they have left us only brief glimpses of native political activity. For example, they recorded their participation in a ceremony held at the huge Pare assembly house, Nanu, but, besides describing a ritual episode suggestive of peacemaking and noting that it was attended by large numbers of persons, including Ariois, their account is uninformative. In their journal record for January 31, 1798, after describing the day's prayer service and the progress made on a new building is the following sentence: "We have, in some measure, been the happy means of preventing Pomere from going to war with the Teeahroa" (I, 25). And that is the only reference to what was probably a most critical episode!

On March 6, 1798, there began a series of incidents that was to bring to a climax, and a resolution, the rivalry between Pomare I and his son. As the missionaries themselves were directly involved, their reports, as preserved in the LMS Transactions, are somewhat fuller and more intelligible. On the date in question there arrived at Matavai a small vessel out of Macao; the *Nautilus* (Captain Bishop commanding) was headed toward South America to pick up sealskins. The ship was badly in need of food supplies, but as it had only muskets and powder to barter the missionaries provided food from their own stocks in exchange for the understanding that no guns or ammunition would be left with the Maohis — a hoped-for assist for peace and security, which however turned out to be quite the reverse.

Inevitably, knowledge of the missionaries' maneuver became public, and the chiefs who had hoped to replenish their arsenals were resentful. This appears to have been particularly so of Pomare II, whose feelings were probably intensified by his irritation at the favored treatment characteristically accorded his father by the missionaries. The resentment finally culminated in an attack made on some missionaries at the end of March 1798. One morning, as four of them were returning home from Pare, where they had sought the help of Pomare I, his son, and Teri'irere-Temari'i in recovering some *Nautilus* seamen who had jumped ship, they were manhandled and relieved of their clothes by a gang of natives. The reaction of Pomare I (and 'Itia) to the affair seems to have been one of genuine surprise, regret, and annoyance. Pomare II also expressed his concern, but in a manner hollow enough to raise doubts even among the credulous missionaries.

The effect of this encounter upon the missionaries was electric. After putting themselves in a "posture of defense" they solemnly voted (after prayer) "that from the recent occurrence, and present appearance of things, a removal of the Society off the island seemed necessary" (I, 37). Four days later the *Nautilus* departed for Australia, carrying all but five of the unmarried missionaries, and all the married ones save Brother Nott and his wife (the latter having been considered either too infirm for the voyage, or too elderly to invite molestation). Those left on the island turned over most of their remaining goods to Pomare and 'Itia in order to be relieved of the risk of further injury to themselves by covetous natives. Pomare I's reactions to the attack were more forceful: "March 30th. Heard this morning that Pomere was avenging our cause, on·some of the people of Opare, and that he had killed two, who either were the principals, or assisted in stripping the four misisonaries" (I, 42).

Two weeks later, word reached the remaining missionaries that the neighbors and relatives of the men killed by Pomare were determined to avenge their death and had declared war against both Pomare I and his son. Aroused by this challenge to their authority (the declared enemies were residents of Pare itself), the two chiefs descended upon their adversaries and drove them into the mountains, meanwhile burning forty to fifty of their houses and killing ten men and two women. According to the missionaries' tally, as reported in the LMS Transactions: ". . . with the two men killed before, and one that died of his wounds, make fifteen lives lost since the brethren were stripped of their clothes at Opare, and which was the foundation of this slaughter. We have not heard of any of Otoo's party being slain." (I, 49)

Much was to happen between the clothes stripping incident and the missionaries' retrospective comprehension of it; but this will be described later on.

In July the remaining missionaries recorded a rumor that Teri'irere-Temari'i was about to make war against Matavai, but shortly thereafter a report reached them that the threatened attack had been called off as a result of Pomare I having made an atonement offering (*tarae hara*) to Teri'irere-Temari'i in the form of a live pig and a young plantain tree: "The cause of Temaree's anger, it is said, originated from some unbecoming jest that had been put upon one of his family. As we do not hear that the offence was given by Pomere, we cannot tell how he came to atone for it." (I, 54–55.) No further explanation is to be found for this puzzling episode, but it does serve to confirm that relations between Teri'irere-Temari'i and Pomare I were anything but friendly. However, the unfriendliness of the former was not to last very long.

On August 30, the missionaries were asked to hurry to Pare and minister medically to a person injured in a gunpowder explosion. On arriving there they found the patient to be none other than Teri'irere-Temari'i, who had burned himself critically while testing the effectiveness of some gunpowder acquired from a visiting vessel. Brother Broomhall, the "surgeon" among them, applied medicine to the wounded man's skin and returned to Matavai. On visiting the patient the next morning he found him in a worse condition, his body covered with a paste made of the scrapings of yams. Having suffered much pain from the missionary's previous medication, Teri'irere-Temari'i and his associates, including Pomare II, were ominously angry. After a threatening encounter with Pomare II the missionaries managed to reach home in Matavai, where Bromhall summed up their thoughts in the following words:

I thought the scene of March 26th [the stripping incident] was again about to be acted, only in a more tragic manner; inasmuch as the natives' suspicions then were small when compared with the present. At that time they suspected we had prevented captains Bishop and Simpson, of the Nautilus, from bartering with them for musquets; but *now* they believed we had cursed the medicine, that it might kill the patient, and *that* the greatest man on the island, he being closely allied with Otoo against his father and mother. (I, 77–78)

Pomare I appealed to the missionaries to treat Teri'irere-Temari'i with medicine that would cause no pain, but, as that was impossible, nothing further was done by the missionaries, who described the situation in a statement notable for its increased understanding of Maohi politics:

The king, queen, Pomere, Edea, Mannemanne, are to the westward, anxiously waiting the issue of the late calamitous visitation. We have reason to believe Orepiah's death would be the cause of great secret rejoicing to Pomere, Edea, and others, who seem to stand in much dread from the close union subsisting between Otoo and Orepiah: the latter being the uncle of the former, has acted as a kind of guardian to him during his youthful days. Though the wheels of political government are not so many in this as in our native island, yet they are more in number than any would conceive from the rude and barbarous state the nation is in. They have their plots and court intrigues, their parties and partisans, as well here as in England; and they are as important in their way as in the most refined court of Europe. (I, 78–79)[9]

Teri'irere-Temari'i finally expired. While embalming and funeral proceedings were in progress Pomare I found it convenient to withdraw to Tetiaroa, and it was announced (presumably by Pomare II) that the corpse would be sent on a tour of the island, to receive the expressions of respect traditionally accorded the remains of individuals of such high rank-status and political power. The response to this announcement from Matavai was admirably candid — but fatally foolhardy: according to the missionaries it consisted of ". . . some improper expressions said to be uttered by Pomere's [the father] orator and others, concerning the corpse of Orepiah [i.e., Temari'i]; namely, that the king [Pomare II] should not bring the corpse of Orepiah to Matavai, but throw it into the sea" (I, 84).

The reaction of Pomare II to this insult to his late friend (and undoubtedly to himself) was swift and deadly. His forces swept through Matavai, driving out most of its inhabitants and killing four of them. The missionaries were again spared of any molestation, but this encounter between Pomare II and his father's closest supporters opened missionary eyes still further to the real issues involved:

Pomere is at the Motoo [Motu, i.e., Tetiaroa], ignorant of the transactions of the day. We have more than once had occasion to notice a disunion between Otoo and his father, and a strong attachment between the former and the deceased chief Orepiah. The providential destruction of Orepiah, though it has deprived Otoo of a powerful ally, may have nothing lessened his disaffection to his father: indeed, the occurrences of this day seem to be a proof it has not, or we suppose he would never have treated his father's friends as he has done, for the imprudent speech of one or more persons. Edea is in Opare indisposed with the rheumatism: how far she approves of her son's conduct we know not. The chief of Tiaraboo (Otoo's younger brother) threatened some time ago to make war upon Otoo; and we have some reason to apprehend there is a league formed between him and his father Pomere, and his uncle Vitua, against Otoo. Thus we see men are the same in Otaheite as in Europe, and other parts of the world: "their feet are swift to shed blood: destruction and misery are in their ways, and the way of peace have they not known." The ties of consanguinity are no more binding here than any where else where men have not the fear of God before their eyes. (I, 84)[10]

Such then was the line-up. Pomare I, 'Itia, Vaetua, and Teri'i na Vaho Roa (now Vehiatua)[11] against Pomare II and the latter's chief counselor, Ha'amanemane. With Pomare I absent and taking the "cure" on Tetiaroa, Pomare II and Ha'amanemane moved swiftly to exploit their advantages:

A little after morning service we heard, that Otoo and Manemanne had usurped the power over all the larger peninsula, and turned Pomere out from exercising authority in any part of the same. The districts of Opare, Tataha, Attahooroo, Papara, &c. (all the lands to the westward, and running round to the isthmus on the south) have declared for Otoo. The land of this district, from the river before us, to the eastern boundary, Otoo has given to Mannemanne, reserving the westernmost part for himself. If the districts on this side of the island, to the isthmus, shall refuse to acknowledge the sovereignty of Otoo, we are informed, war will be declared against them, and their submission extorted by force of arms. Something like this we expected, but did not imagine it would be put into execution so soon, since Temaree, who appeared to be at the head of the faction, was so suddenly cut off. Pomere's absence proved a favourable opportunity, and the indiscreet expressions of some of the inhabitants of this district, respecting the corpse of Temaree, the cause of embracing it. Not long after our settling on the island, we were told of there being two parties, that were meditating the destruction of each other; hence arose the great eagerness of the chiefs to get musquets and ammunition into their hands, from every vessel that has touched here; as also the desire of encouraging seamen to quit their ships, and reside among them: knowing, by former experience, one musqueteer is sufficient to terrify many natives armed with clubs and spears. The Swede and seamen are on Otoo and Mannemanne's side; so that, judging after the manner of men, and forming our conjectures from human reason and probability, we suppose the king and his party will carry all before them. (I, 85)

Vaetua remained in Ha'apaino'o in a state of siege, with too few forces to counter his nephew's moves:

The two brethren found Vitua encompassed with a few adherents, the greatest part of his people being fled beyond the reach of supposed danger. The chief behaved with his accustomed civility. Vitua appeared much incensed against Mannemanne (perhaps he considers him as the principal instigator of the king to the present disturbance) and was preparing to send off a canoe to Tatooroa, to inform Pomere of all particulars, and excite him to come and revenge his cause. But, it is probable, Pomere will not do this; it is said, he is personally a great coward; and as Otoo and Mannemanne have the three Europeans with musquets (the very sight of which strikes terror in every breast) on their side, it is likely he will quietly submit to what is done, till a more favourable opportunity occurs. (I, 87)

True to expectations, Pomare I sent word from Tetiaroa ceding authority over Matavai to Pomare II (including access to the goods which had been turned over to him by the missionaries), and even 'Itia appeared to reconcile herself with the new turn of events, and was "upon the whole . . . sociable with her son" (I, 89). At the moment, then, peace seemed secured, with Pomare II and Ha'amanemane wholly successful.

But within the week rumors reached the missionaries that Taiarapu, Ha'apaiano'o, and rest of Aharoa were determined to war against Pomare II and Ha'amanemane — in the midst of which there came the news that Ha'amanemane himself had been slain. On the heels of this, 'Itia arrived at the missionary settlement to announce that the threatened war would not take place:

Edea came to brother Eyre's door (she had a cartouch box buckled round her waist, a musquet, she had been seen with in her hand a little before, was now laid aside) with a settled air of triumph on her brow, she shook hands in a friendly manner with the Swede, saying unto him, "It is all over"; meaning the war, and retired immediately to the point. (I, 90)

Two days later, the missionaries learned what had transpired:

Heard Edea was gone to Opare, upon the horrible business of sacrificing a relation of Mannemanne's to her devil god. The prevailing account of Mannemanne's death is this: Pomere sent word in a private manner, to Edea, to have him killed. Edea went twice or thrice to Otoo, to draw him to consent to his death; at first he was unwilling, but at length yielded, and assented to the desire of his father and mother. Early yesterday morning Mannemanne set off for Opare, and was followed by Fareroa, the man Edea cohabits with, and one of the Sandwich islanders; they overtook the old priest at the bottom of One-tree-hill, on the west side, and after a little conversation with him, Fare-roa smote him on the head with a stone. (I, 91–92)

The end of Ha'amanemane called forth from the missionaries a résumé of the island's recent political history, which deserves quotation in full:

Mannemanne was a native of Oryateea, of which island he was once chief, but his subjects revolting expelled him the island. He then sought shelter on Otaheite, and obtained it, and has here exercised the office of chief priest for many years; under this character he has been guilty of much slaughter, shedding torrents of human blood in sacrifice to abominable idols and devils. He was esteemed, by all ranks, as a man of great knowledge, so that it was thought he had not his equal on the island. It appears, a jealousy has long subsisted between the deceased and Edea and Pomere, upon what account we know not. Pomere seemed to stand in fear of the priest (who was related to him) and had a kind of persuasion respecting him, similar to that the king of Moab had of Balaam, namely 'Whom he blessed was blessed, and whom he cursed was cursed.' Many were led away with the delusion that Mannemanne had great influence with their gods. It is evident to us, the casting out Pomere from having any power, driving out the inhabitants of the district, and dividing it between Otoo and himself, were projected and chiefly effected through the instrumentality of the priest; and for which, some of us thought, he would draw upon himself what he really has. Mannemanne, though far advanced in years, and almost blind, was, notwithstanding, very active and full of animal spirits; he was always attended with many females, as before observed, who only stayed with him while he could gratify them with gifts. Whether Mannemanne had any foresight of the gathering storm, that was to crush him, and wanted to avoid it, or whether he thought he was now near the time of putting a long devised plan into execution, (and for which purpose, the obtaining of musquets, and making friends with Europeans, for their assistance, were his constant arms) for regaining the chiefship of his native country, we cannot tell, but a small vessel, of about twenty tons, was to be equipped with all expedition, with which he, and the three Europeans, were going with haste off the island. And early on last Sabbath morning, Mannemanne went into brother Eyre's apartment, as soon as he was up, to beg an axe; brother Eyre informed him it was our Sabbath, and that we did not meddle with such things on that day. With this reply he was satisfied, and said no more. He then groped his way to the bed (sister Eyre being asleep) and began to feel the curtains, and to measure them with his arms, in their length and depth: brother Eyre observing him, conceived he wanted them for sails to his boat. Having satisfied his curiosity he retired from the room, and never entered it more. The old man's conduct toward us has always been friendly, and free from that deceit which others have practised, but he was a perpetual beggar. What may follow the late judgment we know not, every thing at present looks very dreary. (I, 92–93)

Their appraisal of Pomare II's role in the recent events was perhaps just as realistic:

The conduct of Otoo, in consenting to the death of Mannemanne, at the time he was in close alliance with him, opens the character of the man in a conspicuous manner, and confirms us in a suspicion we have long entertained, but knew not how to account for, concerning the stripping of brothers Broomhall, Jefferson, Main, and W. Puckey, at Opare. When that circumstance took place we seemed assured it was done by the king's authority, but when Otoo afterwards joined his father in punishing the poor people for the same, we could not readily reconcile his authorizing the action and then destroying those that did it. But we had seen so much of him since, that we believe he is capable of committing any wickedness the devil, his carnal mind, and blood-thirsty followers may excite him to, if God did not restrain him; we therefore think the true cause of that event was this, Temaree, the foster-father of Otoo, was in close connection with him, and clearly appeared to be meditating some great blow, by which they would exclude every other person from having authority on the island but themselves and followers. To effect this they were extremely desirous to get into their hands musquets and ammunition. When the bark Nautilus arrived, finding that she had a large quantity of these articles on board, but that they were deterred from obtaining them through our interference, they were offended, and determined to be revenged. Accordingly, when the Nautilus arrived the second time, and the two seamen escaped from her, and took refuge with Otoo, and the four brethren were dispatched with an endeavour to recover them, the king, thinking it a favourable opportunity to execute his revenge upon the society, secretly gave orders for their being plundered. Otoo and Temaree, though powerful, were not sufficiently strong at the time to oppose Pomere, who shewed displeasure at what was done; and though, no doubt, he was acquainted with the true authors of the action, yet from prudent motives, it may be, vented his anger upon the instruments rather than the movers of them; while Otoo and Temaree, to hide their crime, joined Pomere in so doing. What wicked policy! (I, 93)

The announcement of a peaceful settlement to this whole affair was, characteristically, quite premature. Pomare I and 'Itia appeared to remain reconciled to the new dispensation, and the inhabitants of Matavai returned home after due expression of subservience to Pomare II; but some local skirmishing continued between Taiarapuans and Teri'irere-Temari'i's former supporters in Vaiari. Meanwhile, the whole area from Ha'apape to the isthmus served as a refuge for enemies of Pomare II, and reports reached the missionaries that Atehuru and even Papara were ". . . in great confusion among themselves." In fact, the situation reached a point so unsettled that the missionaries were moved to report: "It appears upon the whole, the inhabitants of the island do not know what they are doing, or what they would be at." (I, 95.)

Nothing however developed from these alarms — not immediately at least — and when Pomare I finally returned from Tetiaroa six months later the island was enjoying what the missionaries earlier called "a great degree of outward peace," and father and son met with mutual displays of amity (I, 115, 123). Meanwhile Pomare II's everyday behavior reached heights of arbitrary arrogance, which even the long-suffering missionaries remarked to be extreme.[12]

"DISAFFECTION OF THE COMMONALITY"

The reconciliation between Pomare II and his father was followed almost immediately by signs of hostility toward both of them. As usual, the center of opposition was Atehuru, where someone had burned the house of Peter the Swede, and thereby issued a challenge to the latter's protectors, the Pomares, that they could not ignore. The cause of the impending war, as represented to the missionaries, was ". . . that the inhabitants of that district have resented the tyrannical and oppressive conduct of the chiefs [i.e., the Pomares], who exercise, with an high hand, their authority over those subject to their power." (LMS Transactions:I, 143)

As an indispensable move in preparing for war the Pomares stepped up their human offerings to 'Oro; the fact that the god's principal image was in Atehuru (i.e., at 'Utu'aimahurau, Pa'ea) seems to have induced the Pomares to offer an increased number of propitiating sacrifices to it:

Heard that five human sacrifices have, within a few days, been brought over from Eimeo, to this island — Also that many of the inhabitants of Opare (of the poorest sort), have fled to the mountains, to avoid being seized for human sacrifices . . . It appears that these things are preparations for the proposed war, and that Pomere is doing what other blind heathens have done before him, labouring to bribe his idol-god to be propitious to him, and to forsake the district of Attahooroo. (I, 143)

Within a few days, the number of human offerings had exceeded ten, Pomare I having demanded some from each district believed to be loyal to him and his son (I, 145).

In the midst of these preparations the missionaries received assurances from Pomare I regarding their own safety; the direct bearing of this message on the subject of this chapter warrants quoting it:

Nov. 30th . . . About noon, Michael Donald [a beached seaman in Pomare I's retinue] came to us from Pomere, the purport of whose message was, that we should be under no fear of danger to our persons, that we should consider *him* as our protector, and that he considered *us*, by the property we had put into his hands, as his protector (that is, we apprehend, Pomere considers his power and authority, and consequently his safety, greatly augmented and established, by the vast addition of wealth he has derived from us). (I, 153)[13]

Meanwhile European vessels began to call at Tahiti (usually Matavai) with increasing frequency: the *Betsey* (and a Spanish prize) in December

1799 and the *Eliza* in January 1800. From these vessles the Pomares were able to add to their European manpower and to increase their arsenals, including an "eighteen pound carronade, . . . several muskets, and a great deal of ammuniton" (I, 169).

But Atehuru, and now Papara, continued to threaten the Pomares, and Hitia'a served as a base for the latter's enemies. Even within their own home district of Pare, Pomare I and 'Itia were, according to the missionaries, ". . . so much afraid as to have a guard around them at night" (I, 201). In October 1800, Pomare I summed up the current situation in a statement of remarkable candor:

> To-day the chief, &c. visited us. In a conversation a brother had with Pomere, the chief gave him to understand, that there is a probability of war upon the island, but not directly. He did not seem to know who were his friends, or who his foes, but acknowledged the general desire of the people is a suppression of a monarchical form of Government, and the re-establishment of independency in each district. It was observed to him, that the arbitrary proceedings of Otoo, were probably the cause of the present discontent. He did not deny it. Pomere wished much for a ship of war to arrive, which he supposed, by an interference in his favour, would restore tranquility, and confirm his and his son's authority. Or if a number of Englishmen like ourselves were to join us, and continue their residence among them in the manner we have done, he said, he was sure there would be no war. (I, 202–203)

Similar sentiments were expressed by Pomare at the beginning of 1801 in a letter to Philip King, Governor of New South Wales:

> May it please your Excellency,
> Your letter and present I kindly accept. I love king George and his subjects, and will, while I live, be a protector to those of them who put themselves under my care; but I must tell your excellency, I at this time stand in fear of the commonality, many of them being disaffected towards me, and their disaffection, I fear, is encouraged by some seamen who are on the island; and therefore I wish your excellency to present me with a few fire-arms, whereby my authority may be maintained, and the peace of my kingdom preserved. (I, 213–214)

Despite all these preparations for war, formal visiting continued between the chiefly adversaries, including some solemn (and obviously hollow) peacemaking ceremonies. One such meeting was held at Pare during 1801, attended by all the island's principal chiefs and probably most of its fighting men as well. I cannot discover the declared purpose of this meeting, nor can I fathom the Pomares' private reasons for holding it and thereby bringing so many of their enemies to their own district. In any case, the meeting appears to have gone well for the Pomares, as the result of two episodes. The first was the arrival in June of the *Porpoise*, an armed vessel from Port Jackson, with gifts and a letter to Pomare I, which were presented with an impressive show of military ceremony and force.[14] In commenting on this event the missionaries wrote:

By intelligence that we have received, it seems that the arrival of the Porpoise is a very providential interference, as the affairs of this country were brought to such a crisis, that a few days, if not hours, would have either dethroned Otoo, or established him in his authority; this could not have been done without much bloodshed, the effusion of which, we hope, is now stopped, and Otoo and family will be permitted to retain quiet possession of their dignity. The Lord does all things well. (I, 229n)

The second advantage secured to the Pomares during this lengthy meeting was the death, at Pare in August, of Teohu, chief of Hitia'a. Teohu had been the Pomares' most outspoken opponent, and his district had been a rallying place for dissidents from elsewhere. He had brought with him to the meeting a formidable force of his own, augmented by the fighting forces of Mahaena and Tiarei, who seem to have accepted his leadership. Teohu appears to have been sufficiently constrained by the show of English support for the Pomares to have concluded a peace settlement with the latter (the terms of which are, however, not clear), but he still constituted a threat. Recognizing this, the Pomares made plans to kill him immediately after the "peace" ceremony, but he saved them the trouble by dying of illness instead.

The Pomares' position received additional strengthening with the arrival, in July 1801, of another contingent of English missionaries together with another supply of goods which, in the nature of things, would eventually in large part find their way into the Pomares' hands (Newbury 1961:32ff.).

On December 12 of that year the climactic session of the greatly heralded meeting took place at Pare; unfortunately for the historian of that crucial period, the information about its proceedings is limited to the following terse entry in a missionary chronicle: "Decr 12th it was said the meeting was to commence five of the misss went down to Pare, to see how things were likely to turn out, and in the evening returned with the good news that the great meeting was likely to terminate peaceably" (Newbury 1961:41).[15]

Characteristically however, within a month a missionary historian had to report that war alarms had been renewed. The general cause of dissension continued to be the widespread hostility to the Pomares' arrogance and pretensions. And on their side, the Pomares — and particularly the son — continued to press the Oropa'a to give up the "Papara" image of 'Oro, which the latter had held on to, perhaps viewing it as the one remaining check to Pomare II's ambition for absolute power.

This raises again the question concerning the advantages accruing from actual physical possession of this particular image of 'Oro. Because of the deep and widespread faith that seems to have been entertained about 'Oro's decisive effectiveness in warfare, this issue evidently had immensely important political implications. Over the course of time it seems to have become the principal, or perhaps even the *sole*, 'Oro image of Tahiti-Mo'orea into which the great god could be induced to enter — at least, for the purpose of receiving human offerings. Along with this, however, there appeared to be a generally accepted and widely honored agreement concerning the *supratribal* status of the god — that is, even in time of intertribal tensions the tribe within whose boundaries the image happened to be lodged usually permitted potential enemies access to it. On the other hand, in view of the efforts made to obtain, or maintain, physical possession of the image, one must infer that there were additional advantages in actually having it, either in terms of prestige, or easier physical access, or both. As we shall see, the Pomares were allowed access to it at 'Utu'aimahurau even during a period of extreme tension; perhaps their enemies suspected, with good grounds, that a similar right of access would not be extended to them if the image were in Pomare hands.

THE IMAGE OF 'ORO

In March 1802 the Pomares and a large force of their followers went to 'Utu'aimahurau, ostensibly to present human and other offerings to 'Oro, but evidently also to negotiate further concerning physical possession of the god's image. The missionaries who witnessed these events gave the following account of them:

Tuesday, March 30. Left Hafaena, and came on to Attāhooroo, near the place where the ceremony is held, which commenced this day. Passed the great Marrai: saw several large hogs upon the altar, and several human sacrifices hanging on the trees. When we arived at the meeting the ceremony for the day was over. Pomarre was offering as a present five or six large hogs to their great god Ooro on board a sacred canoe on which the ark or residence of Ooro is placed. Informed Pomarre that Jehovah is the true God; and there is none else; that hogs are not acceptable to him, that he is offended at them for killing men, and that Jesus Christ is the only atonement for sin. He was also told that Christ would come to raise the dead, judge the world, and turn the disobedient into the fire. At first the Chief seemed rather unwilling to hear, but those around him continued the conversation by asking questions, and at length Pomarre said, that he would attend to our religion.

Wednesday, March 31. This forenoon a strange heathenish ceremony was performed on the beach. Their great god Ooro was laid upon a long stool covered with cloth, and the king, with several of the priests were sitting by, praying or chanting something to Ooro which we could not understand. They seemed to keep time with their drums and conck-shells. The natives stood so as to form a circle round the idol, to which several of them were exposing themselves in the most shameful manner, and every now and then calling out "Māévā-aré." This continued several hours, during which time a native, who pretended to be inspired by Ooro, was seen, with the most strained distortions of countenance and limbs, giving them directions for their future proceedings.

Thursday, April 1. This morning the fleet moved down to the Great Marrai, where several large canoes were hauled on shore with great quantities of cloth upon them for a present to Ooro. The fleet kept about one hundred yards from the shore, while the priests were performing prayers in the Marrai, with the king and their god Ooro; the drums beating as yesterday. This continued some hours, and then orders being given, all the fleet shouted, saying, "Māévā-aré, Māévā-aré." After this, Ooro was carried upon mens' shoulders backwards and forwards along the beach, some of the natives running before the throng exposing themselves, and calling out as above, the fleet answering them in the same manner. After this a council was called, and Pomarre, with the king, and all the principal rātérā's met in the Marrai. The people of Attāhooroo sat on one side of the ring, and the king and Pomarre on the other, and the orators on each side spoke by turns. The purport of the meeting was to consult upon the manner how they should proceed in what they had to do. The king, after the people of Attāhooroo had refused to give up Ooro, who was in their possession, spoke himself, and demanded him. He was answered immediately by their orators in the negative. Pomarre then addressed himself to his son the king, in behalf of the Attāhooroo people, and requested him to yield to them, and suffer them to keep the god, as it seemed that they did not wish to keep him long, but only till a certain ceremony was performed. The king then directed his speech again to the Attāhooroo people and said, it should not be as his father had requested, and insisted upon their delivering up the god directly: But he was still refused. After asking a long time, he rose up in anger, and ordered all his party that were present to draw back. Immediately the cloth upon the canoes was plundered, and a number of the king's people took hold of Ooro and rescued him from the hands of the Attāhooroo people and ran to the sea side. It was then expected that the Attāhoorooans would pursue to take Ooro from them again, and so war thereby commence; the fleet, therefore, was commanded to advance towards the shore, and all the muskets were loaded. However, the Attahooroo people were afraid and made their retreat into the valley. Orders were then given not to pursue them, and Pomarre, Edeā, with several of the principal men stood on the beach, charging the people to go to their canoes: but notwithstanding all that they could say, many pursued them inland, and dared them to return and fight; but they refused. Pomarre continued to send messengers to order his people to come back, which at length, through fear of offending, they did. He then directed the fleet to return to their quarters, which was complied with. Numbers of the people returned by land, and plundered the deserted huts as they went: all arrived at the place of rendezvous about sun-set. We were informed that the king as soon as their god Ooro was taken from the people of Attahooroo, commanded a human sacrifice to be sought for, lest Ooro should be angry at such treatment. Accordingly one of his own servants was killed upon the beach soon after the fleet got on shore.

Friday, April 2. Quietness through the night. Early this morning the fleet sailed to Papparra on their route towards Towtérāin Tyarabboo, where the ceremony closes and where Ooro is to be deposited according (as they suppose) to his desire. Before the king's party sailed, they set fire to the temporary houses they had erected for their convenience during the continuance of the ceremony.

This day we came on to the west end of Oparre. Saw but few people they being gone with the fleet. (LMS Transactions:II, 63–65)[16]

The fleet's destination was Tautira's marae Taputapuatea, at which, according to one account recorded earlier, the cult of 'Oro had been first introduced to Tahiti.[17] (I am not certain about Pomare II's reasons for depositing this image at Tautira, rather than at his own Tarahoi in Pare.) The passage just reproduced implies that the location was the god's own choice — and perhaps that was indeed the politically disinterested revelation of some 'Oro priest on the Pomares' staff. But if political considerations did enter into the choice, as I firmly believe, Pomare II's interest would probably have been considered better served by this strengthening of his base of influence in distant and still uncertain Taiarapu than by concentrating one more token of authority and influence in Pare itself. In other words (and I consider this to be a most important feature of Maohi politics in general), locational centralization had not yet become the dominant strategy for aggrandizement; the ambitious individual extended his authority and influence not solely by increasing the sanctions behind specific statuses, or by eliminating rival statuses, but also by occupying *more* statuses — *including especially those having territorial bases elsewhere.*

If any further evidence were needed on the degree to which the Maohis were influenced by their religious beliefs, as contrasted with an objective appraisal of physical strength and military skill, the Pomares' behavior during the ensuing weeks could provide it. While warning the missionaries that the Oropa'a would probably attack, to avenge their recent setback at 'Utu'aimahurau, the Pomares went on to Tautira and proceeded to install the 'Oro image there with ceremonies lasting several weeks, during which the Oropa'a were devastating Fa'a'a and Pare. (Even the force of several hundred Mo'oreans which the Pomares sent for could not withstand the Oropa'a attack.) After this the Oropa'a, joined by forces from Papara, Vaiari, and Vaiuriri, attacked Tautira itself, with such success that the Pomares and their supporters had to flee for their lives.[18]

At this juncture, the victors could probably have made an end to the Pomares with ease, but instead, quite characteristically, they tarried in Taiarapu killing and pillaging, and then returned home, their fury evidently spent. Needless to say, they recaptured the 'Oro image and reinstalled it at 'Utu'aimahurau. (Newbury 1961:47–51)

Meanwhile the Pomares remained at Pare repairing their losses and girding for another attack. They even revived enough resolution and support to help put down a threatened "revolt" on Mo'orea; the precise nature of the issues involved in this "rebellion" are not reported, but its center was in Afareaitu and neighboring districts. (Thomson, History, p. 54)

On June 26 there arrived from New South Wales the *Nautilus* (Captain Simpson commanding), with news that other vessels were also en route. This appeared to instill new life into the Pomares and their supporters, and Pomare I renewed his pleas for armed support from his English friends, who were by now a sizeable community — including a Captain Bishop, left there by the ship *Venus* to salt pork (for transport to New South Wales); the captain and crew of the *Norfolk*, engaged in the same mission; and now the personnel of the *Nautilus*. To begin with, Pomare I persuaded the captain of the *Nautilus* to send him with an armed escort to Pa'ea in order to make some offerings to 'Oro. This mission was peacefully accomplished, although the Oropa'a obliged Pomare I to make his offering to the god on the beach some distance from the marae.

Thus encouraged, Pomare I again asked his European friends for assistance in putting down the "rebellion," and this time his pleas were sympathetically received. In fact, as a result of the alarms experienced during his six months residence on the island, Captain Bishop urged his compatriots to put an end, once and for all, to the "rebels' " threats. His primary purpose was the security of the English community, and of the Pomares only insofar as this helped the English. After the missionaries themselves agreed upon the desirability of an end to the "rebellion," the project was launched, and on July 2, 1802, the expeditionary force embarked: "The number of Europeans with Capt. B[ishop] was 19 men well armed, a Boat with the first mate and four men from the Nautilus, a four pounder cannon, and all Pomare's forces. Mr. Elder also went to attend as surgeon. The king [i.e., Pomare II], his brother and a few servants staid at Matavai." (Newbury 1961:53)

The missionaries' report of this encounter follows:

The fleet landed in Attahooroo on Saturday, July 3d, at eleven A.M. a small party of the rebels saw their approach, and retired. The enemy was withdrawn to their strong holds, which, on reconnoitering, were found to be almost impregnable, the storming of which, however, must be attended with great loss. Capt. B. and men would have made the attempt; but Pomarre and men could not be brought to venture on so desperate an action. Several shots were fired, which in general fell harmless. One of Pomarre's men was wounded in the chin and throat, by a ball from the enemy; though they fired but few muskets, owing perhaps to their scantiness of ammunition; stones they slung in abundance, and rolled down some from a great height, of several hundred pounds weight. On the following morning, a party of Papparra people, marching to join the rebels, was intercepted by a party of the royalists. The leader of the party and his wife were slain; the rest made their escape. The bodies of the man and his wife were treated in a most inhuman manner. The rest of the day passed without any particular occurrence, till evening, when Capt. B. wearied with the inactivity, irresolution, and want of subordination, that pervaded Pomarre's camp, had actually re-embarked his men, to return to Mattavai. Pomarre also, who thought it not safe to remain there without the Englishmen, was re-embarking his people with all possible speed. The embarkation was nearly completed, and most of the canoes were moving off, when an unexpected event took place, which gave a new turn to affairs.

A young man who has been with the Society some years, and who had taken to himself the name of *To-morrow-Morning*, had shewn a most active and courageous spirit, and performed such feats of bravery as astonished our countrymen, and excited the admiration of his own. This young man at the time of embarking, was up with one more, at the enemy's entrenchments, braving them to appear and fight, and firing at them, as he saw opportunity. At this season a heavy shower of rain came from the mountains. The rebels deeming this a favourable time, seized, as they thought, the golden moment, and, in great numbers rushed out, armed with musquets, spears, clubs, and slings, and chased *To-morrow-Morning* and the other down to the fleet; they at times firing upon him and he on them.

The noise of the musquets attracted the attention of the people embarked, and stopped their further proceedings. *To-morrow-Morning* came in sight, and gave notice that the enemy was come. In the twinkling of an eye, a few of Pomarre's musqueteers, not yet in their canoes, sprang forward to the combat. A successful discharge of their pieces obliged the rebels to turn their backs and fly. In the mean time the seamen and soldiers re-landed, and joined in the pursuit of the flying foe; who, in a very peculiar manner, after running some space, in a moment rallied, and faced their pursuers. Some of Capt. B.'s party were sufficiently near for the attack. The sight of the Europeans overpowered the rebels; their spirit failed them, and they now fled in different directions.

This circumstance proved highly advantageous for Pomarre, as God gave into his hands seventeen of the rebels, who were killed upon the spot; all fighting men, and among them one of the principal ringleaders of the rebellion. Many others were wounded, but escaped. Though we may be thankful to God for the subduing of those who delight in war, and are averse to peace, yet, we find much cause to lament the extreme depravity of man's nature, which admits no bounds to cruelty, when resentment is roused, and power obtained to execute it. Each of the seventeen bodies was treated in the most wantonly barbarous manner: — pierced with spears, beat with clubs, dashed with stones, derided, scoffed, and otherwise maltreated, as if now susceptible of pain, or affected by their taunts.

Pomarre thought the rebellion was crushed, and that he should have nothing more to do the next morning than to go and take possession of their strong holds, and wreak his unpitying anger on those who should fall into his hands. Captain Bishop seeing such a sudden change of circumstances determined to remain the night, and give the finishing blow to the war.

On Monday morning they marched up to the entrenchments, which are about four miles and a half from the beach; but how great was their surprize, when, instead of finding them abandoned, they saw every part as well manned as before. They could do no more than discharge several musquets upon them, and return to the fleet. A woman, an ambassadress, was permitted to pass between the parties. She carried an account to the rebels of those who had been killed, and how they were treated. They received the intelligence with seeming indifference; said that they did not know them; and as for the slain chief, they supposed that he had been carried away by the river, and not slain by the royalists. The surviving ringleader of the rebellion, a relation of Pomarre's, named Tahtahaee, bade the ambassadress acquaint Pomarre, that when they had done to him as they had done to Rooa (the name of the chief killed) then, and not till then, there would be peace in the land.

Capt. Bishop knowing that Capt. Simpson could not be detained longer from prosecuting his voyage, returned with the boat, leaving fifteen men with Pomarre. Brother Elder also returned. Pomarre has not lost in the expedition any man killed, and but four wounded: one of whom was by his own party, by mistake. On Tuesday Pomarre sent the Europeans home, and removed his fleet about twelve miles nearer Mattavai, and there encamped.

Upon the whole, this short campaign, through the mercy of God, has tended very much to destroy the strength of the prevailing commotion. The two chiefs above named (one of whom is dead) may be considered as the life of the rebellion. Their fighting men remaining are but few. As for the body of the people, on both sides, they are always spectators; and prepared to fly, or plunder, and exercise cruelties on the wounded or slain. (LMS Transactions:II, 115–118)[19]

Thus were repeated the events of twelve years earlier, when a handful of Europeans armed with muskets and conditioned to military order won a victory for the Pomares over their traditional enemies, the Oropaʻa, and thereby rescued the Pomares from political mediocrity or even physical extinction.

This chapter of Tahitian history ended fourteen months later when Pomare I died,[20] only a few months after the death of his aged father, Teu, and of his younger son, Teriʻi na Vaho Roa, the Vehiatua of Seaward Teva. The character of this Pare *ariʻi* was summarized in a passage written by the missionaries, who had every reason to know him well:

Sept. 10th. — It may perhaps be expected, that we give some account of Pomarre's character, so far as it came under our cognizance, which we shall do as follows: — Respecting his family, his father was an Otaheitean; but his mother a Ryatteean. He was born in the district of Oparre, where his corpse now is, and was by birth chief of that district, and none other. The notice of the English navigators laid the foundation for his future aggrandizement; and the runaway seamen, that from time to time quitted their vessels to sojourn in the island, especially that part of his Majesty's ship Bounty's crew, which resided here) were the instruments for gaining to Pomarre a greater extent of dominion and power, than any man ever had before in Otaheite.

We suppose the deceased chief to have been between fifty and sixty years of age. In person, he was the most respectable man we have seen since living here; tall, stout, well proportioned; grave in countenance, majestic in deportment, and affable in behaviour. As to his morals, he was a poor untaught heathen, under the dominion of a reprobate mind; and, according to his religion, nothing was sin with him but neglecting praying and sacrificing to his gods. In these things he was exemplary. Satan surely never had, (and we pray God he never again may have) another like him among these heathens who supported his interest with his whole power, and whose study, (from the servile fear of death) was to gain his favour, whatever it might cost. The marais built, and the altars reared at his command all over the island, are not a few, on which hogs and fish were profusely offered; and several hundreds of his subjects he has, in his time, caused to be murdered, and presented as costly sacrifices to the powers of darkness, besides the innumerable gifts of canoes, clothes, &c. &c.

As a governor, if we may judge by the complaints every where made, he was oppressive: but it is probable, that, with the Otaheiteans' present sentiments of right and wrong, those who have complained loudest of him, if in his situation, would not have been less oppressive. He was a peaceable man; and it is generally agreed, that the island has enjoyed a far greater degree of tranquillity, during his reign, than it had even while every district was an independent state. He was an active man. If every subordinate chief had followed his example in this respect, Otaheite would have exhibited a much more pleasing prospect than it now does. Erecting houses, building canoes, and cultivating ground, were employments in which Pomarre appeared to take great delight, and for which he deserves to be well spoken of. It is surprising, all things considered, how he was able to carry on such works as he did; works, that an inconsiderate Englishman, accustomed to behold the labours of art of his own country, would look upon with contempt; but which, notwithstanding, are such as bespeak the greatness and power of an Otaheitean chief, beyond any of his predecessors, and which will perpetuate his memory to long succeeding times.

Pomarre always shewed a fondness for foreigners, especially Englishmen; so that he was sure to give encouragement to any seaman that would elope from his vessel; and he often inveigled them himself: but this proceeded from policy. He supposed that every Englishman was expert in the use of fire-arms, the engine of destruction that carries terror with it all over the island; and he hoped so to engage them on his side, as to have them at his command, to come, and go, and do as he desired. The characters that he has had to deal with (since we have been on the island) have been, generally, the most abandoned, and they have disappointed his hopes and expectations. But had it been otherwise, the chief was not a grateful man: he could forget the services of those who had obliged him, and take no farther notice of them.

His behaviour towards us has always been friendly; which, without doubt, was regulated in a very great measure, if not solely, by the pecuniary advantages he has derived from our residence on the island. The vast acquistion of wealth that he gained at our first coming, and at different periods since, served to bind him to us. But latterly he did not, we think, behave so well to us as he did before the arrival of the Royal Admiral. Perhaps, the great and unexpected calls that he has had upon his attention, by the confused state of his own affairs, and the frequent arrival of vessels, may be some reasons for this change. We have also, for many months past, been enabled to open our commission, and have given him and his countrymen to know the true reason why we quitted our relatives and friends, to come and live with them: and, as the Gospel is so inimical to Satan's kingdom, we are certain that the chief could be no friend to us on account of our religion; and that he ridiculed our preaching (though he would sometimes hear, and use his power to collect his people about him to hear) and counted it foolishness, is not unlikely; and we have heard that he did so.

Upon the whole, as the Otaheiteans in general conceive Pomarre to be the greatest king they ever had, so we believe that he has not left his equal on the island. We have cause to be thankful to God, for the peace we have enjoyed under him, and that he has never debarred us the privilege of endeavouring to plant the Gospel in this island, or in any other, within his jurisdiction. (II, 295–297)

CHAPTER 31 *FALL OF THE POMARES*

At the beginning of 1804, Pomare II was "King" of Tahiti-Mo'orea in fact as well as in name;[1] no effective opposition to him was anywhere evident, and he was again in physical possession of the principal image of 'Oro (although the image itself was left at 'Utu'aimahurau — apparently as a token compromise with the deep feelings expressed by the Oropa'a). But, only five and a half years later, he was forced to flee for his life to Mo'orea, with only a handful of supporters; even his faithful European friends, the English missionaries, had left the island fearing for their lives. What happened to bring about such a radical change in the position of this man?

First, I list the more palpable occurrences of this period, without attempting to explain them. In September 1803 the missionaries reported that Pomare II was residing near the 'Utu'aimahurau marae, with an unidentified new "wife." He seemed at the time "but little affected with his father's decease," his principal preoccupation having been fear of the latter's ghost: "he was so terrified with the apprehension of his father's apparition, that he called for an attendant to sleep by him." (LMS Transactions:II, 294–295)

For a few months he remained mostly in Atehuru, carrying out unspecified rites involving use of the 'Oro image, then in May he moved to Mo'orea — evidently to Varari — with the image and a number of hangers-on; the reason for his move is not known.

The next time we hear of Pomare II was in July 1804, when the missionaries reported a rumor that

. . . the people of Atehuru were coming to make war on the Districts of Matavai, by orders of the king, who was angry because some man of the District had cursed him. The miss. were alarmed, and kept a watch thro' the night. Next day it was found the Raatiras had killed a man, as a sacrifice, to be conveyed to Eimeo to appease the anger of the king &c. (Newbury 1961:72)

A curious turn of events, with Atehuru acting for Pomare II against Matavai — but I very much doubt that any large segment of the Oropa'a was so engaged.

More interesting, politically, was another incident reported shortly thereafter:

There was a report of a war having been kindled in Moorea or Eimeo, on account of the people refusing to acknowledge the king's half-sister (daughter of Idia and Otihe [i.e., Tenania, the Huahine *ari'i*]) as their governor, several were killed and the muskets of the people in general were seized by the kings orders. Peace was however soon restored. (Newbury 1961:73)

The half-sister in question could not have been more than a young girl at the time, but that, of course, would not have disqualified her for a Title; and her parents or half-brother were entirely capable, and perhaps more than willing, to assume the "regency." But the affair does raise questions concerning the Mo'orean succession, and the relations between Tahiti-Mo'orea and Huahine at this time.[2]

Regarding the office of Mo'orean head chieftainship, I noted that upon the death of Mahau in 1792 the (tribal) office had devolved upon his son, Tetuanui (whose mother was Auo, sister of Pomare I). Twelve years later, assignment of the office to Pomare II's half-sister is reported, with no further information concerning the fate of Tetuanui. However, intriguing (and insoluble) as this question may be in terms of intrafamily arrangements, the events themselves had little apparent effect upon wider political developments; for, whoever may have occupied the de jure office of Mo'orean chieftainship, the Pomares firmly held onto de facto coercive authority over the island.

Of considerably more importance, politically, is the question this affair raises regarding relationships between Tahiti-Mo'orea and Huahine, as exemplified by the "marriage" between 'Itia and Tenania.

During Cook's last visit, in 1777, the person having the highest rank-status on Huahine was a youth named Teri'itaria, the son of Mato and Fatuarai. A quarter of a century later that preeminence seems to have rested with Mahine (also known as Teheiura, or Puru) who was Tenania's younger brother (the two, it may be recalled, were Mato's sons by his second wife). The only explanation I have uncovered concerning the transfer of office from Teri'itaria to Tenania and Mahine is found in Chesneau-Marcantoni's circumstantial (but not necessarily accurate) reminiscences. After Mato had left Fatuarai, to marry the daughter of Mo'ohono ("high priest of Huahine"), and had by the latter sired Tenania and Mahine (and a daughter, Rereao), "Moohono asked Tehaapapa (i.e., Fatuarai) to transfer to his grandsons, Tenania and Mahine, the "royalty" of Maiao [a dependency of Huahine]; upon her refusal to do so he attacked and defeated her forces, dethroned her, and transferred her royal office to his two grandsons." After Mo'ohono's death, Fatuarai made five unsuccessful attempts to win back the office for her son. Finally, this account continues, when Tenania went to Tahiti and married 'Itia, he turned over to Mahine the office of tribal chieftainship of Huahine and Mai'ao. (Chesneau 1928:81–82)

No explanation is offered for the ultimate fate of the deposed Teri'itaria, but his sister, Turaiari'i, is recorded as having married the Ra'iatea-Porapora chieftain Tapoa.

Pomare II remained about nineteen months on Mo'orea, where two of the missionaries visited him and found him ''. . . as much, if not more than ever given to the ava drinking & we add, perhaps to those vile affections & the commission of those things that are not seemly to mention.'' He also suffered from an unspecified disease which he would not discuss in public, ''it being counted a reproach to be afflicted with any disorder.'' (Bicknell & Henry, Journal, 24 January 1805, LMS Archives)

In January 1806 Pomare II accompanied the 'Oro image back to Tahiti. The movement was marked by ceremonies involving throngs of people (including a large number of Ra'iateans [Jefferson, Journal, 20 January 1806, LMS Archives]) and huge collections of offerings to the god, including several humans. During the passage, and for some time thereafter, the channel between Mo'orea and Tahiti was prohibited to all canoes not connected with the official procession (Jefferson, Journal, 25 November 1806, LMS Archives). Three months later the 'Oro image was carried to Tautira and reinstalled there; then, for some months thereafter, there took place an almost uninterrupted series of ceremonies which had the purpose of validating Pomare II's status as ''King'' of Tahiti[3] — including the parallel supremacy of 'Oro, the god whose principal ''seat'' (*nohora'a*) — the *to'o* — was once again in Pomare II's physical possession. Before the *to'o* was transported to Tautira (in a canoe paddled mainly by Hawaiians left on the island by visiting ships) it was kept in Pomare II's own marae, Hetemahana, near Point Venus.[4] At this new depository were enacted a ''marae renewal'' ceremony as well as the awesome *paiatua*, the refurbishing of 'Oro's image, and of other images with feathers from it — all accompanied by lavish expenditure of human offerings.

One of the more secular ceremonies enacted during this period was the presentation of tribute (i.e., food, bark cloth, human offerings) to Pomare II by various tribes and subtribes.[5] Those from Aharoa traveled to Matavai to make their contributions, but Pomare II himself went to Pare and Atehuru for the presentations from those places. In connection with his visit to Atehuru he and his retinue went well armed, as acknowledgment of the hostility toward him still prevalent there. (Similar tribute-rendering ceremonies were later accorded Pomare II in Seaward Teva, but I can find no report of any such having been rendered by the Landward Teva — although their contributions may well have been made while Pomare II was receiving the tribute from Atehuru.)

Of even greater importance, symbolically, was the series of kin-Title-investiture ceremonies that culminated during this period. (Such ceremonies had apparently been going on for some time, but had escaped the notice or comprehension of the missionaries.)

Today the people of this District presented the king with 20 Hogs, some English and Taheitean cloth, two Breastplates &c. &c. It is part of an Oroa or ceremony called Bure toto or Fa Eree te Eree, that is, making the king chief of this District, by investing him with the ancient chiefs name of Teepa by certain prayers &c. — therefore it is said to be a confirming him king of Matavae. This Oroa is a part of the ceremony for the king, that has been performing for several years past, and is to be observed in most if. not all the Districts in the Island — some have had it performed, in Pare he is called Tunue-ai-te-tua, in Faa he is called Te Eree vae-e-tua, in Attahuru he is called Te-vahe-atua, in Taearabu he is called T'Eree-navaho-roa, and in Eimeo he is called Punua-te-rae-e-tua. These names given to the King, signify his authority as being invested with that power, which in old times belonged to the several Chiefs who presided over the different Districts, and are used on particular occasions. (Davies, Youl et al., 24 May 1806, LMS Archives)

With the image of 'Oro were transported to Tautira the images of five other deities: Hiro, Tane, Temeharo, Ruahatu, and Huiima'o. (The last two were shark-gods, and Temeharo was the principal familial tutelar of the Pomares.) These other images evidently served as a kind of honor guard for 'Oro, as it was reported that they were to be returned to Mo'orea after 'Oro's image had been installed at Tautira (Jefferson, Journal, 28 January 1806, LMS Archives).

One should not conclude from my brief statements that the flow of goods between Pomare II and the populace was always in his direction. Some of the so-called tribute was evidently redistributed, either in the form of allotments to tribal chiefs and subchiefs or of free-for-all "scrambling." Also, on some occasions, Pomare II acknowledged, and thereby publicized the eminence of, the principal chiefs by making special gifts to them and calling out their names (or Titles?) (LMS Transactions:III, 172). And, following upon some human offerings he had small portions of the victims' bodies cut off and sent to the chiefs of some tribes as confirmation of friendship — a token which the missionaries described as having been received with much satisfaction (LMS Transactions:II, 322).

During September 1806, an especially large meeting, a *tavau*, was held in Pare which evidently included representatives from *all* the island's tribes. Food and other objects passed to and from Pomare II, and some ten days were spent in feasting and in making plans for a solemn ceremony scheduled to be held later on at Tautira. According to Davies' version the coming ceremony was to be a *pure ari'i*, or "worship for the king" (Newbury 1961:87),[6] and it was to require five more human offerings: one each from Mo'orea, Aharoa, Seaward Teva, Landward Teva, and Atehuru — a most telling indication of current political geography (Youl, Bicknell et al., Journal, 30 September 1806, LMS Archives). The absence of Porionu'u from this levy was probably due to its having been Pomare II's own tribal unit.[7]

At this same meeting a demand was voiced for a large tract of land to be set aside for the exclusive use of 'Oro:

> One of their principal Prophets has for some time pretended at be inspired and says that Oro must have the land on the North and Eastern sides of Taearabu to himself, (which extends to the Isthmus from the Rocks, about 20 miles in length) and therefore all the people who reside in the several Districts within the said boundary, must leave their lands and houses, and go to the south side and dwell. The principal Chief of Taearabu asked the king leave for the people to continue on their land, but he gave no answer. And it is said that if they refuse to obey, they will incur the gods anger and may terminate in a war between them and the King. (Youl, Bicknell et al., Journal, 30 September 1806, LMS Archives)[8]

Before this meeting, Pomare II's wife died. Her written obituary is brief:

> This morning about nine O Clock the Queen departed this life, she was (we suppose) about 23 or 24 years of age — her person was of the middle stature, of a delicate constitution — affable in her behaviour — She possessed little more than the name of queen, having no Authority. All the children she has had have been killed, as it is said, they were by common men, Owo her mother — Edea — Taepoto the chief of Aemeo and two other women according to the custom of Tahaite, cut their heads with sharks teeth, and lamented over the deceased; the King appeared affected, as also some of the people about him. (Davies, Youl et al., Journal, 21 July 1806, LMS Archives)

In late May 1807 the peace that had settled on Tahiti during several months past was suddenly broken by a fierce and unhearalded attack upon Atehuru by Pomare II and his warriors. Eight or so persons were slain in the first assault and the rest driven into the mountains, where many more were also slain, including the two most "disaffected" subchiefs. The immediate cause of the assault was described as follows: "The cause of the offence it seems was the conduct of the people of Teoropa, in taking the bones of Mateha, a chief killed by them in the last war, and making fish hooks of them. This had been done as an expression of contempt for the king who was related to the late chief." (Thomson, quoted in Newbury 1961:97n; see also Adams 1901:149–150.)

When the Paparans and other Landward Teva people sought to aid the Oropa'a they too were attacked, their warriors driven into the mountains, their settlements plundered and burned, and their crops destroyed. (The Seaward Tevans showed an inclination to join with their neighbors against Pomare II, but were so impressed with the speed and ferocity of Pomare II's forces that they joined with the latter instead — though evidently not in time to win ultimate exemption for themselves.)

For several weeks thereafter Pomare II's forces ranged through the defeated areas searching for survivors to kill and property to seize or destroy. Some missionaries traveling through the area at this time on a mission of mercy found almost total desolation, and great numbers of corpses left to rot or destined for the Tautira marae. Throughout September the work of destruction was extended to Taiarapu and would probably have gone to the limits reached in Atehuru and Landward Teva but for an illness that overtook Pomare II.

Sometime during this war some prominent leaders, including Te To'ofa,[9] surrendered to Pomare and were granted refuge by him, only to be eventually slain. Supposing his illness to be a supernatural visitation in consequence of this act of treachery, Pomare II ordered an end to the slaughter and declared a general amnesty.[10]

For the moment, then, all effective opposition to Pomare II was put down; but the "King" himself knew how temporary such victories tended to be and warned both his mother and the missionaries to be prepared to flee the island in case he should die.

In October another great meeting was held at Pare, reportedly ". . . for the purpose of dividing the lands of the conquered Districts viz. Atehuru &c. and appointing their respective chiefs" (Newbury 1961: 104). The missionaries have provided a colorful account of the ceremonial proceedings of this event and of the clothing worn by the principals. They also reported at length on the fact that one small portion of Puna'auia land was granted to themselves — a tract called Outumaoro near Tata'a Point. But concerning the politically important aspects of this extraordinary event — the specific units into which the conquered territories were divided, and the identity of their new proprietors — not one word was reported! (Newbury 1961:104; Davies, Journal, 12 October 1807, LMS Archives)

Ten months passed without the occurrence of any major political upheaval, but there did take place events that had some bearing on the political situation. In March 1808 Pomare II lost another loyal supporter with the death of Auo, the last survivor of his father's siblings, and the mother of his own first wife. As wife of Mahau, Auo had played a prominent part in the Mo'orean Succession War, and latterly had been Pomare II's appointive chief of Ha'apaino'o. Then, in May, 'Itia and her husband Tenania removed to Huahine; 'Itia seems to have had less influence upon her son than she had had upon his father, but her absence certainly did not serve to strengthen Pomare II's cause.

Meanwhile, Pomare II made a lengthy visit to Mo'orea; when he returned to Pare in early May he was very ill and evidently very anxious about his political fortunes, not to say about his life. When an explanation was sought for the cause of his illness, the principal 'Oro *taura* thereabouts, a man named Metea, could not (or would not) offer one. Instead, a *taura* inspired by Tepa, the healing god, declared that it was Tepa who had stricken Pomare II, in consequence of this god's having been ill-used some months previously. The report of that occurrence warrants reproduction on several counts:

> Yesterday a man was killed in Pare for a sacrifice, and we find today that this was the real cause of Pomare's coming here, he had given orders for the man to be killed but did not like to be present at the time, at first we supposed it was a sacrifice to Oro on account of Pomare's late illness and recovery, but we were mistaken the cause of the sacrifice is said to be as follows; some years ago, when the people of Atahuru &c. had rebelled and made war upon the king and his Father, every method was then used by Pomare's party to make the gods propitious, as is common in such cases, but one of the gods, called *Tepa*, did not display his power, nor do that for the protection of his votaries that was expected from him, this exasperated Paraha the late chief of Pare to such a degree, that he resolved to use the god in a similar manner to what some of the Negroes in Affrica are reported to do when their gods disappoint their expectations. Paraha took the Too or image representing Tepa, broke it to pieces and put it in a basket called Habora, the same as those human sacrifices are put in, and then he took the Habora, and the broken image in it, to the Marae and offered it a Sacrifice to the god Oro. Thus was Oro magnified at the expence of poor Tepa, however the despised god was (as the Taheeteans think) meditating a severe revenge for this spiteful way. Paraha was taken ill of the Dropsy, and died some months ago, and now Tepa has inspired one of his worshippers who declared in the name of the god that Tepa had already killed Paraha the chief of Pare and that he would also lay his hand upon the king, except his anger was quickly appeased by offering him a human sacrifice, and in consequence of this the man yesterday was killed and offered to Tepa . . . and some say that he must have more human victims. (Davies, Journal, 23 October 1808, LMS Archives)

According to the *taura*, Tepa would withdraw Pomare II's illness only upon assurance of receiving some human offerings and a certain piece of land on which would be built a marae for him. Pomare II promised to do these things, so that his recovery, which occurred shortly thereafter, was attributed to these actions, thereby serving to rehabilitate the offended Tepa to a position of near-rivalry to 'Oro himself.

QUALIFIED DEFEAT

In August 1808 there began the series of events that culminated in the defeat and temporary eclipse of Pomare II. The facts, as reported by the missionaries, were as follows:

> On Sunday last a number of people from the District of Hedea [Hita'a] arrived at Matavae, bringing with them some Cocoanut leaves, which they laid at Pomare's feet, these leaves were called Rahere, and the meaning of the Ceremony seems to be, an acknowledgement of Pomare's sovereignty over the Hedeans. This transaction gave a great offence to the people of Pare, they look upon it as an indignity to them to have the ceremony performed in Matavae instead of Pare the kings own

District. Today brothers Eyre and Scott went down to Pare . . . they found almost all the people of Pare gathered together at the big house at Papaoa, dressed and armed for war, and talking about falling upon Matavae but they were waiting for one or two of their principal chiefs who were absent. The brethren therefore returned without having an opportunity of speaking to them. The people of Matavae are much alarmed today, they took a large hog as an atonement to the king, but they say they are innocent and that all the fault is the kings. The king sent several messengers to the people of Pare, and there is a probability that the affair will be amicably settled. (Davies, Journal, 9 August 1808, LMS Archives)

And so it seemed to be — for the moment, at least. But there was evidently more to the affair than the missionaries were aware of, for their Matavai neighbors voiced the suspicion that ". . . the king has some evil design against them, and that the occurrence mentioned was a preconceived scheme of his" (Davies, Journal, 13 August 1808). And on his part, Pomare II warned the missionaries to be on guard against the Matavaians, because of their talk of war against the missionaries and himself (Davies, Journal, 3 October 1808).

Like most other inhabitants of Tahiti, the Mahinans had ample grounds for their hostile feelings toward Pomare II — feelings that he was undoubtedly aware of — so they were probably correct in suspecting him of contriving a *casus belli*. In any case, although the Hitia'a affair was settled with a prompt *tarae hara*, the mutual bad feelings simmered on. The Matavaians were further incensed by Pomare II's taking of another human offering from among them, and Pomare II's feelings were inflamed by the revelation received from 'Oro, through the *taura* Metea, urging war on the Mahinans. Matters came to a head in November:

Novr 6th. About 11 at night some of the king's people alarmed the miss. with a report that a great number of the people of Matavai, were armed and assembled by the sea side at Hitimahana (less than a mile from the miss. residence) apparently with some hostile intention.

The king was then on board the brig drinking, and unacquainted with the state of affairs. Messengers were dispatched to tell him, and bring him on shore. In the meantime, the king's people gathered together and armed themselves, and went towards Hitimahana, but soon returned without doing anything.

The king came on shore drunk, and assembled his people near the large house of the miss. where they were for some time deliberating upon the measures they should pursue. The king wanted to go and fall immediately upon the Matavaians, but his uncle *Taipoto*, the chief of Eimeo, dissuaded him from it, representing the necessity of prayers &c first. But while they were thus deliberating, all the Matavaians fled over Tapahi to Paperipo, first the women and children, then the warriors. Not an individual was left behind, except the servants of the miss. and a few that lived by the sea side close to Pomare's people. Messengers were dispatched to bring up the people of Pare, and also those of Faaa &c to the westward. The people came up just as it was daylight and then they, and Pomare's servants, scattered themselves thro' the District, plundering and destroying, some few houses were burnt, all the canoes seized, and also all the hogs they could catch.

Had Pomare's plan been adopted of falling upon the Matavaians immediately, it is probable the rebellion would have been soon crushed; but so infatuated were the king's people, and so bound by their superstitions that they would not stir a step beyond the usual routine of prayers, sacrifices &c. The priests went to their prayers, and sacrifices to engage Oro on their side, and a man was killed immediately to be a sacrifice to him, was put [in] a canoe in a haapora (basket) and sent by the way of Papara and the isthmus to Tautira. This delay afforded time for the disaffected to assemble together, and get the people of Hapaiano to join them, and also to send messengers to the Districts to the eastward. They also endeavoured to get Oro on their side, killed a man to be a sacrifice to him, and sent him to Tautira the eastern way. Each party appeared to be in earnest to get the god on their side.

In the evening the miss. heard there was little doubt of all the eastern side of the island joining the rebels, the king had sent messengers to the chiefs on that side but had received no answer. This was perhaps the most gloomy Sabbath day ever spent by the miss. tho' they had been in very trying circumstances often before. They could hardly meet for public worship for noise and confusion about them, tho' they attempted to meet together for prayer &c.

Novr 7th. The miss. had had little sleep the past night most of them kept watch not knowing what might happen. They heard in the morning that the rebels were encamped in Hapaiano, waiting for those of the Districts to the eastward to come and join them.

Pomare sent a messenger to them to signify if they were for Peace, he was not for war, he also requested that two of the Raatiras, one belonging to Matavai, and the other to Hapaiano, would come to him.

By the time however that the king's messenger had reached the camp, Vaiturai, the young chief of Tiarei (the present Hitoti) with his party had arrived at the camp all talk of peace was therefore at an end. The two Raatiras sent for would not come to the king, and it was expected that in the afternoon, *Taute* the chief of Faena and all his people would come, as also Teohu the chief of Hitiaa. And it was expected Taute would head the whole party. The miss. dreaded this Taute more than any man on the island, as he was courageous and enterprizing, and many instances of his treachery and cruelty had occurred. He had been called *Mr Pit* by foreigners and had been Pomare's chief counsellor, had lands given to him after the conclusion of the late war, and was under many obligations to Pomare, and yet it now appeared that he was the very soul of the rebellion.

The king also and his people, on learning how Taute was likely to act, and that he was apparently at the head of the rebellion, were much discouraged. Pomare observed to the miss. that Taute was a warrior, and knew how to act, he advised therefore that the wives and children of the miss. should by all means be sent on board the ship then in the harbour. As it was not at all improbable that Taute and warriors would come to Matavai that night. This was also their own opinion, they thought the party now under the conduct of Taute would come and attack the king and in that case they knew not what to expect. (Newbury 1961:116–118)

One circumstance that happened on the passed day (the 7th) deserves to be mentioned, as it had a great effect on the minds of both parties. *Meetia*, the prophet of the god Oro, was said to be inspired, at which time he happened to have a dispute with a prophet of *Tipa*, as they were disputing he suddenly started, and ran away over the rocks and precipices of the hill Tapahi towards the rebel camp at Hapaiano. Some of the king's people attempted to detain him, but in vain. He proceeded to the camp and joined the rebels. This discouraged Pomare's people very much, and as much elated the other party, for it was looked upon by both parties as the action of the *god* not of the *man*, who was well known as Pomare's friend. (Newbury 1961:118)

This threatening situation prompted the majority of the missionaries to leave the island, and they went aboard the brig in order to take passage to Huahine.[11] Their version of the war continues:

In the afternoon, there was a report there should be peace, and the king in public talked as if peace had been made, but called some of the miss. aside, and said secretly there was no real peace, that he was afraid of his own people, that the Porionuu or people of Pare upon whom he depended most, had already shown themselves inclinable to betray him. Temaehuatea their principal chief had secretly sent several messages to the rebels, and evidently intended to espouse their cause. (Newbury 1961:119–120)

In the afternoon [Nov. 9] at the request of Pomare, two of the miss. Messrs Nott and Scott went to Hapaiano to the rebel camp to speak to the disaffected chiefs, and endeavour to persuade them to come to Matavai and have an interview with Pomare. The chiefs received them in a friendly manner, said they were sorry for the miss. and inquired if it was true they were going away? Being answered in the affirmative they were earnest in persuading them not to go. And there was no doubt some of them had a friendly regard for the miss. though not on account of their religion; yet in case they should prevail against Pomare, they had no power to protect them against the wild rabble that followed them.

The miss. endeavoured to persuade Taute and the other chiefs to come and have an interview with Pomare. But to this they made many objections, mentioning several instances of treachery that had occurred during the late war, and saying they had apprehensions of being served in the same manner as others had been. A(t) last they agreed to come to Matavai with their men, and that Pomare also might bring his men, and that the wariors on both sides should remain behind their leaders at a distance, then the chiefs to advance to the middle, and meet Pomare there with as many of the miss. as would come. Mr S(cott) then returned to acquaint Pomare with these terms, leaving Mr N(ott) with the chiefs to conduct them to Pomare. The king being made acquainted with those agreed to them and advanced with his people to Hitimahana, thinking the others were coming. After the departure of Mr S(cott) the chiefs hesitated, and would not come that day, but sent to Pomare they would come the next. Mr N(ott) then returned to his brethren, and Pomare began now to hesitate about going in the ship, thinking if he left the island he would lose all at once, but by staying there might be a chance of recovering his affairs, but he said perhaps the people would cut off his head as the people of France had done with their king. (Newbury 1961:121)

Other sources provide somewhat different accounts of this episode:

The outrage of June, 1807, had exhausted the last remnants of patience in the islanders, and this time the whole island rose, determined to make clean work of Pomare and all his surroundings. For this purpose they needed a warrior, and as a warrior Opuhara had no superior. So Opuhara became chief of Papara, and soon afterward head chief of the island; for he and his army advanced to Papenoo in 1808, and there, on December 22, Pomare attacked them, and was totally defeated. Pomare and his household, and the whole missionary establishment, without waiting for further notice, abandoned the island, and fled to Eimeo. (Adams 1901:153)

Success had made the conquerors insolent; they indulged in unspeakable atrocities and cruelties, but all the more unbearable was that these (conquerors) for the most part were strangers from Huahine, Ra'iatea, Taha'a, etc., who came to the aid of Pomare and who made up a large part of his army.

Their imprudent conduct produced discontent, which despite the conquered being downtrodden, soon resulted in another war, which failed to remove Pomare's power permanently. This (war) broke out for such an unusual reason in this country, that it is worth describing.

Metouave, a common man but very courageous, had a wife renowned for her beauty and whom one of the principle officers of the king wished to have. The husband and the wife both rejected him. A few days later, she was wrested from her home by force. The husband, furious, ran to announce everywhere the violence of which he was the victim; and so by these speeches he shared his indignation with the people and stirred them up to revolt.

In a few days a large number of discontents met at Hirahouraia or Tire, under the orders of Pafai, who was still living, and at Oahouio. They marched against Pomare, who was at Papara, coming from the North, while the inhabitants of Papara and the Aroopas, who lived in the southeast, came from the other side. All the island rose up. No one remained loyal to the king except strangers, who, attacked from everywhere at once, had many losses and could not hold up. He himself was forced to leave the island and to retire to Eimeo with what was left of his army. (Moerenhout 1837:II, 447–448)

In the end, Pomare II remained at Matavai with four bachelor missionaries and his more loyal followers, while his adversaries continued at Ha'apaino'o; and such was the state of affairs when the brig sailed for Huahine taking the other missionaries along.

The following April (1809) two of the missionaries who had remained at Matavai made their way to Huahine with information about the state of affairs on Tahiti:

They reported, that there had been a cessation of hostilities between Pomarre and the rebels, from the departure of the Missionaries, in the Perseverance, to the 22d of December; on which day, Pomarre being infatuated by the predictions of the prophet Metea, rashly attacked the rebels in the district of Onowhea. The enemy had not only a superiority of numbers, but also greatly the advantage of ground. Pomarre's party was repulsed, and fled to Nanu, some of his principal men were killed, and many muskets fell into the hands of the rebels. The four Brethren, as soon as they heard of this defeat, sailed for Eimeo. In the meantime, the rebels overrun the district of Matavai, Pare, &c. and committed great devastations. The picture of King George, which was sent from England to Pomarre, was also taken by them to the Marao, and offered to Oro. Pomarre, after staying three weeks at Nanu, followed the Brethren to Eimeo, where Messrs. Scott and Wilson left him, with the Brethren Nott and Hayward. (LMS Transactions:IV, 335–336)

In September 1809 there occurred another event which signaled the end of this chapter in Tahiti's history. The first European ship to anchor at Matavai after departure of the *Perseverance* was the *Venus*, a twenty-ton schooner from Port Jackson. It was forthwith captured by some Tahitians, its mate killed, and its master and all the crew made prisoner. Forty years earlier the pioneer *Dolphin* had been attacked by Tahitians, and more recently the castaway company of the *Matilda* had been relieved of some of their property, but otherwise Europeans had suffered little more than thievery or ridicule from their Maohi hosts. And, to underscore the radical nature of this turn of political events, the hope and patience of the long-suffering missionaries finally ran out and most of them embarked for Port Jackson, believing their mission to have failed.

Some discussion is called for to review and try to explain the events that led to this radical change in the political fortunes of Pomare II, only a few years after he had reached the pinnacle of rank-status and of force-sanctioned authority. The measures used in reaching that pinnacle — mostly by Pomare II's father, by his great-great-uncle Tutaha, and only in small part by himself — were as follows:

winning and maintaining European military support, both in terms of an almost complete monopoly of firearms and of active military aid;

securing an almost monopolistic supply of other European objects and distributing them among other Maohis in return for political support;

adding luster to their established rank-status preeminence through prestige-enhancing associations with European leaders;

skillful use of established kinship connections, along with the formation of valuable new ones;

and, gaining most influence with, and most direct access to, the island's most powerful god, 'Oro.

As we have seen, Pomare II continued to utilize these strategies, along with some new ones; so why, one may ask, were they less successful than before?

During the five-and-a-half-year period now under consideration twenty European vessels visited Tahiti, some more than once, and Pomare II continued his forebears' policy of courting the visiting Europeans[12] — but such efforts were nowhere near as rewarding as they had been in the past. For, by this time firearms were in the hands of nearly every one of the island's principal chiefs. Although many arms originally acquired by others eventually found their way into Pomare II's arsenal (LMS Transactions:III, 36), a large enough number was outstanding to render his advantage less overwhelming.

As for other objects of European origin, nearly everyone on the island now had some iron and some article of European dress, so that gifts of such items were no longer as productive of political advantage as they once had been. Moreover, it appears that Pomare II, unlike his father, kept for himself most things received from Europeans. Despite his requests, during this period, Pomare II was never once successful in influencing Europeans to fight his battles. Besides, by this time, many Tahitians were themselves skilled in the use of firearms, and most of them had lost their awe of an armed European.

Nor was there much advantage to be gained, in tangible ways, from close association with Europeans. Many if not most Tahitians had come to harbor hostile feelings toward Europeans in general (though not apparently toward all European individuals) on account of the sicknesses that were so widespread — sicknesses that they almost universally, and bitterly, attributed to Europeans. (LMS Transactions:II, 328–330)

In other words, the awesome wonder that was formerly associated with everything European was most definitely a thing of the past, and the earlier advantage enjoyed by the Pomares as a consequence of such association became in some measure a liability.[13]

Another measure utilized by Pomare II's forebears in support of their aspirations was the exploitation of old kinship connections, and the establishment of new ones. Pomare II also utilized such measures, but to far less extent and to considerably less advantage. In terms of politically profitable alliances, Pomare II (probably through no will of his own) was married to his own first cousin, and his younger brother to the latter's sister; thus, considerations of rank-status eugenics were allowed to overrule those of political *alliance*. Actually, these considerations appear to have been pushed so far that, according to one presumably "official" view, after the death of Pomare II's first wife there remained but one female on Tahiti-Mo'orea of sufficiently high rank-status for him to marry, and even that union did not take place (LMS Transactions:IV, 185). Moreover, Pomare II failed to sire any offspring by his first wife and thereby lost the opportunity for acquiring the means of forming politically useful alliances through an offspring's marriage.

Pomare II did, it is true, attempt to exploit his kinship connections on two different occasions: once, when he forced the Mo'oreans to accept his infant half-sister as their ruler, and again, when he appointed his female cousin to the chieftainship of Ha'apaino'o. In both cases, however, he did so over the strenuous objections of the appointees' new subjects. In the case of Mo'orea he had to put down an armed opposition to gain his point; and in the case of Ha'apaino'o his appointee died soon thereafter, before the political objectives of his action could be achieved.[14]

In fact, there remained very few close kinfolk for Pomare II to lean upon, even had he been so inclined. All siblings of his mother were dead, and the last remaining sibling of his father died during this period; even his mother, the once formidable 'Itia, left his side to go with her husband to Huahine.

So, instead of the kinfolk — who, despite temporary differences, had provided such political strength for his father's regime — Pomare II found himself surrounded and dependent upon a motley of parasites, including the mischief-making Metea (the principal 'Oro *taura*), and a crowd of Ra'iatean Ariois and bloodthirsty Hawaiian castaways, whose time (in the words of the missionaries) ". . . appeared to be taken up in feasting and merriment."[15]

As events were to demonstrate, support from persons like these tended to melt away in times of stress. And, although the preceding pages have made it abundantly clear that kinship among the Maohis was no warranty of loyalty, it did transcend ruthless self-interest more often than did other kinds of relationships known to them.

The most substantial, and eventually most effective, type of support courted by Pomare II was in the persons of chiefly Leeward Islanders. His mother's second husband, Tenania, was, as we have seen, a high-ranking Titleholder and co-chief of Huahine; and Pomare II was reported on one occasion to have organized an expedition to send presents to Ra'iatean chiefs (Youl, Bicknell et al., Journal, 20 August 1806, LMS Archives).[16] His preference in that direction is also evident in his patronage of an immigrant Ra'iatean named Paraha,[17] described in one report as "the most thriving man on the island"; "He [Paraha] has lately been made a *rattera* of Oparre & his favour is much courted in tht. district. If anything should happen to the king, he is likely to be made of much consequence. He is a distant relation of Pomerre's & is from Ryatteea." (Jefferson, Journal, 24 January 1805, LMS Archives)

Pomare II also adopted his forebears' strategy for gaining and maintaining political power by the process of eliminating the opposition — and if anything he was more uncompromising in that than they. I need not repeat the passages describing his many ruthless military campaigns, or the instances of unprovoked and even treacherous murder carried out at his behest. Many of the killings ordered by him were phrased as offerings to the insatiable 'Oro, but the bitterness and vengefulness engendered by them were evidently no less intense. Even Pomare II himself appears to have recognized that he had overreached the limit in this regard, as witnessed by his self-acknowledged guilt in the treacherous slaying of the defeated chiefs who had sought refuge in his camp (Davies, Journal, 7–16 September 1807, LMS Archives).

But Pomare II did not restrict himself to physical measures in eliminating opposition. It is reported, for example, that on one occasion he brought about the death of a Mo'orean by prayer:

The story is thus told: Otoo was at his worship, and while employed, was disturbed by some one's beating a drum. He sent to order the person to desist; but his order was not obeyed, and the man continued beating; on which the king said, "Let him alone": and that same night the man expired. This is esteemed by the natives as an infallible proof of the power of their god Oro, and of their king Otoo. (LMS Transactions: II, 317–318)

Under Pomare II's regime some actions traditionally regarded as trivial errors, or no errors at all, came to be treated as crimes of lese majesty. For example, the chief of Tiarei was banished from his lands for eating part of a turtle, a delicacy which formerly had been accessible to any male tribal chief or high-ranking Titleholder (Jefferson, Journal, 28 February 1805, LMS Archives). Again, for garbling a message from Pomare II to some priests, an aged messenger was condemned to death (Davies, Journal, 29 July 1808, LMS Archives).

Indeed, so encompassing did the presence and will of Pomare II come to be that many reversals formerly put down to the vindictiveness of miscellaneous spirits came now to be attributed to acts (deliberate or otherwise) of lese majesty. For example:

Tuesday, 20. There have been for several weeks upwards of thirty sailing canoes, waiting for a favourable wind to go to Te-tea-roa; they have several times made the attempt, but have been compelled to return. The Taheiteans are easily made to believe that the cause of their miscarriages, in the general, is on account of the god' or the king's anger. The present disappointment, they say, is on account of the king being angry with them, and that while his anger remains, the wind will continue against them. They went to Edea for advice, which was, to take a *tara-ae-hara* to the king, to which they agreed, and yesterday they took a young pig for an atonement to the king, who is at Hapaeano. (LMS Transactions: IV, 183)

The severity with which Pomare II countered opposition, or even suspicion of opposition, may have served to secure immediate political objectives, but there is much evidence for concluding that it produced an almost universal residue of ill feeling toward him and his regime.

Like his father before him Pomare II also courted the favor and support of the god 'Oro for what appear to be political objectives. But unlike his father he went so far in this direction that his attentiveness to the god eventually worked against his political interests. Consider, for example, the numbers of persons slain to provide offerings to 'Oro. An exact count of such victims is impossible to make, but my estimate is that several scores met that fate during the period now under review — not including those slain in wars and afterward presented to the god. One does not have to fall back on "human nature" to explain attitudes of recrimination on the part of the victims' kin and friends. I give but two modest examples from the LMS Transactions:

May 1st. Hear that the inhabitants of Fwhaa were very near coming to blows with the king for the murder of the man for a sacrifice yesterday. They resented it because it was a young and useful man that was killed. (II, 304)

When we have endeavoured to persuade the people, in public and private, to turn from their vanities, and worship the true God, they have frequently replied, by asking, Whether any of the rulers have believed, and turned unto the Lord? They frequently mention Pomarre's killing men for sacrifices, and tell us to go and preach to the king and him. The generality of the people are dissatisfied with his conduct in this particular: and, in some, we have seen a disposition to retaliate. One man was heard to say that Pomarre came to his house seeking a sacrifice, and had his friend, who was sitting by him been killed, he had his spear by him, and would, be said, have killed the man who killed his friend, or Pomarre. (II, 327)

Dispossession of land for 'Oro worship was probably only slightly less popular a measure than loss of a kinsman or friend. There is no report of people having been dispossessed to make way for the uninhabited district dedicated to 'Oro on Mo'orea, but opposition is recorded to the proposal to set aside a twenty-mile stretch in Taiarapu for that purpose (Youl, Bicknell et al., Journal, 30 September 1806, LMS Archives).

Pomare II's almost slavish dependency upon 'Oro was manifested in certain other ways that adversely affected his political fortunes. The extent of that dependency is attested in several passages in the missionaries' journals, such as the following:

Last night the Prophet that has been attending Pomare all the time since the commencement of the late war, came to him in a great fury, being inspired as he pretended by the god Oro, he declared in the name of the god that he had raised up Pomare from his late illness, blamed him for his remissness concerning certain prayers and sacrifices that he has not attended to as he ought to have done, as also his neglect of causing some houses to be built, he threatened to lay his hand upon Pomare again if he did not speedily observe those things. Pomare appeared alarmed, and it seems he has determined to comply, and for that reason will go down in a day or two to the District of Pare, and some say the god must have a human victim, perhaps more than one. (Davies, Journal, 7 October 1807, LMS Archives)

On some occasions Pomare II was persuaded by 'Oro *taura* to undertake irresponsible military adventures against recognized odds, and with disastrous consequences. (See for example the raid against the Oropa's in 1809.) And on other occasions military advantages derivable from prompt action were allowed to lapse while Pomare II was carrying out the ceremonial accompaniments of warfare dictated by 'Oro's clergy. (See for example the Oropa'a's devastation of Pare, while Pomare II and his forces were at Tautira.)

Finally, there is dramatic evidence that Pomare II and his associates had begun to recognize the disadvantages of their exclusive attentiveness to the one god, 'Oro. (I refer to the case of "Tepa's revenge" mentioned earlier.)

As we have seen, most measures undertaken by Pomare II to secure his political objectives were continuations, at intensified levels, of strategies followed by his father. In one respect, however, he went far enough beyond his father to give the appearance of innovation, and that was in his substitution of direct rule for indirect, in territories conquered by him.[18]

The principal action undertaken by Pomare II in this direction was the "division of lands" described earlier, and his appointment of new, and evidently nonlocal, individuals to preside over the conquered territories. As indicated earlier, except for the report that such land divisions and new appointments were made, we are provided with no further information about this momentous event, but it is probably safe to assume that the advantages gained by Pomare II in having his own appointees installed in these territories were more than likely offset by the local resentment engendered by such moves. Moreover, in at least one recorded instance, the appointee eventually turned on his patron and led a large-scale "rebellion" against him. (I refer to the famous Taute, Pomare II's former chief counselor [Newbury 1961:118]. Another action of Pomare II that may be regarded as a substitution of direct for indirect rule, was his personal assumption of several high-ranking kin-Titles traditionally associated with other tribal chieftainships. Multiple kin-Titleholding was of course not a new development in Maohi history, but in the past most such instances involved an individual's succession by purported descent, or by fosterage. It may be that Pomare II was able to justify some of the Title taking he engaged in by reference to legitimate or contrived kinship connections, but there is no evidence that that was attempted or even considered by him to have been necessary.

A question arising at this point has to do with the distinction to be drawn, in Maohi terms, between "ruling" and "governing." I referred to such a distinction when contrasting chieftainship of kin-congregations with that of tribes. As I indicated, I believe that popular expectations regarding such roles did in fact include some differences — although I acknowledged the methodological difficulty of deciding what those differences were. In any case, while I continue to recognize the difficulty in documenting such propositions, I believe that some of Pomare II's behavior did not conform to most Maohis' notions of what constituted a "good chief" or even a "great chief." In his disregard for the welfare of his ordinary subjects he certainly did not live up to what was expected of a chief by members of his own kin-congregation. And there is reason to believe that he exceeded even the broad limits of willfulness in a tribal chief tolerated by members of his tribal unit. I touched upon this matter in my discussion of human offerings, but there were other kinds of excesses as well — that is, actions which even this long-suffering populace considered to be "excessive" — for example:

Such is the rapaciousness of the king and chiefs, that the common people can keep nothing scarcely; for as-soon as they know that they have any thing valuable, it is sent for; and if denied, taken by force: the consequence is, the people are discouraged, which would be prevented if a moderate share was left them, and be an additional comfort and reward for their labour. (LMS Transactions:IV, 184)

As I attempted to show in an earlier chapter, the image of a benevolent leader who spends his time maintaining equities and redressing wrongs among his subjects is hardly applicable to Maohi tribal chieftainship even in a normative sense. Nevertheless, Pomare II appears to have maintained an aloofness from such concerns to a degree that even some Maohis may have found unwarranted. I reproduce below a rambling but revealing account by one of the missionaries:

This morning a barbarous murder was committed by one native on the body of another in a house a few yards distant from us. The murdered man it appears had been guilty of a very petty theft, and for which he lost his life. He was struck a dreadful blow on the nape of his neck with a Tommahawk that almost severed his head from his body & his right shoulder was horribly cut with repeated blows. The perpetrator of this savage act walked about afterwards with the Tomahawk in his hand, with as much unconcern as if he had been splitting up fire wood, & behaved very insolently when spoke to about it. The person killed belongs to Paheete's jurisdiction, who is now in Oparre; but it is apprehended that no notice will be taken of the matter whether by him or Pomarre (to whom the other man belongs) as he was accounted a person but of little worth, & his murderer is a man of consequence. This same man who has so inhumanly destroyed his countryman for a mere trifle we have reason to suspect of having plundered us of various valuables. Towards evening Paheete arrived in the district. He made some enquiries concerning the above murder, and ordered the corpse which its murtherer had buried to be digged up & to be placed within view of him in Edeea's house on the point where he is fled for refuge. It appears that this is held by the natives as a mark of abhorrence of the act, & what is very unpleasant to the guilty person. There is some talk among our neighbours, that the inhabitants of this district & Hapyano will revenge the murder & even burn Edeea's dwelling in which the man has sheltered himself. If this shd. be done it will certainly produce a war. The servants of Edeea removed her property from the point into br. Nott's apartment for fear of the worst.

12.24: Nothing has this day been done towards avenging the murder. It is said that Pomarre has been made acquainted with it, and justifies the deed, and has given directions that nothing be done to the man.

12.25: Missionaries agree to ask Pomare to remove the murderer from the district, & to inform him of the law of civilized nations regarding such crimes.

12.27: Brs. Eyre & Elder . . . found Pomarre in Nannoo bay and declared their message to him. . . . He directed them to Edeea, alledging that the man belonged to her, & therefore application shd. be made to her from his removal from Matavai. After some time the chief acknowledged that the man had been unjustly killed but either did not or would not understand that no one of his subjects had right to avenge himself after such a manner, & that it belonged to him as governour of the Island to judge between man & man & punish the guilty. Nor did he seem to take any notice when told that the law of God had been violated by cruelly shedding blood. Some of his attendants were more candid than Pomarre on the occasion & confessed that the crime was to insignificant for which the man had been killed & that the murderer deserved banishment & advised the chief to banish him. He said at length that he shd. be removed out of the district, but he spoke this so cooly that there is reason to doubt his word & also still recommended that application should be made to Edeea. As Edeea is in Attahooroo the brethren did not think it meet to proceed without knowing the Society's mind, & the Society did not see it necessary to pursue the matter further at present. (Jefferson, Journal, 23–25, 27 December 1802, LMS Archives)

It might be argued that some of Pomare II's popularly adjudged excesses or shortcomings were offset by the attention he devoted to enhancing the trappings of high rank-status and great political power — for such he did to a surpassing degree, in the form of rituals and feasts and other assemblies of many kinds. In fact, an uninformed observer might have concluded that life in Tahiti consisted entirely of, and was about equally divided between, wars and ceremonies. Such of course was not the case, but under Pomare II's regime his activities (and inactivity) were ceremonialized considerably more than those of his father or other known forebears. The question becomes, Did this frequent and highly acclamatory *symbolic* acknowledgment of Pomare II's preeminence serve his more tangible political objectives?

The answer was eventually provided by events themselves, for when his enemies began to gather on Tahiti against Pomare II he was found to have no friends outside his home district of Pare. Evidently the dramatization of social rituals was no substitute for genuine personal loyalty, or even for effectively applied coercive force. The excitement and entertainment provided by festivals may have served momentarily to raise the spirits of these sick and generally dispirited people, but even that is likely to have been offset by the cost of the festivals, which as usual was borne mainly by the populace at large.

CHAPTER 32 *AND RISE AGAIN*

HAU MANAHUNE

The next five years of Tahiti-Mo'orea history have been labeled, quite inappropriately, the period of the *Hau Manahune* — government of commoners; as we shall see, there was not much "government" in evidence, and what there was was exercised by people of commoner origin only episodically. During this period Pomare II divided his time between Mo'orea, where as "King" he continued to be respected and in general obeyed, and Tahiti, where his presence was tolerated, but only as tribal chief of the district of Pare. Meanwhile, politically significant events in the two islands developed in markedly different ways.

The period began with an unsuccessful attempt by Pomare II to reestablish himself as Tahiti's "King." The occasion was the expedition from Mo'orea to Tahiti, by the captain of the brig *Hibernia*, to recapture the schooner *Venus*;[1] Pomare II joined forces with the Europeans, but whereas the latter succeeded in their mission, the former failed dismally. Here is the story of this enterprise, as it was reported by the missionaries still on Huahine:

. . . Pomare and party sailed from Aimeo for Taheete in company with Capt. C., [and] while the Capt. was endeavouring to retake the vessel, which they had towed to the isthmus in her way to Tearabu, Pomare and fleet made the District of Faena where the rebels had collected their forces and canoes, but being suddenly surprised by the unexpected arrival of Pomare they left their canoes by the sea side and fled up the valley. A party of Pomare's people, consisting chiefly of those from Huaheene, pursued them, the rebels rallied and faced the pursuers, trusting to a party that lay in ambush of which Pomare's people knew nothing till they were fired upon, the royalists were put in disorder and forced to retreat with the loss of 24 men, some of them noted warriors. The rebels pursued them in their turn to the sea side where P. and party saved themselves by getting on board their canoes. They, however, succeeded in seizing and taking away all the rebels' canoes. P. and fleet then sailed for the District of Pare, and Capt. C. having recovered the vessel and the men belonging to it sailed for Aemeo, and few days after for this harbour [i.e., Fare, Huahine]. From this account it is evident that the affairs of P. are as bad as ever; he is waiting with great anxiety the arrival of the chiefs from these islands [i.e., Huahine, Ra'iatea, Taha'a, Porapora], and apparently not able to act on the offensive till then, and from their long delay it appears very doubtful whether they will give him any assistance before it be too late. Pomare and his people are forced by the famine in Aemeo to endeavour to keep their station at Pare in Taheete where there is at present abundance of food. (Im Thurn 1925:122–3)

The wonder is, of course, that Pomare was permitted even a foothold on Tahiti, but this he managed to maintain, perhaps because Tahiti itself remained as divided as it had been decades previously; and added to this were certain other circumstances that may have militated against vigorous common action against the self-styled "King" (Newbury 1961:135–136; Moerenhout 1837:II, 449–450).

If one may place any confidence in missionary estimates, the population of Tahiti during this period probably numbered no more than 9,000, and possibly considerably less.[2] In other words, the population as a whole was still subject to the same kinds of influences that had brought it to that nadir during the preceding decade, including especially sicknesses that reduced fertility and cut off lives before they reached reproductive age. While we cannot assume that such a situation was socially "demoralizing" in any way (a condition as difficult to define as it would be to assess), one is certainly justified in assuming that the manpower available to Pomare II's principal chiefly adversaries was not sufficient to encourage them to undertake hazardous military adventures.

Another factor that might have contributed to the Tahitians' disinterest, in general, in uniting to drive Pomare II off the island again was the widespread addiction to the new (for Tahiti) kind of alcoholic beverage mentioned earlier:

Intemperance at this time prevailed to an awful and unprecedented degree. By the Sandwich Islanders, who had arrived some years before, the natives had been taught to distil ardent spirits from the saccharine *ti* root, which they now practised to a great extent, and exhibited, in a proportionate degree, all the demoralizing and debasing influence of drunkenness.

Whole districts frequently united, to erect what might be termed a public still. It was a rude, unsightly machine, yet it answered but too well the purpose for which it was made. It generally consisted of a large fragment of rock, hollowed in a rough manner, and fixed firmly upon a solid pile of stones, leaving a space underneath for a fire-place. The but-end of a large tree was then hollowed out, and placed upon the rough stone boiler for a cap. The baked *ti* root, *Dracanæ terminalis*, macerated in water, and already in a state of fermentation, was then put into the hollow stone, and covered with the unwieldy cap. The fire was kindled underneath; a hole was made in the wooden cap of the still, into which a long, small, bamboo cane, placed in a trough of cold water, was inserted at one end, and, when the process of distillation was commenced, the spirit flowed from the other into a calabash, cocoa-nut shell, or other vessel, placed underneath to receive it.

When the materials were prepared, the men and boys of the district assembled in a kind of temporary house, erected over the still, in order to drink the *ava*, as they called the spirit. The first that issued from the still being the strongest, they called the *ao*; it was carefully received, and given to the chief; that subsequently procured, was drunk by the people in general. In this employment they were sometimes engaged for several days together, drinking the spirit as it issued from the still, sinking into a state of indescribable wretchedness, and often practising the most ferocious barbarities.

Travellers among the natives experienced greater inconvenience from these district stills than from any other cause, for when the people were either preparing one, or engaged in drinking, it was impossible to obtain either their attention, or the common offices of hospitality. Under the unrestrained influence of their intoxicating draught, in their appearance and actions they resembled demons more than human beings.

Sometimes, in a deserted still-house might be seen the fragments of the rude boiler, and the other appendages of the still, scattered in confusion on the ground; and among them the dead and mangled bodies of those who had been murdered with axes or billets of wood in the quarrels that had terminated their dissipation. (Ellis 1829:I, 229–231)

While one need not subscribe fully to this missionary judgment concerning the prevalence and effects of ti drinking, the practice was, nevertheless, very widespread and undoubtedly quite deleterious in terms of the ordinary work of living and war making. A drunken mob might have been easily roused to rush into battle, but could hardly have sustained a lengthy campaign.

Still another factor — both symptom and cause — prevalent in the social disarray of this period had to do with peoples' relations with their gods. Although concrete evidence for this thesis is scattered and fragmentary, it seems quite clear that the more organized means of communicating with spirits, through "official" tribal or kin-congregation priests, was giving way increasingly to the revelations of *taura*. Moreover, there were signs in some quarters that belief in 'Oro was beginning to be complemented, or even superseded, by belief in Jehovah. (This last was firmly evident in Mo'orea, as we shall see; and it seems to have been occurring in Tahiti as well.)

Meanwhile, the political boundaries of Tahiti had been reconstituted to their locations of five decades earlier, that is, into the separate tribes or close tribal coalitions of Seaward Teva, Landward Teva, Oropa'a, Aharoa, Porionu'u, and possibly Fa'a'a.[3] With the exception of Papara, where Tati and then his brother Opuhara ruled, there is little or no information available concerning the identity of the chiefs of these various tribes.[4] In any case, none of them was of sufficiently high rank-status to exercise or even affect claims to *maro ura* associated rights.[5] In other words, with the exception of Pomare II, there was during this period no other conspicuously eminent individual in terms of rank-status among Tahiti's several *ari'i*, and this seems to have been true of the political side of intertribal relations as well.

Indeed, according to one reconstruction of the history of this period, the actual tribal chiefs were partly eclipsed by certain *taura*:

There was at this time at Tahiti an unusual man, the prophet Tino who was called Taramea, when he was in his natural state, and Oro, when he claimed to be inspired by this god. Since, during Pomare's exile, there was no *ari'i rahi* at Tahiti, it was really he who ruled the island, not exactly as chief or king, but as prophet or rather as god. He had begun to play his role even before that year and his power extended because of the calamities of the island, into recent times. He lived in Southwest Tahiti at a point called Mara, in a marae where he was brought offerings and provisions from everywhere. His authority was despotic; he did almost anything he wanted, having been feared in such a way that his slightest threat was tantamount to the most positive order. Should he have to go somewhere? Everything was prepared to receive him; women gave lavishly of their favors to him. Perhaps there has never on earth been an individual so highly honored, so powerful; his slightest wishes were irrevocable laws; the chiefs themselves did not dare to resist him; but he did not directly interfere with warfare, since his good graces were solicited insofar as his displeasure was feared. His moments of inspiration were moments of triumph. Everyone trembled then. Each side dreaded some fatal prescription; and if he had cried "War!" all would arm themselves without question. (Moerenhout 1837:II, 450–451)[6]

Eventually Tino was superceded by another "prophet" who came to exercise an even more fateful influence upon events — but more about this later on.

REINFORCEMENTS

On Mo'orea, where Pomare II again resumed residence in July 1810, two developments of major political importance began to take shape. One was his "conversion" to Christianity, which reached the point of public profession in July 1812; the other was the build-up of his military forces, mainly through reinforcements from the Leeward Islands.

Previous to this Pomare II's links with the Leeward Islands were traced mainly through his father's mother, Tetupaia (who was the daughter of Opoa's *ari'i rahi*, Tamatoa III), and through his mother's recent marriage to Tenania of Huahine. Tenuous as these connections may seem, they were substantial enough to induce the Leeward Islands' most powerful chiefs to lead large contingents of reinforcements to Mo'orea and Tahiti to help restore Pomare II to power, or perhaps to fish in Tahiti's troubled waters.[7]

Among the first of the Leeward Island chiefs to arrive was Tamatoa IV, of Opoa (Ra'iatea), along with his second daughter, Terito o Te Ra'i (later, Tere Moemoe).

The first wife of Pomare II, it will be recalled, was his father's sister's daughter, who died leaving no offspring. Shortly thereafter, 'Itia appears to have undertaken negotiations for a new wife for her son (this may in fact have been the principal reason for her move to Huahine). The woman selected for this important role was Tamatoa IV's daughter, Teri'itaria, whom Davies described as having been "the proper chief (of) the whole Island" (Newbury 1961: 126). This arrangement, however, did not work out.

According to Davies, soon after Tamatoa IV and his second daughter, Terito, arrived on Moʻorea, the former proposed that Pomare II marry her instead; whereupon Pomare II ". . . ascertaining that she was both younger and more handsome than the sister who had been previously proposed at once consented, and she became his wife" (Newbury 1961:137). (Thus, Pomare II's personal, aesthetic preferences were permitted to overrule the usual requirement that a person of superior rank-status be mated with one as comparably high-ranking as possible.) Then, continued Davies, "to soften the disappointment of the elder sister, she was still allowed the name of Pomare vahine wh(ich) she retained for many years afterwards." (What rights, and so forth, this entailed I cannot say; but as will be seen, Pomare Vahine proved to be a most useful ally to the man whose name she bore but whose sleeping mat she evidently did not share.)

As a sign of further changes to come, the marriage between Pomare II and Terito evidently took place without any of the ceremony traditionally associated with the linking of kin-Titles as important as theirs.

Accompanying Tamatoa IV to Moʻorea-Tahiti was also a considerable force of fighting men, but, before discussing that aspect of the Leeward Island aid to the embattled Pomare II, let us examine the nature of the social reinforcement represented by his marriage to the daughter of Tamatoa IV. To begin with, who and what was Tamatoa IV in terms of Maohi social hierarchies?

In her versions of "Royal Tahitian Genealogies" Henry listed Tamatoa IV as the third offspring of Veteʻa-Raʻi Uru by his second wife (his first wife having had seven offspring, and his third wife two); Veteʻa-Raʻi Uru was identified by Cook as "Ooroo" [O Uru], who during Cook's visit to Raʻiatea was highest in rank-status,[8] but who was politically subordinate to the Poraporan, Puni. Despite his birth-order position Tamatoa IV appears to have succeeded to his father's preeminent rank-status, but what that status carried in terms of coercive authority over all Raʻiatea is uncertain. Also, one will recall a statement by Vancouver reported earlier concerning Mauri (Haʻamanemane), the "high priest" expatriate from Opoa and brother to Tetupaia, who designated his grandnephew Pomare II as successor to his (Mauri's) Opoan Title, which was characterized as having been as high-ranking as Pomare's *maro ura* one (Vancouver 1801:327). Although Vancouver implied that Mauri himself enjoyed little influence at Raʻiatea, despite his high-ranking Title there, this does raise questions concerning the nature of that Title. In other words, according to one set of reports, the highest-ranking Opoan kin-Title passed from Tamatoa III to his son, Uru, and on to the latter's son, Tamatoa IV; while , according to another reconstruction, it passed from Tamatoa III to his son (and Uru's half-brother), Haʻamanemane, and then on to Pomare II. It may be, of course, that the reports are of two separate Titles, or that Ha'amanemane had forfeited his claims to the Opoan kin-Title upon leaving Ra'iatea, or even that it was in active dispute. In any case, the marriage of Pomare II to Terito (along with the ambiguous link between him and Terito's elder sister) served to reinforce any claim to the Title that Pomare II may have acquired from Ha'amanemane. By his marriage to Terito, Pomare II also reinforced his connections with Huahine's chiefly family, since Terito's mother was a daughter of Mato and his first wife, Fatuarai (and hence half-sister of Tenania and Mahine).

Other Leeward Island chiefs who traveled to Mo'orea during this period were Mai, Tefa'aora, Fenua Peho, Mahine and his son Ta'aroanui, Tenania (with 'Itia), and Tapoa. Mai and Tefa'aora were associated with Porapora's famed Marotetini marae, and are shown on an Emory genealogy as having been first cousins; their relationship to Pomare II, if any, is not known to us. Tefa'aora was described simply as chief of Taha'a. Mahine was Tenania's brother, and co-chief of Huahine.

Tapoa (also Teri'i Noho Rai), the most formidable of this company, is also the most difficult to place.[9] Among his antecedents were both Tamatoa II of Ra'iatea and Puni of Porapora, and his sister was the wife of Huahine's Mahine. In some accounts he is identified as chief of Ra'iatea, in others as chief of Porapora; both attributions were probably correct as far as they concerned kin-Titles, but whether he also exercised coercive chiefly authority over both islands at any time I cannot discover. (His main tribal base seems pretty clearly to have been Porapora, where his most serious political rival was Mai.)

In any case, even though Tapoa's kinship connections with Pomare II were quite remote — Tamatoa II having been their common great-great-great-grandfather — his presence in Pomare II's camp was considered the *sine qua non* for the latter's political (i.e., military) comeback.

Along with these Leeward Island chiefs went hundreds of their male subjects, but some of the actions of this impressively large force are more suggestive of peaceful pilgrims than of battle-eager warriors. For example, Davies reported that Tapoa (or was it Tamatoa?) brought with him from Opoa the sacred canoe of the Opoa 'Oro image, along with a "deputy" image made from the 'Oro image's bark cloth and feathers, and with these a company of priests. Then, "after many ceremonies at the principal maraes on Mo'orea it [the Opoa 'Oro objects] was sent to Tautira, calling on their passage at several maraes and offering many prayers" (Newbury 1961:137). Indeed, the whole expedition turned into something of a festival:

In January 1811 Pomare and the leeward islanders went over to Tahiti. But peace having been established they were well received by all. The rebels came to Papeete to meet Tapoa and prepared a great feast for the stranger the food for wh(ich) was brought from every district on Tahiti. Previous to the arrival of this reinforcement the two hostile parties seem to have been of about equal strength and now that at least 700 more had joined Pomare it appears strange that no attempt was made to recover his lost kingdom. It was very generally supposed that Tapoa, although he had joined Pomare with many of his people, was yet not very hearty in the aid wh(ich) he had so tardily rendered, and this impression may have prevented Pomare from endangering a peace wh(ich) had secured to him one of the five districts of the island. Instead of fighting their time was spent in feasting and dissipation, and after a few months numbers returned to their own island. (Newbury 1961:138)

In fact, however, the very presence of this force probably served to discourage the enemies of Pomare II from attacking him again.

CONVERSION

The second development of major political importance to take place at this time was the "conversion" of Pomare II to Christianity. "In July 1812," Davies wrote, "King Pomare acquainted several of the brethren with his full determination to cast away his false gods, and former evil practices, and that it was his sincere desire henceforward to embrace the Christian Religion as the only true one; to receive Jehova as his God, and Jesus Christ as his only Saviour and atonement; and that if they thought proper, they might write down his name as a candidate for Baptism; he desired also they might pray for him" (Newbury 1961:153).

This was not the first intimation of the change in Pomare II's public attitude toward religious matters. I noted earlier the circumstance of his marriage to Terito having taken place without traditional religious practices. Somewhat later the death of the young daughter of 'Itia and Tenania brought forth an even more positive response. During the child's illness so many prayers and offerings were made to the native gods that her death moved some influential people to angry recriminations, and led Pomare II to announce his intent to forsake their "false and foolish" gods and thenceforth worship Jehova (Newbury 1961:138).

One could speculate endlessly, but still more or less fruitlessly, concerning the circumstances and motives behind this change in Pomare II's outward behavior. (I shall not even begin to conjecture about its sincerity and depth, mentally and affectively.) His bountiful train of human and other offerings to 'Oro may have accompanied some of his former successes, but had not saved him from disaster in the end. Also, one could not continue forever to ignore the reality and potency of a god (i.e., Jehovah) whose devotees were obviously so numerous, so knowledgeable, so affluent, and so militarily unconquerable. In any case, it is evident that when circumstances encouraged Pomare II to become more preoccupied with these misgivings and reasonings, the missionary Nott was there to reinforce them. (The missionaries began to arrive back in Mo'orea in 1811, but it was Nott who had remained more closely and continuously associated with Pomare II during the Moʻorea "exile," when the latter's profession of belief took place.)

As one would expect, Pomare II's public declaration of belief in Jehovah led many other persons to profess, including some of the visiting chiefs. In addition, the missionaries reported signs of "conversion" among people who cannot be viewed as emulators of Pomare II. I shall not attempt to chronicle or explain at any length the tide of public "professions" that began to rise with that of Pomare II, in 1812, and ended some three to four years later by engulfing the whole population. Frustration with the old gods played a part, as did "miracles," missionary exhortation, genuine emulation, and, of course, political expediency. One of the most dramatic, and probably influential, episodes in this movement occurred at Papetoai, Moʻorea, in February 1815, when Patiʻi, the local high priest of ʻOro, committed all the images in his care to flames.

The sincerity of most of the "conversions" did not entirely satisfy the missionaries' Calvinistic standards in terms of personal behavior,[10] but the *pure-atua* (the pray-to-God people), as the converts came to be called, had by 1813 increased so much in number, and were so widespread, that they became a factor in intra- and intertribal politics. In some areas on Tahiti the *pure-atua* were threatened and attacked by pagan tribesmen, and thus they constituted a divisive element, locally. On Moʻorea and Pare, on the other hand, they became the official party; so the process of conversion became more or less identified with the movement to restore Pomare II's political fortunes.

Soon after he made his public profession of belief at Moʻorea, an emissary arrived from Tahiti inviting Pomare II to resume his residence there. The only report on this noteworthy event is contained in Davies' *History*:"Soon after the above circumstance [i.e., the public "profession"], some of the chiefs of Tahiti came over to fetch the King, professing their desire of restoring him to his government, at least to a part of it, and promising to use their endeavours for that purpose" (Newbury 1961:154). No single clue as to the identity of these chiefs is provided, and no word written as to the circumstances that led them to extend this fateful invitation.

Moerenhout, too, found this development puzzling: ". . . a démarche for which no reliable explanation has yet been discovered" (1837:II, 455). After canvassing the opinions of Tahitians, many years after the event, he reported as follows:

Some, jealous of Oupoufora [Opuhara], said that those who came to make these propositions to him were sincere, others pretended that this was only a trap; while an opinion more generally shared is that they wished to maintain the old religion, by preventing Pomare from becoming Christian. . . .

Needless to say, Pomare II accepted the invitation, and with him went to Tahiti his Leeward Island chiefly visitors and most of their men (whose numbers by this time had increased to almost a thousand). A little further along in Davies' *History* the report is amplified somewhat:

As to the natives, it has been already observed, that Pomare's government in Tahiti had not been restored. He had been invited over, by some of the chiefs, and the District of Matavai and some others were in a manner given up to him, but he had reason to suspect the sincerity of those concerned in the gift, and war was still agitated among the different chiefs. Pomare had been residing for some time on the little island at Papeete (or Wilks harbour) and was there by sufferance as it were for it does not appear the District of Pare was truly given to him. The strong party of the Leeward islanders that were with him, kept his enemies in awe and fear of attacking him; and on the other hand, he had some hope of regaining his authority without commencing hostilities. The former religious services, sacrifices to the gods &c had been entirely abandoned on Pomare's side, and though *Tapoa* and others of the Raiateans would have had recourse to their former heathen customs, they dared not set about it in present circumstances. (Newbury 1961:158)

The year 1813 passed without any new major political developments. Pomare II remained at Pare with some of the Leeward Islanders, while the rest of the Leeward Islanders remained on Mo'orea. Conversions continued apace at both locations, so much so that when an 'Oro *taura* of Tahiti visited Mo'orea he was met, according to Davies' *History*, "with unexpected ridicule and contempt everywhere" (Newbury 1961:156). Even where the *pure-atua* were in a small minority, the *History* continues, although "several of those things [i.e., pagan practices] were still kept up in some measure, tho' the circumstances of the Island at that time had greatly deranged the system. Many of the people everywhere seemed to doubt about the efficacy of their prayers and sacrifices, [11] and the various [Christian] truths which had been so often and so long promulgated among them seemed at times to come to remembrance." (p. 158)

In October 1813 a *tavaru* was held at Pare. Since participation in such tribute rendering was indicative, traditionally, of the shape of political or at least rank-based hierarchic structures, it would be illuminating indeed to learn who attended and how the objects were transacted; but the only information recorded is that it was attended by the co-chiefs of Huahine with their people, along with 'Itia, and by most of the people then residing at Mo'orea (Newbury 1961:168).

In January 1814 'Itia died, and shortly thereafter her husband too; earlier this would have represented a significant political setback for Pomare II, but with his connections with Huahine now firmly established, these deaths were for him more of a personal than a political loss.

In July, Tamatoa, Fenuapeho, and most of the Ra'iateans (and presumably most Taha'ans) left Tahiti and Mo'orea for home.[12] Shortly thereafter Pomare II removed to Mo'orea, probably because of the insecurity of his position in Pare resulting from the departure of the main forces of Leeward

Islanders. In fact, despite steady increments to the ranks of the *pure-atua*,
on the surface at least it appeared for a time that Pomare II's political fortunes
were again in decline. Then there occurred one of those series of
"accidents," so characteristic of Maohi political history, that wholly reversed
the trend of events.

JEHOVAH VERSUS 'ORO

In May 1814 a flotilla of canoes arrived at Mo'orea bearing Pomare Vahine
and a retinue of Huahine people. As eldest child of Tamatoa IV and as
one-time consort-designate of Pomare II (whatever that signified!), her visit
was of extraordinary ceremonial consequence. She and her following
remained for a year on Mo'orea, where most of them became "converted,"
and then continued to Tahiti to carry out a grand tour. Less than two months
later, the party hastily returned to Mo'orea, accompanied by many Tahitian
pure-atua. The following weeks brought other canoe loads of refugee *pure-atua* from Tahiti, along with reports of conflict among the pagans themselves.
The missionary version of these events was provided by Ellis. His account
of the episode offsets reports of the glitter of Pomare Vahine's ceremonious
tour of Tahiti:

> When a present of food and cloth was brought to the visitors by some of the
> chiefs of Tahiti, the priests also attended, and, observing the party disinclined to
> acknowledge or render the customary homage to the gods, began to expatiate on
> the power of the gods, and, pointing to some bunches of *ura*, or red feathers, which
> were always considered emblematical of their deities, employed insulting language,
> and threatened with vengeance the queen's companions. One of Pomare-vahine's
> men, the individual who had offered their acknowledgments to God, on the presenta-
> tion of food in Eimeo, hearing this, and pointing to the feathers, said, "Are those
> the mighty things you so extol, and with whose anger you threaten us? If so, I
> will soon convince you of their inability even to preserve themselves." Running
> at the same time to the spot where they were fixed, he seized the bunches of feathers,
> and cast them into a large fire close by, where they were instantly consumed. The
> people stood aghast, and uttered exclamations of horror at the sacrilegious deed;
> and it is probable that this act increased the hatred already rankling in the bosoms
> of the idolatrous party. (Ellis 1829:1, 237–238)

The man credited with this preposterous act (and with the unlikely
phrases that accompanied it) was a recent convert of Poraporan origin. About
him Ellis wrote (with an understatement that surely must constitute some
kind of record): "He was a man of decision and daring enterprise; and
though on the occasion in Tahiti above referred to, he may have acted with
a degree of zeal somewhat imprudent, it was a zeal resulting, not from
ignorant rashness, but enlightened principle, and holy indignation against
the boasting threatenings and lying vanities of the priests of idolatry; to
whose arts of deception he had formerly been no stranger" (1829:I, 239).

As Ellis would have put it, the idolatrous party continued to rankle, and the chiefs of Pare, Mahine, and Haʻapainoʻo formed a project to exterminate every *pure-atua* among them. Ellis continued:

> The influence of the Bure Atua in the nation, from the rank many of them held, and the confidence with which they maintained the superiority of their religion, together with the accessions that were daily made to their numbers from various parts of the island, not only increased the latent enmity against Christianity which the idolaters had always cherished, but awakened the first emotion of apprehension lest this new word should ultimately prevail, and the gods, their temples, and their worship, be altogether disregarded. To avoid this, they determined on the destruction, the total annihilation, of every one in Tahiti who was known to pray to Jehovah.
>
> A project was formed by the pagan chiefs of Pare, Matavai, and Hapaiano, to assassinate, in one night, every individual of the Bure Atua. The persecuted party was already formidable in point of numbers and rank, and the idolaters, in order to ensure success in their murderous design, invited the chiefs of Atehuru and Papara to join them. The time was fixed for the perpetration of this bloody deed. At the hour of midnight they were to be attacked, their property plundered, their houses burnt, and every prisoner secured, to be slaughtered on the spot. The parties, who for a long time had been inveterate enemies to each other, readily agreeing to the proposal, were made friends on the occasion, and cordially assented to the plan of destroying the Christians. The intended victims of this treachery were unconscious of their danger, until the evening of the 7th of July; when, a few hours only before the horrid massacre was to have commenced, they received secret intelligence of the ruin that was ready to burst upon them.
>
> Circumstances, unforeseen and uncontrollable by their enemies, had prevented the different parties from arriving punctually at their respective points of rendezvous; otherwise, even now escape would have been impracticable, and destruction inevitable, as the Porionu, inhabitants of Pare, Matavai, and Hapaiano, would have been on the one side, and in their rear, and the party from Atehuru and Papara on the other. The delay in the arrival of some of these, afforded the only hope of deliverance.
>
> At this remarkably critical period, the whole of the party having to attend a meeting either for public worship, or for some other general purpose, assembled in the evening near the sea. No time was to be lost. Their canoes were lying on the beach. They were instantly launched; and, hurrying away what few things they could take, they embarked soon after sunset, and reached Eimeo in safety on the following morning, grateful for the happy and surprising deliverance they had experienced. The different parties, as they arrived towards midnight, learned, with no ordinary remorse and disappointment, that their prey had been alarmed, and had escaped beyond their power.
>
> A large body of armed and lawless warriors, belonging to different and rival chieftains, thus brought together under irritated feelings, and perhaps mutually accusing each other as the cause of their disappointment, were not long without a pretext for commencing the work of death among themselves. Ancient animosities, restrained only for the purpose of crushing what they considered a common enemy, were soon revived, and led to an open declaration of war between the tribes assembled. The inhabitants of Atehuru and Papara, who had been invited by the Porionu to join them in destroying the Bure Atua, attacked the Porionu; and, in the battle that followed, obtained a complete victory over them, killing one of their principal chiefs, and obliging the vanquished to seek their safety in flight.
>
> After this affair, the people of Taiarabu joined the victors. The whole island

was again involved in war, and the conquering party scoured the coast from Atehuru to the eastern side of the isthmus, burning every house, destroying every plantation, plundering every article of property, and reducing the verdant and beautiful districts of Pare, Faaa, the romantic valleys of Hautaua, Matavai, and Hapaiano, and the whole of the north-eastern part of the island, to a state of barrenness and desolation.

Success did not bring peace or rest to the victorious party. Proud of their triumph, insolent in crime, and impatient of control, the Atehuruans and natives of Papara quarrelled with the Taiarabuans, who had joined them in destroying the Porionu. A battle followed. The natives of Taiarabu were defeated, and fled to their fortresses in the mountains of their craggy peninsula, leaving the Oropaa masters of the island.

Numbers of the vanquished fled to Eimeo, where they were received by the king, or protected by the chiefs, who had taken no part whatever in the wars that were now desolating Tahiti, and who determined to observe the strictest neutrality; or, if they acted at all, to do so only on the defensive, should invasion be attempted. (pp. 239–242)

Moerenhout, drawing his information from Paparan sources some two decades after the fact, provided a different perspective on these events. He began with an account of the tour of Pomare Vahine:

She disembarked at Pare (or Papaoa) with a large entourage. She was greeted most respectfully and, as was customary, was presented with bark cloth and other gifts; however, one of her followers, a convert to Christianity, audaciously aroused the anger of a priest (and of the gods) by his insulting gesture of ripping off some of the red feathers that covered the images and throwing them into a brazier that had just been lit. The populace was surprised and horror stricken, and the humiliated priest cried out for revenge; thereupon commenced a conflict which one can label the *Religious War*, on account of the circumstance that an attempt was made, at the priest's instigation, to slay all the visitors. The chiefs of Matavai and the rest of northwestern Tahiti made up their minds to attack the *pure-atua* — the Christians — but in view of the limited number of the former they prevailed upon the Paparan chief, Opuhara, to join with them in the enterprise. Opuhara immediately set out with the warriors of Papara, along with those of Atehuru as well. With him he also took the well-known *taura* named Taramea, who up to that time had been a center of superstitious awe and who was a deadly enemy of the new [Christian] religion, having seen in it a threat to his own position of power (which, however, was already in something of a decline even before Christianity's rise in influence).

En route to battle it was noticed [among the pagans] that one of their number, a hitherto unknown commoner named Maro, displayed the usual signs of being possessed by a spirit, namely, a solemn expression on his face and a strip of bark cloth wrapped around one arm. Taramea indignantly accused him of imposture, whereupon the latter, instead of replying in words, fixed the former with such a ferocious stare that the frightened onlookers cried out in chorus, "He is possessed! He is possessed!" Opuhara alone seemed not to be taken in by the skillfully acted grimaces, et cetera; he silenced Taramea's objections and walked on, but somewhat apart from the others, for the first time giving evidence of some indecisiveness and lack of energy.

The agreed upon time for attacking the Christian party was midnight. Meanwhile, wholly ignorant of the fate planned for them, the latter remained calm and secure up to the time, at sunset, when a secret message arrived to warn them of their danger. In order to escape they would have to move immediately and in a way calculated to arouse no alarm in the hostile Matavaians and Paparans, who were strong enough to destroy them and who were by then only a short distance away. This they succeeded in doing, having embarked in their canoes and stolen away without being discovered in the act. It is still not known for certain who it was who sent them the warning, but it is thought [by some] that Opuhara himself had done so; although this great, open-handed chief had been on occasion a rival of Pomare's, he would have been unwilling to take part in a conspiracy of this kind — especially one involving some chiefs whom he knew to be unfriendly toward him and whom he detested even more than he disliked Pomare himself.

In any case, it was Opuhara's tardiness in arriving that saved the Christian party. If he had led his men with his customary speed, he would have reached the environs of Papaoa before nightfall, and the Christians would not have been able to escape as they did, unseen. The new *taura*, Maro (or rather, Aretaminu — for so quickly had he taken on a new name), wished to join immediately in pursuit in order to attack Pomare Vahine and her party, promising victory and annihilation of all the Christians; but Opuhara refused to do so, as did the Chief of Puna'auia, thereby indicating that [even the pagan] Tahitians had begun to lose some of their superstitious awe for *taura*. Thus, the queen's canoes were able to make for Mo'orea that very night; in pointing this out, Maro accused the chief [Opuhara] of negligence and threatened him with the wrath of his gods. Opuhara, however, seems not to have been moved by this threat, stating that he had no ill will toward [Pomare Vahine] or her people, and that instead he would turn his attack against his ancient enemies, the Poreonu'u. This he did, having proceeded immediately to Papaoa, chasing after the enemy and killing one of their chiefs. The Poreonu'u retired to Matavai and sent forth an envoy to ask for peace. Maro agreed to their proposal on condition that they would send him a Christian for sacrifice to 'Oro (by whom Maro himself was possessed). The terrified Poreonu'u hastened to comply by killing a young convert and sending his trussed body to Maro at Papaoa. The latter, however, replaced the corpse in the canoe, ordered it to be returned to Matavai, and advised the envoy that if the chiefs of Matavai would set fire to their Arioi lodge house the sight of the blaze would serve as a signal for the Oropa'an army to return home. When the envoy reached Matavai with the sacrificial victim and informed the anxiously waiting chiefs of the wishes of the *taura* they hastened to comply. But then, when Maro saw the flames rising he immediately cried out, "Victory! Victory!" and, explaining the fire signal as a sign of triumph, he urged Opuhara to proceed to Matavai [to finish off the enemy]. Then, as Opuhara and his attacking force drew near them, the Poreonu'u took flight and abandoned everything in their rush to reach their fort in Ha'apaiano'o. Thereupon, the victors laid waste to the district, burning all the houses and massacring all those whose age or infirmities hindered their escape. From there they proceeded to Ha'apaino'o where they remained for four days encamped on the coastal plain. On the fifth day Maro announced that it would be necessary to attack the fort itself, which was situated some distance in the interior. However, the besieged force was so panic stricken that they were almost incapable of resistance, and after a light skirmish they fled into the mountains upon the first attack of the Oropa'a. All told, only a dozen or so people were killed.

The Oropa'a took over the fort and were joined there by the Seaward Tevans, with whom they were then at peace. When the Tevans arrived, Maro was sitting on a high spot of ground close to Opuhara and the other chiefs. As usual he was in a somber mood, seemingly lost in deep thoughts, and appeared not to have seen the Tevans for a while; but then he raised his head and demanded to know who the newcomers were. When told that they were "friends, from Taiarapu," he cried out, "Friends nothing! They are our enemies, and we must attack them forthwith." The chiefs, however, refused to do so, but some of them sought to appease him. Meanwhile, after learning what the *taura* had urged, the Seaward Tevans desired to leave, and despite all Opuhara's reassurances they kept to themselves and on guard. Nothing happened, however, so that they all found courage again and rallied their forces in order to take after the unfortunates who had sought refuge in the mountains. Then, after two days, the victorious forces departed from Ha'apaino'o and went to Papetoare, where they carried the corpses of their slain enemies around the marae, and — on orders from Maro — returned to their homes in Papara and Puna'auia, lest their continued absence encourage the Mo'oreans to go there and attack their women and children.

Scarcely had they arrived at Afaina [?] when many of them, believing peace to have been restored, took off for the mountains in search of the friends and relatives who had sought refuge there during the absence of their chiefs and fighting men. Then, while persuading the refugees to return to their homes they received news that the *taura* Tino (or Taramea), the one who had played such an influential role in former years but who was now eclipsed by Maro, had joined with the Seaward Tevans and they were marching to attack Papara. The only force left [in Papara] to oppose this attack consisted of Opuhara and some thirty of his subjects, plus the *taura* Maro. The chief wanted to retreat before the enemy's superior 200–300 man force, but Maro, on hearing that his archrival was with the enemy, ordered the Paparans to stand fast, telling them that Taramea no longer had any power and that the god 'Oro would fight on their side. And so it happened that Maro, whether out of hatred toward his rival or out of pure enthusiasm, marched at the head of this little troop against the Tevans, even after having been abandoned by Opuhara, who was highly skeptical of his prediction. Whereupon the Paparans actually routed the Seaward Tevans, Maro having killed five or six by his own hands. The rest of the Seaward Tevans managed to escape, and many of them, fearful of further pursuit by the Paparans, went over to Mo'orea to join up with Pomare. (II, 458–464)

In December of 1814 Pomare returned to Tahiti accompanied by his supporters and most of the fugitives from the recent Tahitian wars. I reproduce two versions of the episode, not only because of the climacterical importance of the events themselves but because of the contrasting perspectives on them served up in these different versions. First, the missionary version, as set forth in the Davies' *History*, presents a touching picture of a peace-loving Pomare II returning home merely to carry out his official duties:

After this [the defeat of Taiarapu by Papara] there was a prospect of peace being established; and the people, who on account of religion, had fled to Eimeo to save their lives, were invited to return to Tahiti, and take repossession of their respective lands. This made it necessary for the King and his people, and most of the people about us to go over to Tahiti in company with the different parties of the refugees, and according to an ancient custom of the country, to reinstate them in a formal manner in their old possessions.

On the arrival of the king and those who followed him, at Tahiti, the idolatrous party appeared on the beach, in a hostile manner; seemed determined to oppose the king's landing and soon fired on his party; but by the king's strict order the fire was not returned, and at last apparently issued in peace and reconciliation. In consequence of this, several of the people returned peaceably to their different lands; but still fears and jealousies existed on both sides. This state of things continued till Sabbath day Novr 12th 1815 when the heathen party, taking advantage of the day, and of the time, when the king and all the people were assembled for worship, made a furious, sudden, and unexpected assault, thinking they could at such a time easily throw the whole into confusion. They approached with confidence, their Prophet having assured them of an easy victory. In this however they were mistaken. It happened that we had warned our people before they went to Tahiti, of the probability of such a stratagem being practiced should war take place; in consequence of which they attended worship under arms; and tho' at first they were thrown into some confusion, they soon formed for repelling the assailants; the engagement became (warm) and furious, and several fell on both sides.

In the king's party there were many of the refugees from the several parties who had not yet embraced Christianity; but our people not depending upon them took the lead in facing the enemy, and as they were not all engaged at once, being among bushes and trees, those who had a few minutes respite, fell on their knees, crying to Jehova for mercy and protection, and that he would be pleased to support His cause against the idolatry of the heathen. Soon after the commencement of the engagement, *Upufara* the chief of Papara was killed, this when known threw the whole of his party into confusion and Pomare's party quickly obtained complete victory. (Newbury 1961:191–192)[13]

Moerenhout's version was written from the vantage point of Papara:

Those last conflicts, which were more destructive to property than to life, resulted again in bringing all of Tahiti under Opuhara's sway. But in doing so they made a near-desert out of the island and left the conqueror with only a small force of warriors, most of the defeated ones having escaped to Mo'orea and joined forces with Pomare. As for the latter, when he saw his forces thus augmented day by day, he began to entertain the ambition of conquering Tahiti itself. Meanwhile Opuhara, with what remained of his forces from Papara and Atehuru, made ready the foodstuffs and bark cloth for a *puriri* ceremony (a rite of thanksgiving), or *Te Deum* . . . ; it was during these preparations at the Taiarapu marae [the Taputapuatea marae at Atutira?] that he learned of Pomare's arrival at Pape'ete, on the northeastern coast of Tahiti Nui. At this news the *taura* Maro became highly excited and mobilized the warriors; in a state of possession he predicted the wholesale destruction of the party of Christian converts. Opuhara, similarly aroused by his enmity for his old rival, set forth to battle with all his own warriors and with those recently united to his cause.

Despite their lack of intrinsic interest I have been at pains to record the details of all these petty wars because it was through them that was brought about such a total change in the life of these Islanders, namely, the successful introduction of a wholly new religion. In taking refuge with Pomare on Mo'orea, those defeated in these wars served not only to augment his fighting strength but also swelled the ranks of converts to the new religion — encouraged, as they were, by the example of their new chief and reinforced in their change by their belief that their former gods had forsaken them.

Thus, the army with which Pomare returned to Tahiti was in large measure one of Christians; that is to say, like Pomare himself this army placed its trust in a god said to be more potent than 'Oro or any other gods known to them (whose existences, by the way, the missionaries did not deny, but rather lumped them with their *varua ino* — evil spirits or demons — and in opposition to the True God).

On a Sunday in December [*sic*] . . . Pomare arrived from Mo'orea, accompanied by about a thousand people, and he betook himself to services in the chapel constructed at Nari'i, in WSW Tahiti. Scarcely had the services begun when gunshots were heard, announcing the approach of the enemy, who at the very same moment came into view as they rounded a point of land some distance away — all of which set forth cries of "War! War!" Fortunately, the Christians had armed themselves — although the enemy had planned the attack for that day [i.e., the Sabbath] in the belief that they would have found them to be without arms or other means of defense (or so Maro had predicted). As soon as the enemy came into view most of the Christians became eager to rush into battle but Pomare held them in check, telling them that the prayer services must first be completed — for, the whole outcome would depend on the backing given their side by God. (In this respect, evidently, Pomare had not changed his views: as he had in the past done with 'Oro, he now put all hope and faith in the protective powers of Jehovah.) When their prayer service was finished the Christians drew up in battle formation: the more zealous ones in the front lines, the recent [Tahitian] refugees (whose loyalties were more uncertain) in the center, and the Mo'oreans in the rear.

The enemy advanced to attack in full cry, under the leadership of the courageous Opuhara and urged on by the *taura* Maro, who assured them a certain and easy victory. Some of the attackers wavered when shots from a cannon [of Pomare's], mounted on a small boat and fired by a European, killed a few of them, but their leader brought them back into order, saying: "Those of you who have been killed brought it onto themselves. Can't you see that the enemy's shots usually go either too high or too low? If they fire too high you must lower yourselves, and if too low simply leap into the air. Just look at me in front of you all; they will not hit me.'

The heathens attacked recklessly, and for a time Pomare's forces seemed in danger of losing the fight. The latter fought with unusual bravery, but they lost large numbers of men and gave up much ground, so that it appeared [for a while] that the victory would go to Opuhara. This chief continued to stay out front and to lead the attack, thereby inspiring his troops by example and going to their assistance when needed — until, that is, he himself was felled by a bullet. Opuhara did not succumb immediately, and raised himself enough so that he continued to face the other side. On seeing him struck down several of his companions rallied round him to carry him to safety, but realizing that his wound was mortal he ordered them in a voice still firm with command: "Leave me here; instead, fight on and avenge my death. Over there is the one who has slain your chief," he added, pointing to one of Pomare's men. At this, his companions rushed into the attack — a handful of men against a whole formation of Pomare's best fighters. . . .

Despite the loss of Opuhara his troops continued to fight with great ardor — indeed, the condition of their chief seemed to inspire them to even greater efforts. Meanwhile, however, Pomare's forces were encouraged [by the felling of Opuhara] and held tenaciously to their ground. [From then on] the heathens lost more and more of their leaders on account of the Christians' greater number of firearms; particularly deadly was the firepower directed at them from several boats that were under Pomare's personal command and that struck them on their [seaward] flanks. Finally, the heathens had to give way; and with this their ranks broke in disorder and they turned and fled. Such was the sight that met the eyes of the fallen Opuhara as he breathed his last breath. (II, 464–468)

Considering their reinforcements (from Mo'orea and the Leeward

Islands) and the greater number of firearms in their hands, it is not surprising
that the Pomare forces finally prevailed. What is surprising, however — and
not only to the student of Maohi society, but, evidently, to most Maohis
of that period as well — is the fact that Pomare II held back his followers
from completing their destruction:

> Flushed with success, in the moment of victory, the king's warriors were, accord-
> ing to former usage, preparing to pursue the flying enemy. Pomare approached,
> and exclaimed, *Atira*! It is enough! — and strictly prohibited any one of his warriors
> from pursuing those who had fled from the field of battle; forbidding them also
> to repair to the villages of the vanquished, to plunder their property, or murder
> their helpless wives and children. (Ellis 1829:I, 252)

The final events in this fateful episode are described in the missionary
History, under the date of November 17, 1815:

> Many people returned these days from Tahiti, and brought news that the *Teva
> i uta* and the *Oropaa* viz those of Atehuru, Papara &c who had fled, were come
> to Pomare and had delivered up their muskets, and that it was said all these were
> resolved to embrace the new Religion. Pomare had sent people to destroy the maraes
> and altars and fetch Oro from Tautira, that he also might undergo the same fate.
> [Fig. 32–1]
> Some days after this the king wrote to the miss, if they could make it convenient,
> it would be well if two could come over to Tahiti to instruct the people how to
> proceed in the present new state of things. (Newbury 1961:193–195)

"New State of Things"

With the battle of Fei Pi all effective political opposition to Pomare II was
extinguished in Tahiti and Mo'orea. The monarchy therewith established

FIGURE 32–1. From Missionary Sketches, July 1819. London Missionary Society.

was preeminent in terms of both coercive authority *and* rank-status, and in addition the monarch became head of the official Christian (Protestant) Church.

In 1843 French colonial rule superseded the monarchy's coercive, governmental authority, but the Pomare Dynasty was permitted to retain its ceremonial prerogatives for another four decades. —— But that is another story, better told elsewhere.

NOTES

CHAPTER 25

1   As I acknowledged previously, I am conscious of the difficulties of such an undertaking and am not altogether confident that I have succeeded in carrying it out.

2   Population figures in this section are derived from the Tupaia-based estimates (see chap. 2), and thus are subject to innumerable qualifications.

3   "Tetahah" appears on Cook's map of 1769, and later it was used interchangeably with "Fa'a'a" to refer to the territory between Puna'auia and Pare. It may possibly represent a misreading of "Te Fana," as Newbury implied (1961:xxxv).

4   See chap. 16, section on Tahiti-Mo'orea. According to Rodriguez, Reti's domain extended only *up to* Mahaena on the north (Corney 1919:165).

5   Emory's Papara genealogy, however, equates Te Vahine Moeatua with Purai, and lists Purahi as a younger sister of the latter (Marae Traditions).

6   Morrison identified Ti'itorea as "uncle" of the younger Vehiatua, but the genealogical basis for this is unrecorded.

7   According to Corney's note Bougainville lost six anchors and kedges during his brief stay at Hitia'a: "The anchor recovered by the natives weighed 700 lbs., and was given to Puni, the noted Chief of Porapora who subjugated the greater part of Ra'iatea" (1919:136n).

8   See, for example, Jefferson, Journal, 24 January 1806, LMS Archives.

9   Captain Winnifred Brander, "Society Island Genealogies," manuscript, Bernice P. Bishop Museum, Honolulu, Hawaii.

10 This "Tee" (i.e., Ti'ipari'i) was probably the individual identified as Toppere by J. Forster, who described him as having "the direction of Matavai" (1778:354).

11 Another name prominent in the earliest accounts of Matavai and its vicinity was Robertson's and Cook's "Owhaa" (Robertson 1948:169–175; Beaglehole 1955:75n) and Thomson's "Ofa'a" (Thomson, History, p. 36). Henry transcribed this name as O Hau, which raises the possibility of its having been an official designation for Ti'ipari'i — i.e., as *hau* of this tribe. However, I consider this an unlikely transcription and settle for Thomson's identification of "Ofa'a" as a landed proprietor of Point Venus — in other words, a *ra'atira* of only local consequence.

12 Bligh 1789:I, 372; Vancouver 1801:262, 285; Bligh 1792:125a. It was Poeno

who was custodian of Webber's portrait of Cook, the back of which served as a ship's register for a while.

13   The bases for these conflicting interpretations, which were touched upon earlier, are set forth in Gunson 1963 and Newbury 1961.

14   In his journal of his voyage of 1792, under the date of 29 April, Bligh identified Tutaha as "uncle" of Tu (Pomare I), but his journal of 1789 indicates that he probably intended "great uncle." See also Beaglehole 1955:clxxxii.

15   Beaglehole 1955:95–96; Beaglehole 1962:I, 280–282. It will also be recalled that Tutaha's relations with Hitia'a's chief, Reti, were such that he was able to visit Bougainville there.

16   Tutaha evidently had some proprietary rights in the important Pa'ea marae, Maraeta'ata, but I cannot discover the basis for these rights, except possibly from "Old" Tutaha's mother, who is given in Emory's Tarahoi genealogy as having been a To'ofa, the Title usually associated with that marae.

17   While this list is of Teu's offspring, there is some question as to whether the mother of all of them was in fact Tetupaia. For example, Adams stated that Ari'ipaea (Te Ari'i Fa'atou) was son of another of Teu's consorts (1901:100).

18   My bases for setting the birth years of these first three offspring of Teu and Tetupaia are as follows. Most writers (correctly, I think) identify Te Ari'i na Vaho Roa as the young woman seen by Cook et al. in 1769 in company with Papara's young *ari'i*, Teri'irere (and who was at the time either his wife or his wife-to-be). On that occasion Cook estimated her age at about 18 or 20, and Banks estimated it at 16 (Beaglehole 1955:103; Beaglehole 1962:293), which would put her birth between 1749 and 1753. In December 1772 Boenechea guessed Pomare I to be 20 to 22 years old (Corney 1913:319), and writing in August 1773 G. Forster put his age at 24 or 25 (1777:I, 326). These estimates would locate the young *ari'i*'s birth date between 1748 and 1752. Adams put the date at about 1743 (1901:88) but on what evidence I cannot discover. I have found no observer's estimate of the age of Ari'ipaea Vahine, but, if she was in fact born after Te Ari'i na Vaho Roa and before Pomare I, her birth date must have been as given in my list.

19   Gunson — mistakenly, I believe — identified Morrison's Ari'ipaea Vahine with "Ine Metua" (i.e., Vahine Metua) (1964:64), another famous Tahitian woman whom I shall identify further. Vahine Metua was wife of Teu's second son, Ari'ipaea (Te Ari'i Fa'atou).

20   Pomare I shared his sleeping mat with a number of males as well (Jefferson, Journal, 8 June 1799, LMS Archives).

21   Gunson identified Vavea as 'Itia's father (1964:62), in opposition to the identifications made by Henry (1928:268) and Emory (Marae Traditions).

22   See also Turnbull 1813:280.

23   "Tynah with his Wives, Father and Brothers dine with me every Day. A Cannoe with a Party came over from Moreah to see the Ship, there were some Friends of Whyerreddee for whom Tynah had recourse to my lockers, to satisfy with presents. Tynah is a perfect Fool to this Woman. She rules him as she pleases, while Iddeeah quietly submits, and is contented with a moderate share of influence." (Bligh 1792:133b).

24   In describing Teu's offspring G. Forster listed as number five "T'-aree-Watow
      [who] appeared to be about sixteen years of age [in 1776]; he told us he had
      another name but which I have forgotten, from whence I conclude that this
      which I have mentioned is only his title" (1777:II, 96). Other attempts to
      transcribe Te Ari'i Fa'atou were "Tarevatee" and "Tarevatou."
           Adams identified Ari'ipaea as half-brother of Pomare I (1901:100, 111,
      113) but this is confirmed by no other primary source that I know of.
25   In 1792 Bligh also included Tetaha (along with Pa'ea, his "Taaigh," and
      Puna'auia, his "Paterre") within the "land Division" of Atehuru (1792:166).
26   "Lycurgus" was the nickname given to Tupura'a i Tamaiti by Banks, in admi-
      ration for the effective manner in which he recovered and restored some objects
      stolen by his subjects from the Europeans (Beaglehole 1962:I, 255–258).
27   The Beaglehole edition reads, ". . . one of the Chiefs of Attahourou"
      (1967:198), which may be accounted for by some writers' inclusion of Fa'a'a
      in Atehuru.
28   Bligh 1789:II, 48–49; Bligh 1792:126b, 135.
29   Pohuetea, through this or some other Title, may also have been associated
      directly with the Puna'auia Point Taputapuatea marae just described, but that
      is not clear. In any case, his principal household was some miles away from
      both marae — or so one may infer from the fact that it took Rodriguez several
      hours by canoe to travel from one place to the other (Corney 1919:171).
      Anderson, writing in 1777, described Pohuetea as residing near 'Utu'aimahurau
      (Beaglehole 1967:979) — a somewhat puzzling circumstance inasmuch as this
      would have placed this Puna'auian chief's residence deep within Pa'ea.
30   It was this same Purutihara, it will be recalled, who offered her sexual favors
      to Cook in exchange for some red feathers — presumably before she became
      his "sister"!
31   Called also "Paterre." In some contexts the name Atehuru was used by Euro-
      peans to designate Pa'ea specifically, rather than Pa'ea *and* Puna'auia; but
      whether this was also a Maohi usage is not clear.
32   According to Emory's classification two of the enclosed units corresponded
      to his "inland" type and the third to his "coastal" type (1933:67–69). For
      a more analytical classification see Green et al. 1967.
33   In earlier writings Emory identified the marae complex described by Cook
      et al. and sketched by Webber as Maraeta'ata (1931; 1933; Marae Traditions);
      but later he joined Beaglehole (1967:198n) and Green (Green and Green 1968)
      and myself in identifying it as 'Utu'aimahurau. This correction has an important
      bearing on our understanding of Tahitian political history, and is not mentioned
      merely for the sake of technical accuracy.
34   Adams' designation of proprietorship referred specifically only to Maraeta'ata.
      But then, Adams did not even mention the name 'Utu'aimahurau, not even
      in his long list of marae, consequential and otherwise. From this I am led
      to conclude either that Ari'i Ta'ima'i was ignorant of its existence (which
      seems unlikely), or that she confused or lumped together the two marae (or,
      of course, that Adams himself misinterpreted the old matriarch's recollections).
35   There would seem to be two possible and equally plausible explanations for
      the close connection between Maraeta'ata and 'Utu'aimahurau marae. First,

one of them might have been a direct offshoot of the other — say, 'Utu'aimahurau from Maraeta'ata — with the 'Oro cult having been added to the latter's other functions and buildings over the course of time. Or second, 'Utu'aimahurau could have been constructed *de novo*, as the tradition vaguely implies, and its proprietorship taken over (or indeed sponsored) by the chiefly dynasty already established at Maraeta'ata.

36   "*E parau tupuna no Te-toofa arii no Teoropaa: Outuai te marae.*" (Transcribed by Emory from the Pomare genealogies.)

37   Tevahitua was a fairly common name, separately or as part of a Title — as for example, of Papara's Amo. Patea was recorded by Adams as having been connected with Fa'atoai's (Mo'orea) marae Taputapuatea (1901:38).

38   My basis for this opinion is the display of affection between Teri'irere and Te To'ofa's wife and daughter, witnessed in 1777 by Lieutenant King (Beaglehole 1967:1378–1379).

39   Explanatory notes with this genealogy add that the only offspring of Tavi and Taurua died without issue, and that Tuiterai was Tavi's "younger brother or cousin" — whatever that might signify.

40   The note recording this event, as reproduced in Emory (Marae Traditions), reads: "Maua came to Papara bringing Oro and the Maro Ura, Teraipuatata, connecting Raiatea and Atupii (Huahine)." The significance (and possible historicity) of this event will be discussed later on.

41   One of the sons was also called Aromaiterai, said Adams (1901:38).

42   For example, a great-granddaughter was Ari'i Ta'ima'i, the source of Adams' *History*.

43   As noted above (p. 1190) there is some question about this identification — with implications which will be discussed later on.

44   Henry's Papara genealogy lists only one, Teri'irere (or Temari'i) (1928:270); but Emory (based on notes from Tati Salmon) listed nine (Marae Traditions).

45   In line with this version, of the nine offspring of Amo listed in the Papara genealogy reproduced in Emory's "Marae Traditions," only Teri'irere was borne by Purea. (Adams 1901:110)

46   Teri'irere-Temari'i was hardly the "bachelor" that Henry described him as having been, but as I noted already, he produced no publicly acknowledged progeny, and his kin-Titles and tribal office eventually passed to a collateral. According to Adams, *his* Temari'i Ari'ifa'ataia was at one time married to a daughter of the chief of Matarea (1901:122), a union which could not, however, have added much luster to Temari'i's own glittering kin-Titles, or much political strength to his tribal office.

47   He was a rare exception among Ra'iatean emigrees in Tahiti, for most Ra'iateans on Tahiti who are mentioned in the pages of the sources were alleged to be "princes" or "princesses" from Opoa.

48   The name Metuaro (or Motuaria, or Mahau) also figures importantly in these accounts but appears to be an alternative personal name for a holder of one of the Titles just listed.

49   "[Baldness] . . . a thing rather uncommon in these islands at that age, he wore a kind of Turban and seem'd ashamed to shew his head, but whether a bald head is a Mark of desgrace with them or they thought it was so with

us I cannot say; we judged it was the latter, as we had shaved the head of a Indian we had caught Stealing.'' (Beaglehole 1967:227)

50   In a footnote to this passage Beaglehole registered some skepticism, saying, ''Mahine's lady *may* have been Amo's sister, but there is no trace of a sister in the genealogies I have seen'' (1967:226n3). Evidently Dr. Beaglehole had not seen the Papara genealogy reconstructed by Emory, for this shows Amo to have had ten siblings, including four positively identified as females, and five others not identified as to sex. Also, one will recall the name of another of Amo's sisters, Tetua Unurau, who was mother of the famed Purahi.

51   According to a missionary survey published in 1818, the (usually uninhabited) islet Tupai was also ''subservient'' to Porapora, but who its proprietors were in 1767 I am unable to discover (*Narrative of the Mission at Otaheite* [London: London Missionary Society, 1818] p. 7).

52   The reference is to hogs sent by Puni to the ship, and to three young women who evidently visited the ship at Puni's command.

53   Chesneau labeled it the Battle of Ho'oroto (Ra'iatea), and asserted that it came about as the result of Mo'ohono's efforts to have his grandsons, Tenania and Mahine, vested with ''sacred kingship'' at Opoa's Taputapuatea marae (i.e., probably meaning, invested with a *maro ura* kin-Title associated with this marae). At this period the principal, locally held *maro ura* kin-Title of this marae was evidently that of Mato's second cousin, Vetea Uru. It is reasonable to suppose that Mato might have claimed it also, on the basis of his grandfather Ari'imao's primogenitary rights over those of Vetea Uru. (The latter's incumbency probably derived from his father.) In any case, the question of succession was evidently open enough to encourage counterclaims.

54   The account states that the location of this site on Taiarapu was near Point Ta'atua at a previously built marae called Te ahu rua tama. I am, however, unable to locate any point or marae so named. As for Taputapuatea, the name of the marae built to house the image, there was a well-known marae of that name at Tautira, which later became (or resumed being?) the principal 'Oro image depository for the whole island — but, of course, *all* marae serving that function were so named.

55   I called attention earlier to the peculiar discrepancy between two versions of this story. In Adams' version, which was based on Ari'i Ta'ima'i's account but translated by her daughter Marau, the lover was a shark-god of ''the race of arii rahi,'' and the girdle in question was a *maro tea* (1901:12–14). In the Handy version, however, which the author reportedly obtained from Marau herself, several decades later and after the death of Ari'i Ta'ima'i, the lover is specifically identified as an Opoan chief (though also a fish god), and the girdle was of red feathers — i.e., a *maro ura* (1930:68).

CHAPTER 26

1   The personnel of Bougainville's expedition, which anchored off Hitia'a in April 1768, were similarly unaware of what was then taking place at Papara, 25 kilometers to the west.

2   This version, which I shall label the ''Adams' version,'' is really a hodge-podge

of "facts" put together (and without entire consistency) from Georg Forster's journal, Wilson's "Missionary Narrative," etc., and from oral traditions said to have been transmitted — twelve decades after the events — by Ari'i Ta'ima'i herself.

3   According to the Emory genealogies, Teihotu's wife was Vavea, and this couple had only three offspring: 'Itia (principal consort of Pomare I), Pateamai (first married to Vehiatua III, later to Pomare I), and Mahau, the embattled claimant to Mo'orea's principal chieftainship. Teri'i Vaetua was one name of Teihotu's father, and may have been an alternative name for some other member of the Ahurai family, possibly for Te Pau "B" (fig. 25–1), but I can find no confirmation of this on any genealogy known to me.

4   Cook's "Tarevatoo" was indeed Pomare I's brother (or half-brother), Te Ari'i Fa'atou, and not Teri'i Vaetua.

5   Undoubtedly, a great deal of politically relevant information is encapsulated in this cryptic formula, but I shall resist the temptation to try my hand at interpreting it.

6   Beyond pointing to some traditional conflicts, such as the one between Tavi and Tuiterai (Adams 1901:22ff), I cannot account for this antagonism in specific terms. Perhaps we see here a predictable process in Maohi-like societies — namely, the typical (but not inevitable) development of friction between two more or less evenly matched tribes having a common boundary. This is, of course, far too large a matter to consign to a note, and I do so only to call attention to the question.

7   Adams quoted a dramatic song which was said to have been composed by Paparans in memory of this blow to their tribe and which identifies Purahi as the principal mover of it (1901:57–59).

8   *Journal of a Voyage round the World in H.M.S.'s Ship* Endeavour (Dublin, 1772) pp. 93–95. Beaglehole referred to Tupaia's intrigues against Tutaha, but provided no reference for this information (1955:117n).

9   Wilson 1799:xii–xiii; d'Urville 1834–1835:I, 544.

10 This is only one of several *totally different* versions for the origin of marae Teahupo'o.

11 This seems to refer to Vehiatua's part in the Papara debacle. G. Forster's error in having Tutaha view this as an insult to his family was based on his mistaken notion that Tutaha and Amo (and Teu) were brothers.

12 This refers to the time since their departure at the end of the first visit of the second voyage.

13 It will be recalled that Vehiatua I's spouse, the famous Purahi, did in fact "marry" a man named Ti'itorea after her husband's death, and that her new partner became "prime minister" to her elder son, Vehiatua II.

14 I refer here to the statement in Adams linking Tutaha with Maraeta'ata in Pa'ea (1901:74).

15 On this point Adams stated: ". . . Otoo was not allowed to wear the Maro without a protest. In order to receive full recognition, he was obliged to take a seat and wear the Maro-ura in the great Marae of Maraetaata in Paea. This Marae had three heads: (1) Pouira, the Tevahitua i Patea; (2) Tetooha, the

Taura atua i Patea; and (3) Punuaaitua. Tevahitua protested, and refused to allow Otoo to take his seat and wear the Maroura on his part of the Marae. The other two made no objection, and the reason was characteristic of Tahitian society. Otoo's great-grandmother, Te-fete-fete-ui, was the daughter of Tevarua hoiatua, a chieftess of Ahurai and Punaauia, and as such had the right to a seat in Marae Maraetaata.'' (1901:75)

CHAPTER 27

1   In a footnote commentary on King's statement above, Beaglehole wrote: "This is not a very intelligible account. The name of the brother of Vehiatua here referred to seems to be an attempt at Teri'itetua-ounu-maona; but this person was himself Vehiatua 1775–90, and was the boy whom King has already mentioned (17 August). He never settled on Moorea. There seems to be no other reference to such a battle." (Beaglehole 1967:1382n1.) Evidently, Beaglehole missed de Barreda's and Bligh's references to "such a battle," as well as Bligh's reference to a third brother.

2   Although the actual nuptial rites formalizing these two marriages may not have been finalized for some time after the beginning of this era, the understandings regarding the alliances were probably already in effect by the time of Cook's second voyage, when the succession issue came to a head. The link between Vehiatua III and Pateamai (and hence between Vehiatua III and Mahau) is likely to have reinforced Seaward Teva's hostility toward Mahine, and was conceivably formed with that in mind.

3   See also Beaglehole 1967:977, 1064–1065, 1315–1316, 1376.

4   The situation described earlier concerning the nonhostile reception accorded some visiting Mo'oreans at Tautira could count as another example of this "Police" — although it is of course possible that the visitors in question were not from Mahine's territory. (See Corney 1919:116.)

5   See also Beaglehole 1967:214. This would appear to indicate that a Seaward Teva contingent, possibly under Vehiatua III, accompanied Te To'ofa's and Pohuetea's in the expedition against Mo'orea. This accounts for the reference to "another Chief" in Cook's passage about the expedition (p. 210), and for the reported presence of a Seaward Teva chief at the "peace" ceremony yet to be described.

6   In blaming Te To'ofa for the stalemate, Old Teu, Pomare I's father, was giving vent to a narrowly partisan sentiment, but the very exiguity of his view might indicate that his own family's interests were particularly damaged by terms of the truce. Among other things, he seems to have assumed that had Te To'ofa waited a while to attack Mahine, Cook himself might have been persuaded to intervene on the side of the Tahitians.

7   Except for the *Lady Penrhyn* (Lieutenant Watts, commanding), which anchored at Matavai for a fortnight during July 1788, en route to Australia.

8   According to Vancouver, Mahine was killed during the Battle of Atehuru, but this conflict took place in September 1791, three years after Bligh wrote of Mahine's death in the earlier campaign, a fact also overlooked by Adams (1901:102).

9   This young woman, who was also called "Alredy" (Ariti?), was estimated
        to be about sixteen years old in 1791, and thus born circa 1775 (Edwards
        and Hamilton 1915:103).

10   I am somewhat puzzled by this so-called friendship between Pomare I and
        Te Pau "B", since Fa'a'a appears not to have aided Pomare I during the
        attacks of Te To'ofa, Mahine, and Vehiatua III. Actually, this seems to confirm
        a situation noted earlier — i.e., although Te Pau "B" had succeeded to his
        father's Title, de facto tribal authority had rested in the hands of Te To'ofa.
        Of course, with Te To'ofa dead, the friendship between Te Pau "B" and
        Pomare I could blossom, for the moment at least.

11   However, the Wallis *maro* seems to have been still at 'Utu'aimahurau marae
        at this time.

12   This individual was only about seven years old at the time of Bligh's *Bounty*
        visit, and he did not assume the Title of Pomare "II" for some time to come;
        but I shall refer to him throughout by this label in order to spare the reader
        some of the confusion involved in trying to keep track of Maohis' name
        changes.

CHAPTER 28

1   Strictly speaking Morrison was not one of the *Bounty* "mutineers," as he
        was subsequently cleared of culpability in the mutiny, but I shall continue
        to refer to him and all his companions by this term.

2   For example, in February 1790, Morrison witnessed a solemn ceremony at
        which offerings were made and shoulders bared to a portrait of Captain Cook,
        just as to a living sovereign (1935:85–86). One will also recall the use made
        of the *Dolphin*'s pennant in the Wallis *maro*.

3   Henceforth for convenience I shall refer to the immediate family of Pomare
        I and II as the Pomares, although the Title applied only to the incumbents
        themselves.

4   Hitihiti's ("Odiddy," "Oedideedee," "Hedeedee") native hearth was
        Porapora and he claimed kinship with that island's famous old chief Puni.
        In 1773 and 1774 his age was put at seventeen or eighteen, and he was a
        useful and universally liked member of Cook's crew. After that expedition
        he settled at Pare in the service of Pomare I. Cook met him there in 1777,
        but this time he was described as "foolish," "clumsy," and kava-addicted,
        but evidently still skillful enough with firearms to make himself a valuable
        ally. According to G. Forster his original name was Mahine, but this was
        exchanged with a Mo'orean chief when the two became friends. As for the
        report that he was married to Tetupaia's sister, Te Pau, I find no such sister
        listed in the genealogies to which I have access, but that does not necessarily
        discredit this attribution. (Beaglehole 1961:lxxiii, 426n; 1967:1375, 1058–1059;
        Bligh 1789:II, 68.)

5   Adams reconstruction is vitiated in part by his assumptions that Temari'i and
        Teri'irere were half-brothers, and not alternative names for the same individual,
        and that Temari'i — the one under discussion — had been born about 1772

(whereas Morrison judged him to be twenty-seven or twenty-eight years old in 1791). Moerenhout also offered a reconstruction of this complex of relationships, but it is even more ill informed and confused than Adams', and does not warrant further consideration here.

6 Adams claimed that Ari'ipaea was also Temari'i's "guardian," having been made so upon the death of Amo; but Temari'i was already about twenty-five years old when these events took place, and, as we shall see, Amo was still alive (1901:110ff.). According to Moerenhout, Ari'ipaea "betrayed his trust" as guardian to Temari'i by turning over his seat in the Papara marae to Pomare, which was tantamount to transferring the sovereignty to all Papara (1837:II, 417ff.). This account was accepted as factual by Adams, who, however, added that the transaction took place without the consent of Temari'i or the people of Papara, and was never considered by them to be binding (p. 114). I am unable to accept or reject these reconstructions written so many decades after the events they are supposed to describe, and by such partisan chroniclers.

7 As we saw previously, although Pomare II, and before him his father, had been permitted access to the Wallis *maro* and the Paparan image while they had been deposited at 'Utu'aimahurau, he did so only with the consent of that marae's proprietors, and subject to constraints that he evidently considered to be distasteful.

8 Thus, Amo was still alive in October 1790, contrary to Adams information (1901:111).

9 For a description of marae Tarahoi, including its new addition, see Green and Green 1968.

10 As an example, I refer the reader to Hamilton's account of his encounters with the custom of "wife-hospitality," which provides, among other things, a somewhat different view of the character of two of our leading personalities, Mahau, principal chief of Mo'orea, and his wife, Auo, who was sister of Pomare I. (Edwards and Hamilton 1915:109–110)

CHAPTER 29

1 Some idea of the nature of this expedition's relations with their hosts (and hostesses) may be gained from the information, as reported by Vancouver, that only one member of the entire company of both ships was a married man!

2 In telling Bligh about one of these vessels, in July 1792, a native informant described it as ". . . a Miserable vessel and the Commander as a great Rascal" (1792:168b).

3 Other members of this expedition who left accounts of some value were Tobin, Portlock, and Flinders; Tobin particularly deserves credit for the series of watercolors he produced (figs. 29–1 through 29–5).

4 See chapter 28. According to Vancouver this expedition was carried out by the mutineers themselves (1801:323–324), but if one accepts Morrison's on-the-spot report, the trip to Mo'orea by some mutineers took place *after* Hitihiti's successful campaign, and was merely a peaceful sight-seeing tour. Vancouver

also recorded, mistakenly I believe, that Mahine was killed in the battle of Atehuru, whereas other evidence places his death sometime earlier.

5   As I observed concerning an earlier period of this era, I am not entirely certain about the political geography of Mo'orea, or about the degree of authority exercised by its successive chiefs. Although Mahau may not have exercised the same amount of control over all parts of the island, since the defeat of Tairihamoetua (?), in 1790, Mahau and his immediate successors were undoubtedly the island's most powerful and influential tribal chiefs.

6   Vancouver's detailed amount of this event, which occurred during Mahau's visit to Pare, is one of the best descriptions we possess of an actual Maohi funeral. As most of the generalities obtainable from it have already been set forth in chapter 3, I shall not reproduce it again. The particularity about it of most present interest is the fact that Mahau's embalmed corpse, after remaining a month in state in Pare, was carried on a tour of Seaward Teva and "some of the Western districts," before being returned home to Mo'orea (Vancouver 1801:297). Another point of interest is the location of the principal funeral rites, which were at Pare's Tarahoi; in fact, no mention is made by Vancouver of Mahau's father's marae, Ahurai, although this principal Fa'a'a marae may have been included in the corpse's itinerary through "the western districts."

7   This is in disagreement with Vancouver's version, which reads as follows: "On the late decease of *Mahow*, his daughter by *Pomurrey*'s sister succeeded to the sovereignty of Morea, under the supreme authority of her cousin *Otoo* [Pomare II]. To this young princess *Pomurrey* [Pomare I] became regent, and in course, the inhabitants of Morea were intirely at his command" (1801: 325–326). I am inclined to accept Bligh's version of this succession; not only was Tetuanui male, and older than his sister, but Vancouver's opinion, which was formed within days of Mahau's death, was superseded by Bligh's by several months' time. Bligh also introduced an interesting complication of this episode, in his reference to a Matuaro, which will be discussed later on.

8   I cannot definitely identify this "Matuarro" with any individual appearing on the Huahine genealogies available to us. The most likely candidate is Teri'itaria, the young boy who was *ari'i rahi* in Huahine during Cook's visit in 1777 (Beaglehole 1967:233), and who was the son of "Queen" Tehepapa and of either her first husband, Rohianuu, or of her second husband (and Rohianuu's brother), Mato.

9   For a description of the conclusion of this ceremony see Bligh 1792:173, which is one of the most detailed eyewitness accounts available of an actual ceremony involving a human offering. To this account Bligh also added the interesting observation that a *maro ura* (probably the Wallis *maro*) had been added to, since he last saw it, with hair from one of the mutineers — "an ostentatious mark of their connections with the English, and not of respect to the Person it belonged to."

10 Even their livestock underwent change: "It is remarkable how the Otaheite breed of Hogs is effectually destroyed. We meet with none but of the European Kind, owing to the Natives prefering them to their own, which were of the

China sort, and another of an inferior kind because they are of a larger size.'' (Bligh 1789:I, 376)

11 For references to diseases allegedly introduced into these Islands during the Early European Era see the following: Beaglehole 1955:98–99; Beaglehole 1961:215; Beaglehole 1962:I, 374; J. Forster 1778:488; G. Forster 1777:I, 370–371; Bligh 1789:I, 388–389, 398, 409, 421; II, 10, 30–31, 60; Corney 1915:51; Corney 1919:30; Morrison 1935:228–230; Vancouver 1801:337; Ellis 1829:II, 272.

CHAPTER 30

1 The Spanish friars who had spent a year at Tautira had moral codes and objectives somewhat similar to those of the English missionaries, but they insulated themselves so effectively from Maohi society that they could not have produced much of an impression of any kind on their native neighbors.

2 The accounts of this encounter, mostly written by the missionaries themselves, are in places so unconsciously ironic — or poignant, or incredibly naïve, or downright hilarious — that I am often tempted to include them, if for no other reason than to lighten my own exposition; but I refrain from doing so in the interests of space. I do, however, recommend the account of the first meeting between this solemn band and a mob of Arioi on the decks of the *Duff*, in which the former responded to an especially lusty greeting by the untrammeled Arioi with a few tunes by Brother Bowel on the German flute (Wilson 1799:73).

3 This ritual condition of Pomare II was also mirrored in the behavior of his father, Pomare I, who at this time was still constrained from feeding himself (Wilson 1799:75).

4 Temari'i also bore the name Ari'ipaea (the missionaries' ''Orypaih'' or ''Oripaia''), which Adams claimed was bestowed upon him as the result of his ''adoption'' by the late Ari'ipaea, brother of Pomare I.

5 It will be recalled that Cook's ''Towha'' (Te To'ofa), the great chief of Pa'ea, left as his successor his own son, who died in 1791, and that the latter was succeeded by his sister's son, whose age was about four at the time; thus he was ten or eleven in 1797, and possibly the individual in question.

6 Tutaha was an alternate name of Ha'amanemane, but appears not to be the one here mentioned.

7 The missionaries reported that Pare's principal marae, Tarahoi, was (again) ''inferior'' to 'Utu'aimahurau (Wilson 1799:211). During their tour of the island in 1797, the *Duff*'s officers visited Puna'auia's marae Tahiti and reported the presence there of a small ''ark'' containing a god's image (pp. 208–209); the identity of the god is not given, and, although it may have been 'Oro, the image itself was evidently of less importance than the one theh deposited at 'Utu'aimahurau.

8 One cannot overlook, as a contributory factor, the extent to which a successor to an important kin-Title was insulated from his parents, and particularly from his father, throughout infancy and childhood. That is to say, the lack of nurturant interaction during those formative years need not have fostered *hostility*

between parent and child but by the same token cannot be expected to have fostered much *affection* either.

9   Further insight into Maohi social relations is provided by the fact that five other (presumably lower-class) persons were also badly burned by the gunpowder explosion, and that the missionaries were not even informed of their painful plight when first asked to treat Teri'irere-Temari'i. In fact, three of the five were not even given native medication. (LMS Transactions:I, 76–77)

10   The events were, however, not without some hopeful expectations on the part of the missionaries: "This shaking of the nation may be only plowing up the fallow ground for the better sowing the seed of eternal life: though many may fall, yet we trust the gospel will not be removed off the island, till thousands have felt it to be the power of God and the wisdom of God for their souls' salvation" (LMS Transactions:I, 84–85).

11   According to one missionary historian a contributing factor to Pomare II's hostility toward his father was the latter's action in naming his youngest son, Teri'i na Vaho Roa, to the local chieftainship of the tribal subdivision comprising Point Venus — an estate which Pomare II coveted for himself. (Thomson, History, p. 27)

12   See, for example, LMS Transactions:I, 11, 115, 120, 124.

13   The occasion of the message was the suicide — or possibly murder — of Lewis, who had been a missionary prior to his "excommunication" from the group (on account of his living with a Tahitian woman). This episode contains a world of poignant human interest, and the almost daily interchange between Lewis and the other missionaries, couched in turgidly biblical prose, reveals much about the Europeans involved. The occurrence constituted such a major preoccupation for the missionaries during so many weeks that their journal for the period contains little else.

14   In describing these events in the LMS Transactions, the missionaries provided an interesting sidelight on the degree to which Pomare I had become reconciled to his role vis à vis his son: "Pomere and Edea having been made fully sensible, that the presents sent by Governor King are for them, and Otoo not considered, began to express their fears, lest Otoo (who, by the custom of the country, is held superior in dignity to his father and mother) should take offence thereat, they expressed a wish that the scarlet dress should be given to Otoo, in preference to Pomere. Capt. Scott being informed of this, consented that it should be so, and, in order to make all things agreeable, employed his tailor to make a scarlet dress for Pomere, and another for his youngest son Teare-navo-roa; and also appointed a white shirt for each of the two chief women, Tatooa-noce, and Tooboo-iote-rye." (I, 229)

15   The missionaries' journal of the period August to January is not extant.

16   In the interest of brevity I offer no comments on the ritual aspects of this important event, and call attention only to one other feature — the fact that Pomare II had now gone beyond his father in sheer ruthlessness.

17   According to my reconstruction the image we are now concerned with was the one originally established at Papara, then taken to 'Utu'aimahurau by Tutaha et al. in 1768, to Pare in 1792, then back to 'Utu'aimahurau. What had hap-

pened meanwhile to the image called 'Óro Rahi To'o toa, the one said originally
to have been at Tautira, I cannot fathom.

18 One person on the Pomares' side who was slain in Taiarapu was Mateha,
a brother of Ra'iatea's chief, Tamatoa IV.

19 See also Thomson, History, p. 57.

20 According to one interpretation, Pomare I was killed by the god 'Oro to punish
him for the sacrilege involved in the forceful removal of the god's image from
'Utu'aimahurau (LMS Transactions:II, 342).

CHAPTER 31

1 In their journal entry of December 10, 1806, the missionaries requested: "If
the Directors should write again to Pomare, we beg them to address him *King
Pomare*, or *Pomare King of Taheite*, &c &c; and not *chief*, as it is likely
to give offence, if continued." (LMS Transactions:IV, 19)

2 The reference also raises interesting questions concerning Maohi "marriage" — in this case, the nature of the relationship between 'Itia and Tenania.
As we have seen, 'Itia was a loyal and helpful supporter of Pomare I to the
end of his days, although she had long since had paramours, perhaps even
while sharing Pomare I's mat. Tenania, however, was a somewhat different
matter. Whereas 'Itia's early lovers had been *toutou*, Tenania held a very high-
ranking Title; and his daughter by 'Itia was evidently considered of superior
enough status to qualify her for the Mo'orean office of "governor." That
is to say, the relationship between 'Itia and Tenania was a "marriage" in
the fullest Maohi sense, and it was in effect long before Pomare I died. (See
Turnbull 1813:134, 145–146.) In other words, in view of 'Itia's continuing
alliance with Pomare I, and in the absence of any indications of a formal
separation between the two, we are confronted in this case with still another
example of the flexibility with which the Maohis defined relationships of
affinity.

3 Pomare II wished himself to be called "King," but this does not imply any
identity between his concept of kingship and the English one which served
as his model. Nor does it imply that other Tahitians held him to be "King."

4 We do not know when or why Pomare II chose to set up a marae for himself
separate from the traditional family one of Tarahoi; perhaps this had been
another move in his previous effort to make himself independent of his father's
control.

5 Perhaps the clearest ritual indication of the extent to which the interests of
Pomare II and 'Oro had come to coincide is to be found in the account of
a *maeae* in June 1806: "Today there was an Oroa at Pare called Ma-e-ae,
this ceremony consists in offering to the god Oro Cloth, Hogs, Ava &c. which
are brought from every district in the Island. After a certain part is divided
out for this purpose, the priests on the canoe (designed to carry the dedicated
food &c. to Oro who is at the Marae at Toutera) blow the conch shell, crying
out at intervals Teie te ma e ae na Oro here is food for Oro to eat — supposing
that the god comes and eats the spirit of the food &c. The greater part of

the presents brought are the Kings which he disposes of at pleasure." (Davies, Youl et al., Journal, 20 June 1806, LMS Archives)

6   A marginal comment by the missionary Nott on this passage in Davies' manuscript described the ceremony as "A kind of investing of their god oro with the royal authority, or making him their king by putting on him the royal *maro ura*, for which ceremony the bure is performed. *Not for King Pomare*." (Newbury 1961:87n2.) If Nott's identification were true — and he was undoubtedly more fluent in the language than were the other missionaries — this would constitute a most intriguing reversal of ritual roles between human *ari'i* and deity.

7   Fa'a'a was rarely singled out as a separate political unit in this or in other accounts of this period. Earlier it was sometimes included with Atehuru, but in later years it was included in Porionu'u.

8   According to Adams, although the land in question was in fact dedicated to 'Oro and his priests, some of its inhabitants refused to leave, thereby giving Pomare II another pretext for his next attack on the south (1901:149–150).

9   This individual is not specifically identified as a leader, but he was possibly the tribal chief of Pa'ea.

10   According to Adams the attack upon Atehuru, Papara, etc., was simply a continuation of the old feud between Purea and 'Itia which had culminated in the Papara debacle of 1768. Specifically, Pomare II's attack was viewed as a measure for wiping out the insult offered to 'Itia by Purea when the former tried to put an end to the *rahui* imposed by Purea on behalf of her son, Teri'irere. (1901:152.) As Adams noted, this is a "more picturesque" version of the war than others that might occur to the reader, but it is not altogether credible. For one thing, why would Pomare II include Oropa'a in his offensive action?

11   Reinforcing the missionaries' decision to withdraw was the lack of any evident sign of success in their mission, and the absence of any communication from the London Missionary Society's directors for some *six years*! (Newbury 1961:116)

12   Pomare II even engaged in pimping in order to obtain gunpowder: "In the evening Pomare sent 8 women to the ship to prostitute themselves to the seamen, giving them charge to get powder to bring it to him" (Jefferson, Journal, 8 April 1803, LMS Archives). This was certainly not a new tactic with the Maohis, but there is no previous record of it having been organized on this large a scale.

13   This disenchantment applied especially to the missionaries, who had few objects to give away, who had shown themselves unwilling to engage in military adventures, and whose ideology was still generally considered to be ridiculous, if not insane.

14   Newbury 1961:73; Jefferson, Journal, 12–22 September 1804; LMS Transactions:III, 43.

15   This merriment included the manufacture and drinking of an intoxicating beverage made from the root of the ti plant — an innovation introduced by the Hawaiians.

16   Some of these chiefs may have been kinsmen, related to him through his paternal grandmother, Tetupaia, but one has the impression that Pomare II's solicitude toward those distant individuals was based more on their chieftainship than on their consanguineal ties to him.

17   One will recall in this connection that other Ra'iatean immigrant, Ha'amanemane, who made such an important place for himself in Tahitian politics.

18   I do not propose that this was a wholly new kind of development in Maohi history. In fact, similar measures seem to have been imposed shortly before this in the Leeward Islands, in connection with Poraporan conquests there, and it is likely that the same kind of development had taken place in the past on Tahiti and Mo'orea — but probably on a much smaller scale.

CHAPTER 32

1   *Venus* was the small schooner captured by Matavaians in September 1809. See pages 1324–1325.

2   See the strictures on missionary ''censuses'' in chapter 2.

3   I am not entirely sure whether Fa'a'a was an autonomous unit during this period, or was allied with Puna'auia and Pa'ea.

4   Tati and Opuhara were grandsons of Amo's younger brother, Manea, and thus legitimate successors to Teri'irere-Temari'i, who left no heirs.

      With no missionaries stationed on the island during this period, such information that was recorded about events and personalities outside Pare was sparse and secondhand. However, had any of the tribal chiefs made much of a political stir, the missionaries would likely have heard of and dutifully recorded it.

5   Although humans continued to be offered to 'Oro and perhaps to other deities during this period, the sacrificial rituals evidently took place without benefit of a feather-girdle *ari'i*.

6   These developments may perhaps represent a local manifestation of a much more generic phenomenon in Polynesian societies: that is, the ascendancy of shamanism over priestcraft in times of social disorganization.

7   It is, of course, impossible to divine all the actual motives that moved these important leaders to travel with scores and even hundreds of their followers to Mo'orea and Tahiti, and to spend so much time there. Aid to Pomare II, the announced reason, was possibly also a sincere one, but political adventuring probably figured, along with an expectation of loot. Nor should one underestimate a desire for the novelty and excitement of travel, so apparent in other situations in Maohi life.

8   Technically, inasmuch as this Uru had already sired a successor before 1777, it was the latter who held the highest-ranking Opoan kin-Titles at the time of Cook's visit — or so I assume from practices elsewhere.

9   One cause of this difficulty is Davies' apparent confusion in some passages between Tapoa and Tamatoa. For example, see Newbury 1961:137.

10   For one thing, although I do not suggest any causal connection between the two, the turn to Christianity took place simultaneously with the widespread consumption of ti-root alcohol. And Pomare II, the missionaries' premier con-

vert and their proudest evidence of success, was described by some observers as having been drunk most of the time.

11   An interesting sidelight on the changes then taking place is revealed in the fact that pagan Maohis had begun to refer to their gods collectively as *Tatani* (Satan). (Newbury 1961:168)

12   In May of 1814 the missionaries received reports that a war had commenced in the Leeward Islands; no details were offered concerning the combatants or causes, but it is likely that this conflict was largely responsible for the return home of the Ra'iateans and Taha'ans.

13   In his more detailed (and doubtless more imaginative) account of the battle Ellis indicated that the most active leaders on the Pomare side were Mahine, "king" of Huahine, and Pomare Vahine herself — Pomare II, characteristically, having viewed the battle from the comparative safety of a canoe (1829:I, 248–249).

BIBLIOGRAPHY

This bibliography contains only those items actually cited in the text. For a more comprehensive, and probably well-nigh complete, bibliography on ancient Tahiti, the reader is advised to consult the extraordinary *Bibliographie de Tahiti et de la Polynésie française*, critically and painstakingly compiled by Patrick O'Reilly and Édouard Reitman — perhaps the finest bibliography of its kind I have ever encountered, and one that would have shortened my labors by a year or more had it been available ten years earlier.

In addition to published works cited in the bibliography much use was made of unpublished documents and manuscripts. Text and bibliographic references should aid the researcher in the use of this material which may be found in the following places:

Alexander Turnbull Library
National Library of New Zealand
Wellington, New Zealand

Bernice P. Bishop Museum
Honolulu, Hawaii

London Missionary Society Archives
London, England

Mitchell Library
Public Library of New South Wales
Sydney, Australia

Public Record Office
London, England

Adams, Henry
   1901 *Memoirs of Arii Taimai E, Marama of Eimeo, Teriirere of Tooarai, Teriinui of Tahiti, Tauraatua I Amo.* Paris: Privately printed.
Ahnne, Édouard
   1923 "Deux légendes tahitiennes: Le grand lézard de Fautaua; histoire des Ainanu, Pipiri-ma." *Bulletin de la Société d'études océaniennes* 1(7): 35–40.
   1924 "Le Lyrisme des Tahitiens." *Bulletin de la Société d'études océaniennes* 1(9): 20–23.
   1925 "Mystérieuse aventure de Ariipaea Vahine, reine de Huahine." *Bulletin de la Société d'études océaniennes* 1(10): 43–46.
   1926 "De la coutume du *pii* et des modifications qu'elle apporta au vocabulaire tahitien." *Bulletin de la Société d'études océaniennes* 2(11): 6–10.
   1931a "La Coutume du *pii* en Polynésie et le *Fady* de Madagascar." *Bulletin de la Société d'études océaniennes* 4:181–182.
   1931b "Turi et Mahu." *Bulletin de la Société d'études océaniennes* 4:168–169.
   1932a "Le Déluge: version tahitienne." *Bulletin de la Société d'études océaniennes* 5:84–87.
   1932b "Proverbes tahitiens." *Bulletin de la Société d'études océaniennes* 5:142–143.
   1933 "Légendes tahitiennes: La légende de Ruanui; la légende de Paiheotuu." *Bulletin de la Société d'études océaniennes* 5:170–173.
   1940 "Origine du nom de Punaauia." *Bulletin de la Société d'études océaniennes* 6:268–271.
Ahnne, P. (?)
   1930 "L'Art du tatouage." *Bulletin de la Société d'études océaniennes* 4:77–80.
Alexander, W. D.
   1893 "Specimens of Ancient Tahitian Poetry." *Journal of the Polynesian Society* 2:55–59.
Anderson, Eugene
   1963 "Tahitian Bonito Fishing." *Kroeber Anthropological Society Papers* 28:87–119.
Anderson, William
   1777 "A Vocabulary of the Language of the Society Islands." In *A Voyage towards the South Pole and round the World* . . . , by James Cook. London: W. Strahan and T. Cadell.
Andrews, Edmund, and Irene D. Andrews
   1944 *A Comparative Dictionary of the Tahitian Language.* Chicago Academy of Sciences Special Publication no. 6. Chicago.
Archer, Gilbert
   1965 *The Art Forms of Polynesia.* Auckland Institute and Museum Bulletin no. 4. Auckland.

Baessler, Arthur
   1897 "*Marae* und *Ahu* auf den Gesellschafts-Inseln." *Internationales Archiv für Ethnographie* 10:245–260.
   1900 *Neue Südsee-Bilder.* Berlin: Von A. Asher.

Barthel, Thomas
    1961 "Zu Einigen Gesellschaftlichen Termini der Polynesier." *Zeitschrift für Ethnologie* 86:256–275.
Beaglehole, Ernest, and Pearl Beaglehole
    1938 *Ethnology of Pukapuka*. Bernice P. Bishop Museum Bulletin no. 150. Honolulu.
Beaglehole, John C., ed.
    1955 *The Journals of Captain James Cook on His Voyages of Discovery*. Vol. 1. Hakluyt Society Extra Series no. 34. Cambridge: University Press.
    1961 *The Journals of Captain James Cook on His Voyages of Discovery*. Vol. 2. Hakluyt Society Extra Series no. 35. Cambridge: University Press.
    1962 *The Endeavour Journal of Joseph Banks 1768–1771*. 2 vols. Sydney: Angus and Robertson.
    1967 *The Journals of Captain James Cook on His Voyages of Discovery*. Vol. 3, 2 parts. Hakluyt Society Extra Series no. 36. Cambridge: University Press.
Bechtol, Charles
    1962 "Sailing Characteristics of Oceanic Canoes." In *Polynesian Navigation* . . . , edited by Jack Golson. Supplement to the *Journal of the Polynesian Society* 71:98–101.
Beckwith, Martha
    1944 "Polynesian Story Composition." *Journal of the Polynesian Society* 53:177–203.
Beechey, Frederick William
    1831 *Narrative of a Voyage to the Pacific and Beering's Strait, to Co-operate with the Polar Expeditions: Performed in His Majesty's Ship Blossom under the Command of Captain F.W. Beechey in the Years 1825, 26, 27, 28*. London: H. Colburn and R. Bentley.
Best, Elsdon
    1917 "Some Place Names of Islands of the Society Group Supplied by Natives of Those Isles at Wellington, in 1916." *Journal of the Polynesian Society* 26:111–115.
Bligh, William
    1789 [published in 1792] *A Voyage to the South Sea, Undertaken by Command of His Majesty, for the Purpose of Conveying the Breadfruit Tree to the West Indies, in His Majesty's Ship the Bounty. Including an Account of the Mutiny on Board the Said Ship*. 2 vols. London: G. Nicol.
    1792 *Journal of the Voyage of H.M.S. Providence*. Unpublished manuscript in the Public Record Office. Reference: Adm. 55/152.
    1937 *The Log of the Bounty, Being Lieutenant William Bligh's Log of the Proceedings of His Majesty's Armed Vessel Bounty in a Voyage to the South Seas, to Take the Breadfruit from the Society Islands to the West Indies*. 2 vols. London: The Golden Cockerel Press.
Bohannan, Paul
    1955 "Some Principals of Exchange and Investment Among the Tiv." *American Anthropologist* 57:60–70.

Bougainville, Louis Antoine de
   1772 *A Voyage round the World. Performed by Order of His Most Christian Majesty, in the Years 1766, 1767, 1768 and 1769, by Lewis de Bougainville*. Translated by J. R. Forster. London: Printed for J. Nourse and T. Davies.
Bouge, L.-J.
   1928 "Pêche par jet de pierres 'Tautai taora ofai'." *Bulletin de la Société d'études océaniennes* 3:73–77.
   1955 "Un Aspect du rôle rituel du 'Mahu' dans l'ancien Tahiti." *Journal de la Société des océanistes* 11:147–149.
de Bovis, Edmond
   1909 *État de la société tahitienne à l'arrivée des Européens*. Papeete: Published by the French Government.
Buck, Peter H. [Te Rangi Hiroa]
   1943 "The Feather Cloak of Tahiti." *Journal of the Polynesian Society* 52: 12–15.
   1944 *Arts and Crafts of the Cook Islands*. Bernice P. Bishop Museum Bulletin no. 179. Honolulu.
Burbidge, George W., and John F. Stimson
   1930 *A New Grammar of the Tahitian Dialect of the Polynesian Language* . . . . 2nd ed. n.p. For the Church of Jesus Christ of Latter Day Saints.
Buschmann, Johann Carl Eduard
   1843 *Aperçu de la langue des îles Marquises et de la langue taïtienne* . . . . *Accompagné d'un vocabulaire inédit de la langue taïtienne par le baron Guillaume de Humboldt*. Berlin: C. G. Luderitz.

Chabouis, Louis, and François Chabouis
   1954 *Petite histoire naturelle des Établissements français de l'Océanie*. Vol. 1: *Botanique*, vol. 2: *Zoologie*. Paris: Éditions Paul Lechevallier.
Chadourne, Marc
   1922 "Le Lyrisme des Tahitiens. . . ." *Bulletin de la Société d'études océaniennes* 1(6): 64–76.
Chesneau, Henri [Le Père Joseph]
   1928 "Histoire de Huahine et autres îles Sous-le-Vent." *Bulletin de la Société d'études océaniennes* 3:57–67.
   1929 "Histoire de Huahine . . . ." *Bulletin de la Société d'études océaniennes* 3:81–98.
Collingwood, R. G.
   1946 *The Idea of History*. Oxford: Clarendon Press.
Cook, James
   1784 *A Voyage to the Pacific Ocean Undertaken by the Command of His Majesty, for Making Discoveries in the Northern Hemisphere, to Determine the Position and Extent of the West Side of North America, Its Distance from Asia, and the Practicability of a Northern Passage to Europe. Performed under the Direction of Captains Cook, Clerke and Gore, in His Majesty's Ships the Resolution and Discovery, in the Years 1776, 1777, 1778, 1779 and 1780.* Vol. 2, book 3. London: G. Nichol and T. Cadell.

Corney, Bolton Glanville, ed.
   1913 *The Quest and Occupation of Tahiti by Emissaries of Spain during the Years 1772–1776*. Vol. 1. London: Cambridge University Press.
   1915 *The Quest and Occupation of Tahiti.* . . . Vol. 2. London: Cambridge University Press.
   1919 *The Quest and Occupation of Tahiti.* . . . Vol. 3. London: Cambridge University Press.
Crampton, Henry E.
   1916 *Studies on the Variation, Distribution, and Evolution of the Genus Partula. The Species Inhabiting Tahiti*. The Carnegie Institution Publication no. 228. Washington, D.C.
Crook, William Pascoe
   1826 "Extract from the Journal of W. P. Crook Containing Particulars of His Visit to the Marquesas. . . ." *Transactions of the Missionary Society, London* (October): 225–238.
Cuzent, Gilbert
   1860 *Îles de la Société*. Rochefort: Imprimerie C. Thèze.

Danielsson, Bengt
   1956 *Love in the South Seas*. Translated by F. H. Lyon. London: George Allen and Unwin.
   1957 "A Unique Tahitian Stone Figure." *Journal of the Polynesian Society* 66:396–397.
   1962 "Étude anthropométrique des habitants de Mai'ao." *Bulletin de la Société d'études océaniennes* 12:46–47.
Davies, John
   1851 *A Tahitian and English Dictionary* . . . . Tahiti: London Missionary Society's Press.
Dening, G. M.
   1962 "The Geographical Knowledge of the Polynesians and the Nature of Inter-Island Contact." In *Polynesian Navigation* . . . , edited by Jack Golson. Supplement to the *Journal of the Polynesian Society* 71:102–153.
Draper, John W.
   1959 *Rhyme in the Pacific*. West Virginia University Bulletin, series 60, no. 2–1. Morgantown.
Drollet, Alexandre
   1954 "Légende du marae de Arahurahu." *Bulletin de la Société d'études océaniennes* 9:336–345.
[Dumont] d'Urville, Jules Sébastien César
   1834–1835 *Voyage pittoresque autour du monde*. 2 vols. Paris: L. Tenré.

Edwards, Edward, and George Hamilton
   1915 *Voyage of H.M.S. Pandora*. Edited by Basil Thomson. London: Francis Edwards.
Efron, D. H., ed.
   1967 *Ethnopharmacologic Search for Psychoactive Drugs*. U.S. Public Health

Service Publication no. 1645. Washington, D.C.: National Institute of Mental Health.

Egler, F. E.
1941 "Unrecognized Arid Hawaiian Soil Erosion." *Science* 94:513–514.

Ellis, William
1829 *Polynesian Researches*. 2 vols. London: Fisher, Son and Jackson.
1831 *Polynesian Researches*. 4 vols. 2nd ed. London: Fisher, Son and Jackson.
1844 *The History of the London Missionary Society, Comprising an Account of the Origin of the Society, Biographical Notices of Some of Its Founders and Missionaries; with a Record of Its Progress at Home and Its Operations Abroad. Compiled from Original Documents in the Possession of the Society.* Vol. 1. London: John Snow.

Ellis, William (Surgeon)
1782 *An Authentic Narrative of a Voyage Performed by Captain Cook and Captain Clerke, in His Majesty's Ships Resolution and Discovery, during the Years 1776, 1777, 1778, 1779, and 1780, in Search of a North-West Passage between the Continents of Asia and America, Including a Faithful Account of All Their Discoveries, and the Unfortunate Death of Captain Cook.* 2 vols. London: G. Robinson, J. Sewell, and J. Debrett.

Emory, Kenneth P.
n.d. *Traditional History of Maraes in the Society Islands.* Unpublished manuscript in the Bernice P. Bishop Museum. (Referred to as *Marae Traditions* in the text.)
1928 "Chant de Pai pour sa lance Rufautumu qui perça Moorea." *Bulletin de la Société d'études océaniennes* 3:170–171.
1931 "The Marae at Which Captain Cook Witnessed a Rite of Human Sacrifice." *Bulletin de la Société d'études océaniennes* 3:194–203.
1933 *Stone Remains in the Society Islands.* Bernice P. Bishop Museum Bulletin no. 116. Honolulu.
1938 "The Tahitian Account of Creation by Mare." *Journal of the Polynesian Society* 47:45–63.
1962 "Report on Bishop Museum Archaeological Expeditions to the Society Islands in 1960 and 1961." *Journal of the Polynesian Society* 71:117–120.
1963 "East Polynesian Relationships. Settlement Pattern and Time Involved as Indicated by Vocabulary Agreements." *Journal of the Polynesian Society* 72:78–100.

Emory, Kenneth P., and Yosihiko H. Sinoto
1964 "Eastern Polynesian Burials at Maupiti." *Journal of the Polynesian Society* 73:143–160.

Finney, Ben
1959 "Fa'ahe'e, l'ancien sport de Tahiti." *Bulletin de la Société d'études océaniennes* 11:53–56.
1962 "Différents noms de Mai'ao." *Bulletin de la Société d'études océaniennes* 12:24–25.

1964*a* "Notes on Bond-friendship in Tahiti." *Journal of the Polynesian Society* 73:431–435.

1964*b* "Polynesian Peasants and Proletarians: Socioeconomic Change in the Society Islands." Unpublished Ph.D. dissertation, Harvard University, Cambridge, Mass.

1966 "Resource Distribution and Social Structure in Tahiti." *Ethnology* 1:8–86.

Firth, Raymond

1936 *We, the Tikopia*. London: G. A. and Unwin.

1940 "The Analysis of Mana: an Empirical Approach." *Journal of the Polynesian Society* 49:483–512.

1961 *History and Traditions of Tikopia*. Wellington: The Polynesian Society.

Fitzroy, Robert

1839 *Narrative of the Surveying Voyages of His Majesty's Ships Adventure and Beagle, between the Years 1826 and 1836*. Vol. 2. London: H. Colburn.

Foltz, J. M.

1835 Appendix to *Voyage of the United States Frigate Potomac under the Command of Commodore John Downes, during the Circumnavigation of the Globe, in the Years 1831, 1832, 1833 and 1834*, by J. N. Reynolds. New York: Harper and Brothers.

Forster, [Johann] Georg Adam

1777 *A Voyage round the World in His Brittanic Majesty's Sloop, Resolution, Commanded by Captain James Cook, during the Years 1772, 3, 4 and 5*. . . . 2 vols. London: B. White, J. Robson, P. Elmsly, and G. Robinson.

Forster, Johann Reinhold

1778 *Observations Made During A Voyage round the World on Physical Geography, Natural History and Ethic Philosophy*. Part 6: "The Human Species." London: G. Robinson.

Fried, Morton H.

1968 "On the Concepts of 'Tribe' and 'Tribal Society'." In *Essays on the Problem of Tribe*, edited by June Helm. Seattle: University of Washington Press.

Garanger, José

1964 "Recherches archéologiques dans le district de Tautira, Tahiti." *Journal de la Société des océanistes* 20:5–21.

1967 "Archaeology and the Society Islands." In *Polynesian Culture History: Essays in Honor of Kenneth P. Emory*, edited by G. A. Highland et al. Bernice P. Bishop Museum Special Publication no. 56. Honolulu.

Gautier, Jean-Maurice

1947 "Tahiti dans la littérature française à la fin du XVIIe siècle." *Journal de la Société des océanistes* 3:43–56.

Goldman, Irving

1960 "The Evolution of Polynesian Societies." In *Culture in History*, edited by Stanley Diamond. New York: Columbia University Press.

Golson, Jack, ed.

1962 *Polynesian Navigation: A Symposium on Andrew Sharp's Theory of Acciden-*

tal Voyages. Supplement to the *Journal of the Polynesian Society* vol. 71. Wellington.

Gougenheim, André
1956 "La Marée de Tahiti; fin d'une légende." *Encyclopédie mensuelle d'outre-mer* (January): 39–40.

Green, Roger C.
1961 "Moorean Archaeology." *Man* 61:169–173.
1967 "The Immediate Origins of the Polynesians." In *Polynesian Culture History: Essays in Honor of Kenneth P. Emory*, edited by G. A. Highland et al. Bernice P. Bishop Museum Special Publication no. 56. Honolulu.

Green, Roger C., and Kaye Green
1968 "Religious Structures of the Society Islands." *New Zealand Journal of History* 2:66–89.

Green, Roger C., Kaye Green, Roy A. Rappaport, Ann Rappaport, and Janet Davidson
1967 *Archaeology on the Island of Mo'orea, French Polynesia*. Anthropological Papers of the American Musum of Natural History, vol. 51, no. 2. New York.

Gunson, Niel
1962 "An Account of the Mamaia or Visionary Heresy of Tahiti, 1826–1841." *Journal of the Polynesian Society* 71:209–243.
1963 "A Note on the Difficulties of Ethnohistorical Writing, with Special Reference to Tahiti." *Journal of the Polynesian Society* 72:415–419.
1964 "Great Women and Friendship Contract Rites in Pre-Christian Tahiti." *Journal of the Polynesian Society* 73:53–69.

Handy, E. S. C.
1927 *Polynesian Religion*. Bernice P. Bishop Museum Bulletin no. 34. Honolulu.
1930 *History and Culture in the Society Islands*. Bernice P. Bishop Museum Bulletin no. 79. Honolulu.
1932 *Houses, Boats, and Fishing in the Society Islands*. Bernice P. Bishop Museum Bulletin no. 90. Honolulu.

Handy, W. C.
1927 *Handcrafts of the Society Islands*. Bernice P. Bishop Museum Bulletin no. 42. Honolulu.

Hawkesworth, John, ed.
1773 *An Account of the Voyages Undertaken by the Order of His Present Majesty for Making Discoveries in the Southern Hemisphere and Successively Performed by Commodore Byron, Captain Wallis, Captain Carteret and Captain Cook, in the Dolphin, the Swallow, and the Endeavour; Drawn Up from the Journals Which Were Kept by Several Commanders and from the Papers of Joseph Banks, Esq.* 3 vols. London: W. Strahan and T. Cadell.

Henry, Teuira
1893 "*Te Umu-ti*, a Raiatean Ceremony." *Journal of the Polynesian Society* 2:105–108.
1894 "The Birth of New Lands." *Journal of the Polynesian Society* 3:136–139.

1895 "Te Parau a Honoura. The Legend of Honoura." Collected by John Williams. *Journal of the Polynesian Society* 4:256–294.
1897 "A War Song of the Oparaa Clan of Tahiti." *Journal of the Polynesian Society* 6:211–212.
1911 "More on the Ari'is of Tahiti." *Journal of the Polynesian Society* 20:4–9.
1912 "The Tahitian Version of the Names Ra'iatea and Taputapuatea." *Journal of the Polynesian Society* 21:77–78.
1913 "The Oldest Great Tahitian Maraes and the Last One Built in Tahiti." *Journal of the Polynesian Society* 22:25–27.
1928 *Ancient Tahiti*. Bernice P. Bishop Museum Bulletin no. 48. Honolulu.

Hertz, Robert
1960 "The Pre-eminence of the Right Hand: a Study in Religious Polarity." In *Death and the Right Hand*, translated by Rodney and Claudia Needham. New York: The Free Press.

Hervé, François
1926 "Légende des Teva." *Bulletin de la Société d'études océaniennes* 2:110–111.

Highland, Genevieve A., R. W. Force, Alan Howard, Marion Kelly, and Yosihiko H. Sinoto, eds.
1967 *Polynesian Culture History: Essays in Honor of Kenneth P. Emory*. Bernice P. Bishop Museum Special Publication no. 56. Honolulu.

Hilder, Brett
1962 "Primitive Navigation in the Pacific — II." In *Polynesian Navigation* . . . , edited by Jack Golson. Supplement to the *Journal of the Polynesian Society* 71:81–95.

Hill, S.
1856 *Travels in the Sandwich and Society Islands*. London: Chapman and Hall.

Hoebel, E. Adamson
1949 *Man in the Primitive World*. New York: McGraw-Hill.

Hooker, Sir Joseph D., ed.
1896 *Journal of the Right Hon. Sir Joseph Banks . . . during Captain Cook's First Voyage in H.M.S. Endeavour, in 1768–71, to Terra del Fuego, Otahite, New Zealand, Australia, the Dutch East Indies, etc.* New York: Macmillan and Co.

Huguenin, Paul
1902–1903 "Raiatea la sacrée, îles Sous-le-Vent de Tahiti, Océanie française." *Bulletin de la Société neuchâteloise de géographie* 14:1–256.

Im Thurn, Sir Everard F., ed.
1925 *The Journal of William Lockerby*. London: Hakluyt Society.

Jacolliot, Louis
1954 "Une Genèse tahitienne." *Bulletin de la Société d'études océaniennes* 9:307–312.

Jacquier, Henri
  1944 "Le Mirage et l'exotisme tahitiens dans la littérature." *Bulletin de la Société d'études océaniennes* 7:1–27, 50–76, 91–114.
Jaussen, Mgr. Florentin Étienne [Tepano]
  1898 *Grammaire et dictionnaire tahitiens*. Paris: Neia I Te Nenei Raa No Belin.

Kooijman, Simon
  1964 "Ancient Tahitian God-figures." *Journal of the Polynesian Society* 73:110–125.
Koskinen, A. A.
  1960 *Ariki the First Born. An Analysis of a Polynesian Chieftain Title*. Folklore Fellows Communication no. 181. Helsinki.

Laguesse, Janine
  1945 "A propos des connaissances astronomiques des anciens Tahitiens." *Bulletin de la Société d'études océaniennes* 7:141–152.
  1947 "Notes au sujet des phases de la lune chez les Polynésiens." *Bulletin de la Société d'études océaniennes* 7:292–294.
Lavaud, C. F., ed.
  1928 "La Création. Hiro. Tradition diluvienne. Notice Sur Teriitinorua. Légende de Maui." Translated by Pierre Gaussin. *Bulletin de la Société d'études océaniennes* 3:78–80, 134–138.
Leach, E. R.
  1961 *Rethinking Anthropology*. London: University of London, Athlone Press.
Lesson, René P.
  1839 *Voyage autour du monde, entrepris par ordre du gouvernement, sur la corvette la Coquille*. Vol. 1. Paris: P. Pourrat Frères.
Leverd, Armand
  1912 "The Tahitian Version of Tafaʻi (or Tawhaki)." *Journal of the Polynesian Society* 21:1–25.
  1918 "Notice sur la pierre 'Anave'." *Bulletin de la Société d'études océaniennes* 1(3):146–147.
Lévi-Strauss, Claude
  1960 "La Geste d'Asdiwal." In *L'Annuaire de l'École des Hautes Études*. Paris: École des Hautes Études.
Levy, Robert I.
  1968 "Tahiti Observed: Early European Impressions of Tahitian Personal Style." *Journal of the Polynesian Society* 77:33–42.
  1970 "Tahitian Adoption as a Psychological Message." In *Adoption in Eastern Oceania*, edited by Vern Carroll. Honolulu: University of Hawaii Press.
Lockerby, William
  See Im Thurn.
LMS Dictionary
  See Davies.
London Missionary Society
  1821–1833 *Quarterly Chronicle of the Transactions of the London Missionary Society, 1815–1832*. 4 vols. London: London Missionary Society.

Lounsbury, Floyd
1964 "A Formal Account of the Crow-and-Omaha-type Kinship Terminologies."
In *Explorations in Cultural Anthropology: Essays in Honor of Murdock*,
edited by W. Goodenough. New York: McGraw-Hill.

Lucett, Edward
1851 *Rovings in the Pacific, from 1837 to 1849; with a Glance at California. By a
Merchant Long Resident at Tahiti*. Vol. 1. London: Longman, Brown,
Green, and Longmans.

Luomala, Katharine
1940 "More Notes on Ra'a." *Journal of the Polynesian Society* 49:303–304.
1951 *The Menehune of Polynesia and Other Mythical Little People of Oceania*.
Bernice P. Bishop Museum Bulletin no. 203. Honolulu.

Malardé, Yves
1930 "La Légende du Maioré (arbre à pain)." *Bulletin de la Société d'études
océaniennes* 4:110–114.
1946 "Maeva, île de Huahine." *Bulletin de la Société d'études océaniennes*
77:247–250.

Malinowski, Bronislaw
1922 *Argonauts of the Western Pacific*. London: Routledge and Kegan Paul.

Marau Taaroa
See also Salmon, Marau Taaroa.
1937 "Légende de Hinaraurea et de la chenille de Papeiha." *Bulletin de la Société
d'études océaniennes* 5:694–699.

March, H. Colley
1893 "Polynesian Ornament a Mythography; or a Symbolism of Origin and Descent." *Journal of the Anthropological Institute of Great Britain and Ireland*
22:307–333.

Marshall, Donald S.
1961 *Ra'ivavae*. New York: Doubleday.

Marshall, Donald S., and C. E. Snow
1956 "An Evaluation of Polynesian Craniology." *American Journal of Physical
Anthropology* 14:405–427

McArthur, Norma
1968 *Island Populations of the Pacific*. Honolulu: University of Hawaii Press.

McKern, W. C.
1929 *Archaeology of Tonga*. Bernice P. Bishop Museum Bulletin no. 60. Honolulu.

Mead, Margaret
1928 *Coming of Age in Samoa*. New York: William Morrow and Co.
1930 *Social Organization of Manu'a*. Bernice P. Bishop Museum Bulletin no. 76.
Honolulu.

Moerenhout, Jacques-Antoine
1837 *Voyages aux îles du Grand Océan, contenant des documents nouveaux sur la
géographie physique et politique, la langue, la littérature, la religion, les
moeurs, les usages et les coutumes de leurs habitants; et des considérations*

générales sur leur commerce, leur histoire et leur gouvernement, depuis les temps les plus reculés jusqu'à nos jours. 2 vols. Paris: A. Bertrand.

Montgomery, James, ed.

1832 *Journal of Voyages and Travels by the Rev. Daniel Tyerman and George Bennet, Esq., Deputed from the London Missionary Society, to Visit Their Various Stations in the South Sea Islands, China, India, etc., between the Years 1821 and 1829*. 3 vols. Boston: Crocker and Brewster.

Morrison, James

1935 *The Journal of James Morrison, Boatswain's Mate of the Bounty, Describing the Mutiny and Subsequent Misfortunes of the Mutineers, together with an Account of the Island of Tahiti*. Edited by Owen Rutter. London: The Golden Cockerel Press.

Mortimer, George

1791 *Observations and Remarks Made during a Voyage to the Islands of Teneriffe, Amsterdam, Maria's Islands near Van Diemen's Land; Otaheite, Sandwich Islands; . . . in the Brig Mercury Commanded by John Henri Cox, Esq.* London: T. Cadell, J. Robson, and J. Sewell.

Moschner, Irmgard

1955 "Die Wiener Cook-Sammlung, Südsee-Teil." *Archiv für Völkerkunde* 10:136–253.

Mühlmann, Wilhelm Emil

1938 *Staatsbildung und Amphiktyonien in Polynesien*. Stuttgart: Verlag Strecker und Schröder.

1939 "Das Parai-Maskenkostüm von Tahiti." *Ethnologischer Anzeiger* 4:219–221.

1955 *Arioi und Mamaia*. Studien zur Kulturkunde vol. 14. Wiesbaden: Franz Steiner Verlag GMBH.

Murdock, George P.

1949 *Social Organization and Government in Micronesia, Final Report*. Washington, D.C.: Pacific Science Board, National Research Council.

Needham, Rodney

1962*a* "Age, Category, and Descent." *Bijdragen tot de Taal-, Land- en Volkenkunde* 122:1–35.

1962*b* "Genealogy and Terminology in Wikmunkan Society." *Ethnology* 1:223–264.

Newbury, Colin

1961 *The History of the Tahitian Mission, 1799–1830, Written by John Davies, Missionary to the South Seas Islands, with Supplementary Papers from the Correspondence of the Missionaries*. London: Cambridge University Press.

1967*a* "Aspects of Cultural Change in French Polynesia: The Decline of the Ari'i." *Journal of the Polynesian Society* 76:7–26.

1967*b* "Te Hau Pahu Rahi: Pomare II and the Concept of Inter-Island Government in Eastern Polynesia." *Journal of the Polynesian Society* 76:477–514.

Nordhoff, Charles

1930*a* "Notes on the Off-shore Fishing of the Society Islands." *Journal of the Polynesian Society* 39:137–173.

1930*b* Notes on the Off-shore Fishing . . . .'' *Journal of the Polynesian Society* 39:221–262.

Nordmann, Paul I.
1943 "Contribution à l'étude de l'infanticide, cause principale de la dépopulation à Tahiti avant l'introduction du christianisme." *Bulletin de la Société d' études océaniennes* 6:337–354.

Oliver, Douglas L.
1955 *A Solomon Island Society*. Cambridge: Harvard University Press.

O'Reilly, Patrick, and Édouard Reitman
1967 *Bibliographie de Tahiti et de la Polynésie française*. Publications de la Société des océanistes no. 14. Paris: Musée de l'Homme.

Orsmond, John Muggridge
n.d. *Notes: Arioi, War, Dictionary*. Unpublished manuscripts in the Mitchell Library.

Panoff, Michel
1965 "La Terminologie de la parenté en Polynésie: Essai d'analyse formelle." *L'Homme* 5:60–87.

Papy, H. René
1951 "Plantes utiles de Tahiti et des Établissements français de l'Océanie." *Revue internationale de botanique appliquée et d'agriculture tropicale* nos. 339–340:94–113.
1954 *Tahiti et les îles voisines. La Végétation des îles de la Société et de Makatéa*. 2 vols. Toulouse: Les Artisans de l'Imprimerie Douladoure.

Parkinson, Sydney
1773 *A Journal of a Voyage to the South Seas in His Majesty's Ship the Endeavour, Faithfully Transcribed from the Papers of the Late Sydney Parkinson, Draughtsman to Sir Joseph Banks, Esq. on His Late Expedition with Dr. Solander, round the World*. London: Stanfield Parkinson.

Piddington, R.
See Williamson 1937 and 1939.

Plischke, Hans
1931 *Tahitische Trauergewander*. Arbeiten der Ethnographischen Sammlung der Universität Göttingen no. 2. Berlin: Weidmannsche Buchhandlung.

Pugeault, Charles
1927 "La Sceptre des reines de Huahine." *Bulletin de la Société d' études océaniennes* 2:219–222.

Pukui, Mary Kawena, and Samuel H. Elbert
1957 *Hawaiian-English Dictionary*. Honolulu: University of Hawaii Press.

Rey-Lescure, Philippe
1936 "Le Piège à poulpe." *Bulletin de la Société d' études océaniennes*. 5: 557–560.
1944 "Analogies dans le langage tahitien." *Bulletin de la Société d' études océaniennes* 6:431–441.

1944 "Essai de reconstitution des moeurs et coutumes de l'ancien Tahiti, d'après le vocabulaire." *Bulletin de la Société d'études océaniennes* 7:28–34.
1945 7:77–85.
1946 7:191–195, 259–263.
1947 7:284–288, 303–307, 356–360.
1948 7:503–505.
1951 8:331–335.
1953 9:82–83.
1946 "Le Chien en Polynésie." *Bulletin de la Société d'études océaniennes* 7:266–272.
1946 "La Coutume du Tavau." *Bulletin de la Société d'études océaniennes* 7:196–205.
1948 "Documents pour l'histoire de Tahiti." *Bulletin de la Société d'études océaniennes* 7:418–422, 461–472.
1949 "La Guerre de Rooua." *Bulletin de la Société d'études océaniennes* 7:568–577.
1951 "De vieux gestes." *Bulletin de la Société d'études océaniennes* 8:220–228, 352–353.
1954 "Légende de Turi." *Bulletin de la Société d'études océaniennes* 9:346–349.
1955 "Le Cerf-volant." *Bulletin de la Société d'études océaniennes* 9:413–414.
1956 "La Mort de Vehiatua." *Bulletin de la Société d'études océaniennes* 9:538–542.

Reynolds, Jeremiah N.
1835 *Voyage of the United States Frigate Potomac, under the Command of Commodore John Downes, during the Circumnavigation of the Globe, in the Years 1831, 1832, 1833, and 1834.* New York: Harper and Brothers.

Rivers, William H. R.
1914 *History of Melanesian Society.* 2 vols. Cambridge: University Press.

Robertson, George
1948 *The Discovery of Tahiti.* Edited by Hugh Carrington. London: Hakluyt Society.

Ropiteau, André
1929 "Légende des deux amies." *Bulletin de la Sociéte d'études océaniennes* 3:289–291.
1932 "Notes sur l'île Maupiti." *Bulletin de la Société d'études océaniennes* 5:113–129.

Roth, Henry L.
1905 "Tatu in the Society Islands." *Journal of the Anthropological Institute of Great Britain and Ireland* 35:283–294.

Roussier, Paul
1928 "Documents ethnologiques taïtiens. . . ." *Revue d'ethnographie et des traditions populaires* 9:188–206.

Sahlins, Marshall
1958 *Social Stratification in Polynesia.* Seattle: University of Washington Press (for The American Ethnological Society).

Salisbury, R. F.
1962 *From Stone to Steel*. London and New York: Cambridge University Press.
Salmon, Ernest
1937 "Les Maximes de Tetunae." *Revue de folklore français et de folklore colonial* no. 1.
Salmon, Marau Taaroa [Queen Marau Taaroa]
1926 "Légende de Tariitaumatatini." *Bulletin de la Société d' études océaniennes* 2:119–123.
1927 "Quelques commentaires sur le *Pii*." *Bulletin de la Société d' études océaniennes* 2:260–271.
Salmon, Tati [Teura i te Rai Tati]
n.d. *The History of the Island of Borabora and Genealogy of Our Family from Marae Vaiotaha*. Printed manuscript in the Bernice P. Bishop Museum.
1910 "On Ari'is in Tahiti." *Journal of the Polynesian Society* 19:40–46.
Sasportas, Léon
1926 "Le Miracle tahitien de la marche sur les pierres chauffées." *Revue d' ethnographie et des traditions populaires* 7:269–276.
Scherzer, Karl von
1861–1863 *Narrative of the Circumnavigation of the Globe by the Austrian Frigate Novara (Commodore B. von Wüllerstorf-Urbair), Undertaken by Order of the Imperial Government, in the Years 1857, 1858 & 1859*. Vol. 3. London: Saunders, Otley, and Co.
Schmitt, Robert C.
1965 "Garbled Population Estimates of Central Polynesia." *Journal of the Polynesian Society* 74:57–62.
1967 "The Missionary 'Censuses' of Tahiti, 1797–1830." *Journal of the Polynesian Society* 76:27–34.
Seurat, Léon G.
1934 "La Faune et le peuplement de la Polynésie française." In *Contribution à l'étude du peuplement zoologique et botanique des îles du Pacifique*. Mémoires de la Société de biogéographie no. 4. Paris: Paul Lechevallier et Fils.
Shapiro, Henry L.
1930 "The Physical Characters of the Society Islanders." *Bernice P. Bishop Museum, Memoirs* 11:275–311.
1943 "Physical Differentiation in Polynesia." In *Studies in Anthropology of Oceania and Asia, Presented in Memory of Roland Burrage Dixon*. Edited by C.S. Coon and J.M. Andrews. Papers of the Peabody Museum of American Archaeology and Ethnology vol. 20. Cambridge, Mass.: Peabody Museum.
Sharp, Andrew
1963 *Ancient Voyagers in Polynesia*. Sydney: Angus and Robertson.
Smith, Bernard
1960 *European Vision and the South Pacific, 1768–1850. A Study of the History of Art and Ideas*. Oxford: Clarendon Press.

Smith, S. Percy
    1892 "The Tahitian 'Hymn of Creation'." *Journal of the Polynesian Society*
        1:31–32.
    1893 "The Genealogy of the Pomare Family of Tahiti, from the Papers of the Rev.
        J. M. Orsmond." *Journal of the Polynesian Society* 2:25–42.
    1910 *Hawaiki: The Original Home of the Maori.* 3rd ed. London: Whitcomb and
        Tombs.
Söderström, Jan
    1939 *A Sparrman's Ethnographical Collection from James Cook's 2nd Expedition
        (1772–1775).* The Ethnographical Museum of Sweden, new series, publica-
        tion no. 6. Stockholm.
von den Steinen, Karl
    1925–1928 *Die Marquesaner und Ihre Kunst.* 3 vols. Berlin: Reimer.
Stimson, J. Frank
    1928 "Tahitian Names for the Nights of the Moon." *Journal of the Polynesian
        Society* 37:326–337.
Stimson, J. Frank, and Donald S. Marshall
    1964 *Dictionary of Some Tuamotuan Dialects of the Polynesian Language.* The
        Hague: Martinus Nijhoff.

Teissier, Raoul
    1953 "Étude démographique sur les Établissements français de l'Océanie, de Cook
        au recensement des 17–18 September 1951." *Bulletin de la Société d'études
        océaniennes* 9:6–31.
    1956 "Île Tupuae Manu ou Maiao Iti." *Bulletin de la Société d'études océaniennes*
        10:517–523.
    1962 "A'ai no te mo'o: la légende du lézard (Ara'i Temauri)." *Bulletin de
        la Société d'études océaniennes* 12:30–34.
    1962 "Note sur l'île Tetiaroa." *Bulletin de la Société d'études océaniennes*
        12:97–102.
Teuinatua, François
    1950 "Légende du cocotier et du mape ou l'histoire de l'anguille aux grandes
        oreilles." *Bulletin de la Société d'études océaniennes* 8:45–48.
Thomson, Robert
    n.d. *History of Tahiti.* Unpublished manuscript in the London Missionary
        Society Archives.
Thornthwaite, C. W.
    1948 "An Approach Toward a Rational Classification of Climate." *Geographical
        Review* 38:55–94.
Titcomb, Margaret
    1969 *Dog and Man in the Ancient Pacific, with Special Attention to Hawaii.*
        Bernice P. Bishop Museum Bulletin no. 59. Honolulu.
Turnbull, John
    1813 *A Voyage round the World, in the Years 1800, 1801, 1802, 1803 and 1804,
        in Which the Author Visited Madeira, the Brazils, Cape of Good Hope, the
        English Settlements of Botany Bay and Norfolk Island, and the Principal*

Islands in the Pacific Ocean. With a Continuation of Their History to the Present Period. 2nd ed. London: A. Maxwell.

d'Urville, Jules S. C. Dumont
See Dumont d'Urville.

Vancouver, George
1801 *A Voyage of Discovery to the North Pacific Ocean, and round the World . . . .* Vol. 1. London: John Stockdale.
Vérin, Pierre
1962*a* "Introduction géographique et ethnographique sur l'île Mai'ao." *Bulletin de la Société d'études océaniennes* 12:3–16.
1962*b* "Prospection archéologique préliminaire de Tetiaroa." *Bulletin de la Société d'études océaniennes* 12:103–124.
Vincendon-Dumoulin, Clément Adrien, and César Louis François Desgraz
1844 *Iles Taïti. Esquisse historique et géographique, précédée de considérations générales sur la colonisation française dans l'Océanie.* 2 vols. Paris: A. Bertrand.
Volk, Winifried
1934 *Die Entdeckung Tahitis und das Wunschbild der seligen Insel in der Deutschen Literatur.* Heidelberg: Kranz und Heinrichmoller.

Wales, William
1778 *Remarks on Mr. Forster's Account of Captain Cook's Last Voyage round the World, in the Years 1772, 1773, 1774, and 1775.* London: J. Nourse.
Walker, Orsmond H.
1925 "Tiurai le Guérisseur." *Bulletin de la Société d'études océaniennes* 1(10):1–35.
1927 "La Légende de Vei." *Bulletin de la Société d'études océaniennes* 2:193–218.
Wallis, Samuel
1767 *An Exact Transcript of Wallis' Journal, June 5–July 29, 1767.* Unpublished manuscript in the Public Record Office. Reference: Adm. 55/35.
Webster, Hutton
1908 *Primitive Secret Societies.* New York: The Macmillan Co.
White, Ralph G.
1967 "Onomastically Induced Word Replacement in Tahitian." In *Polynesian Culture History: Essays in Honor of Kenneth P. Emory,* edited by G. A. Highland et al. Bernice P. Bishop Museum. Special Publication no. 56. Honolulu.
White, Ralph G., and Ariihau a Terupe
1958 *Linguistic Check-Sketch for Tahitian.* Tahiti: Te Fare Vana'a. Mimeographed.
Wilder, Gerrit P.
1928 *The Breadfruit of Tahiti.* Bernice P. Bishop Museum Bulletin no. 50. Honolulu.

Williams, H. W.
    1957 *A Dictionary of the Maori Language*. Wellington: Government Printer.
Williams, John.
    1837 *A Narrative of Missionary Enterprises in the South Sea Islands*. London: J. Snow.
Williamson, Robert W.
    1924 *The Social and Political Systems of Central Polynesia*. Vol. 1. Cambridge: University Press.
    1933 *Religious and Cosmic Beliefs of Central Polynesia*. 2 vols. Cambridge: University Press.
    1937 *Religion and Social Organization in Central Polynesia*. Edited by R. Piddington. Cambridge: University Press.
    1939 *Essays in Polynesian Ethnology*. Edited by R. Piddington. Cambridge: University Press.
Wilson, James
    1799 *A Missionary Voyage to the Southern Pacific Ocean, Performed in the Years 1796, 1797, 1798, in the Ship Duff, Commanded by Captain James Wilson*. . . . London: T. Chapman.

Young, J. L.
    1898 "The Origin of the Name Tahiti, as Related by Marerenui, a Native of Faaiti Island, Paumotu Group." *Journal of the Polynesian Society* 7:109–111.
    1925 "The *Umu-Ti*. Ceremonial Fire Walking as Practised in the Eastern Pacific." *Journal of the Polynesian Society* 34:214–222.

INDEXES

For purposes of alphabetizing, the glottal stop at the beginning of a word has been ignored.

Some Tahitian words are indexed under both old-style spellings (as found in the extracts) and their modern equivalents.

The Place and Name indexes do not contain the detail found in the Subject Index, which we consider of greater importance, given the emphasis of this work.

SUBJECT INDEX

1003; consumption of nut from, 125, 133, 135, 220, 228, 229, 244, 427, 556, 1005; cordage made from products of, 139–142, 199, 289, 319, 390; oil derived from nut of, 155, 244, 435, 479, 1051; origin myths about, 708, 709; ritual use of parts of, 188, 261, 487, 510, 916, 929, 934, 996, 1010, 1032, 1046, 1268, 1320; use of, in construction, 149, 165, 199, 244, 379

Coffins, 507. *See also* Burial

Cognatic stocks, 621, 622, 655, 660–685, 1094, 1097

Colocasia antiquorum. See Taro

Colocasia esculenta. See Taro

Coming-of-age, 437

Conception, beliefs about, 63, 353, 409–413, 442–443, 550, 619–620, 1093, 1139. *See also* Reproduction, human

Conch-shell trumpets, 77, 328, 330, 1006; ritual use of, 261 330, 389, 417, 909, 910, 1018, 1021, 1307

Concubines, 451, 464, 833, 834, 838, 1099, 1145. *See also* Marriage; Semi-marriage

Conjoining, 110

Contraception, 360, 411–412, 617. *See also* Abortion; Infanticide; Reproduction, human

Cookhouses, 44, 162, 173, 228. *See also* Cooking

Cooking, 228–229, 246–247, 250, 251, 274, 276, 325, 606, 824–825; utensils for, 169–170, 221, 225, 236, 244, 245, 1038; while traveling, 196, 279. *See also* Cookhouses; Earth ovens

Coral, 134, 135, 177, 245

Cordage, 135, 139–143, 154, 165, 244, 294, 300; made of human hair, 139, 143, 152, 157, 320, 932, 1058, 1135; manufacture of, 140–143, 166, 289. *See also* Sennit

Cordyline terminalis, 108, 934, 1334

Cotton, native, 23, 530, 550

Council platforms, 46, 887. *See also* Tribal council

Crabs, 25, 282, 307, 308

Crataeva nuts, 535

Crayfish, 294, 308

Creation, 592, 923, 1134; myths about, 49–54, 57, 95, 188, 410, 704–705, 774, 882, 890, 1050, 1134; processes in, 49–50

Cuckoos, 26

Cultivation. *See* Agriculture

Cults, 57, 97, 104, 881–964, 981, 1082, 1105–1106, 1115, 1123, 1207, 1258; of Hiro, 1054–1055; of 'Oro, 57, 666, 671, 684, 909–913, 1151–1152, 1160, 1166, 1174, 1194, 1207, 1213–1214, 1223, 1308;

of Ta'aroa, 57, 882–884; of Tane, 57, 884–890, 1160

Curlews, 25

Cursing, 729, 743, 873, 908, 1314; of children by parents, 719–720, 723, 745. *See also* Sorcery

Cuttlefish. *See* Octopus

Dancing, 332–339, 364, 430, 544, 545, 603, 611, 614, 792, 863, 950, 1076, 1149; costumes for, 337, 338; erotic, 93–94, 153, 332, 334–336, 338, 339, 351–352, 368, 602, 786, 924, 931, 936, 949, 1244–1245; experts at, 359, 365, 435, 864, 880, 914, 923, 937, 938, 945; group coordination required in, 584, 586, 1083; musical accompaniment to, 326–327, 328, 506; occasions for, 109, 262, 263, 336, 344, 397, 447, 483, 506, 514, 703, 997, 1003, 1106, 1153

Daphne, 284

Day, lunar, 128, 130–132, 264, 536. *See also* Ao

Death, 409, 469–472, 485–507, 620, 787; as a supernatural sanction, 594; characterization of, 56, 64; recognized causes of, 473, 555. *See also* Burial; Funeral rites; Mourning

Demigods, 50, 51, 53–54, 56, 62, 95, 222, 327, 412, 532, 537, 597, 648, 678, 729–730, 847, 1079, 1148. *See also* Spirits; Name Index: name of individual demigod

Descent, 65, 688–748, 771–772, 1048, 1093–1098, 1117–1118; bilateral, 449, 454, 617, 619, 624, 694, 721, 805, 841, 1097, 1100, 1125, 1130; traced to gods, 49, 52–53, 65, 442, 867, 901; units of, 65, 617–687, 1093–1098. *See also* Cognatic stocks; Kin-congregations; Kin-Titles, succession to; Marriage

Dioscorea alata, 1003, 1004, 1268

Dioscorea bulbifera, 541

Dirges, 491–492

Diseases, 160, 474, 484–485, 550, 583, 784; indigenous, 42, 243, 1078, 1189; induced by kava, 257; introduced, 39, 485, 1287. *See also* Healing; Illness; Injury

"Districts," 27–28, 30, 31, 357, 970–982, 991; activities engaged in by, 260, 261, 316–317, 322, 336–337, 435; fighting forces of, 27–28, 30, 31. *See also* Tribal polities

Divination, 69–71; events requiring, 188, 384, 395, 397, 488–489, 1026; methods of, 204, 219, 489, 555–556; objects used in, 108, 533; specialists in, 219, 384–385, 756,

774, 799, 863, 1140, 1147; arranged, 453–462, 698, 721–722, 829–830; ceremonies of, 67, 104, 107, 108, 418, 443–444, 447–453, 456, 457, 459, 461, 553, 604, 624, 693, 722, 754, 772, 775–776, 805–807, 819–820, 829–830, 840, 843, 928, 950, 1015, 1022, 1082, 1100, 1115, 1145, 1186, 1187, 1189, 1357; head-freeing completed with, 434, 439, 553, 608, 696; of chiefs, 186, 553, 645, 824, 1022, 1096, 1097, 1363; political motivations for, 447, 454, 465, 553, 658, 807, 979–980, 1099, 1100–1101, 1122, 1125, 1130–1132, 1157, 1192, 1242, 1260, 1293, 1315, 1326, 1337, 1338; suitable partners for, 360, 447–465, 625, 678, 729, 751–754, 755–759, 764, 770–771, 773–774, 805, 965, 1097, 1099, 1101, 1130–1131, 1166. *See also* Concubines; Semi-marriage; Separation, marital
Marriage classes. *See* Classes, social
Massage, 159, 348, 427, 480, 487, 603, 737, 755, 788, 1051, 1144
Mata'eina'a, 31, 32, 176, 626, 654, 750, 966, 968, 969, 973–975, 976, 978, 983, 1002, 1156, 1157, 1209. *See also* Neighborhoods
Matahiapo. See Firstborn
Mates: primary, 464; secondary, 464, 834–838. *See also* Marriage
Mats, 165, 171, 340, 416, 507, 508, 856, 915; use of, as clothing, 380, 384; gifts of, 448, 490, 491, 635, 865; manufacture of, 171, 370, 537, 602, 603; offerings of, 109, 260, 385, 418, 635, 916, 1003, 1005
Maturity, 609, 613, 799, 1113, 1123, 1149
Measurements of distance, 585
Mediums. *See* Oracles
Menstruation, 353, 361–362, 554, 601, 607, 809
Messengers, 627, 761, 852, 980, 1016, 1031–1033, 1034, 1046, 1328; announcements made by, 417, 643–644, 681, 815–816, 989, 1010, 1036, 1050, 1109, 1229, 1243, 1245, 1260, 1264, 1270, 1321; spirit, 57, 77, 114, 115–116, 415, 629. *See also* Standards
Meterology, 218, 299. *See also* Climate
Miro. See Thespesia
Missionaries, 4, 26–27, 46, 48; arrival in Society Islands of, 4, 26, 46, 48, 1288–1313
Mo'a. See Sacred, state of being
Mock combat, 262, 319, 379–380, 382–383, 501–502, 602. *See also* Warfare
Molluscs, 25, 130, 282–283, 284, 304, 602
Monarchy, emergence of, 1171, 1249, 1253, 1280–1281, 1305, 1306, 1349–1350

Moon: god, 57; phases of the,127, 264, 283, 305–308, 543
Morinda citrifolia. See Apples
Mosquitos, 25
"Mourners' masque," 501, 502–507, 798, 929, 960, 1153
Mourning, 488, 516–517, 556, 557, 590, 722–723, 725, 757, 960, 995, 1138; activities of, 226, 311, 488–494, 498–499, 501–507, 510–511, 516–517, 519, 520–521, 832, 1015, 1179; symbols of, 157, 280. *See also* Death; Funeral rites
Mua-muri. See Before-after contrast
Mulberry, 43, 140, 248, 256, 430, 1148
Mullet, 283
Murder, 424, 468, 822, 824, 826, 830, 1053–1054, 1056–1058, 1059, 1065, 1084, 1296, 1331, 1335
Musa fehi. See Plantains, mountain
Musa paradisia. See Plantains
Music, 863, 931, 938, 945, 1076, 1106. *See also* Musical instruments; Songs
Musical instruments, 169, 326–332. *See also* Music; name of particular instrument; Singing
Mussels, 283
Muteness, 484
Myths, 111, 172, 188, 219, 340, 409, 456, 552, 557, 592, 661, 764, 784, 882, 883, 892–900, 903–904, 905–906, 908, 910–912, 944, 954, 992, 1131, 1140, 1150, 1152, 1155, 1209, 1211, 1245; Bible-inspired, 47, 53, 892; local variations in, 48, 530; origin, 235, 704–706, 708, 709, 724, 763, 992, 1050, 1053. *See also* Legends

Names, 581–583, 603, 643, 646, 668; giving of, 419, 424, 449, 581–582, 710, 717, 721, 840; personal, 424, 581, 844, 1080, 1165, *See also* Marae-names
Navigation, 215–218, 281, 539, 1133
Needlefish, 283, 286–287
Neighborhoods, 44–45, 65, 316, 614, 967–970, 976, 978, 979, 1061, 1108, 1156, 1208. *See also* Mata'eina'a
Nets and netting, 142, 151, 170; fishing with, 282, 307
Night-walkers, 869, 871–872. *See also* Priests
Noa. See Secular, state of being
Noddies, 215, 279
Nohora'a, 59
Noho-vao contrast, 767
Nono. See Apples
Nudity, 152, 153–154, 332, 335, 338, 339, 348, 367, 368, 428, 432, 434, 484, 537, 1022, 1023. *See also* Clothing

Pigs, 43, 70, 272, 427, 430, 542, 712, 788, 1058, 1360–1361; association of, with Arioi sect, 898–899, 906, 919–920, 938, 945, 953, 956, 1152, 1153; cooking flesh of, 228; flesh of, denied to females, 224–225, 275; gifts of, 287, 421, 446, 447, 451, 452, 453, 806, 999, 1005, 1031; offerings of, 87–90, 109, 117, 120, 201, 260, 263, 345, 348, 385, 399, 422, 444, 461, 482, 513, 517, 747, 938, 1003, 1011, 1248, 1261, 1265, 1267, 1269, 1299, 1307, 1312; ownership and tending of, 787, 853–854, 1148; trade in, 232, 355, 856; wild, 248, 272, 273, 278, 281, 710–711

Pillows, 168, 172, 213, 1038

Pipefish, 25

Piper methysticum. See Kava

Piripiri, 139, 140, 1530

Plaitware, 149–151, 152, 245

Planets, 536

Plantains, 375; consumption of, 220; cultivation of, 252; preparation of, 274, 1005; ritual use of, 107–108, 117, 261, 263, 313, 317, 345, 348, 399, 422, 490, 497–498, 502, 510, 512, 720, 748, 1246, 1247, 1248, 1267, 1268, 1299. *See also* Plantains, mountain

Plantains, mountain, 25, 146, 247–248, 448, 934, 1003; collecting of, 125, 244, 248, 279, 602, 611, 706, 824; consumption of, 170, 242, 244, 247–248; cultivation of, 43. *See also* Plantains

Plants. *See* Vegetation; name of particular plant

Play, 123, 124. *See also* Games; Sports

Pō, 95, 473, 487, 525, 536, 706, 724, 739, 746, 821, 982, 1041, 1077; as spirit realm, 49, 57, 66, 96, 263, 398, 433, 524, 526, 542, 630, 892; contrasted with *ao*, 585, 1082; equated with night, 128, 132. *See also* *Ao*; Day, lunar

Pō tupapa'u. See Ghosts' night feast

Poetry, 326, 331, 337, 549, 864, 946

Pohue, 537

Poisons administered by sorcerers, 473, 555

Polyandry, 455, 463, 835. *See also* Marriage

Polygyny, 453, 455, 463–465, 642, 694, 808, 828, 833, 1189

Polynesia, comparative studies of, 12, 20, 26, 45, 66, 68, 93, 351, 375, 462, 587, 601, 760, 780, 991, 1126–1127, 1129, 1143, 1365

Polynesians, Maohis compared to other, 41–42, 62–63, 133, 140, 211, 278, 310, 326, 794

Pooling-and-sharing, 229–230, 238, 629, 636,

637, 724, 742, 810, 812–813, 1083, 1084, 1088, 1089, 1095, 1114, 1115

Population, 26–46, 985, 1101, 1123; composition of, 39–40, 554; decrease in, 966, 968, 1143, 1286–1287, 1334; density of, 44, 45, 175–176, 254, 309, 579, 853, 966; estimates of, 26–39

Porcupine fish, 283, 284–285

Porpoise, 225, 275, 283, 299

Portage, 210–211

Possession, spirit, 58, 69, 78–83, 94, 226, 600, 937, 1107; behavior during, 512, 517, 1307, 1344; duration of, 262; individuals subject to, 469, 475, 484, 600, 866, 901, 907, 937, 1048, 1105, 1107, 1291. *See also* Oracles

Prawns, 25, 284

Prayers, 66, 76, 83–93, 108, 323, 326, 395–396, 411, 412, 480, 525, 599, 628–629, 632, 1095, 1321; curing through, 414, 419, 513, 517; harming through, 473, 1327–1328; manner of saying of, 85, 115, 483, 1017; occasions requiring, 69, 124, 127, 192, 311, 414, 419, 434, 444, 448, 450, 474, 479, 481, 624, 1055, 1322; of atonement, 475; parphernalia associated with, 75, 534, 856. *See also* Priests, prayers said by; Priests, training given to

Prayer surrogates. *See* Priests, effigies of

Prayer tallies, 109, 114

Pregnancy. *See* Reproduction, human

Priests, 81–83, 94–95, 148, 411, 475–476, 503, 601, 627, 636, 653, 654, 679, 851, 858, 864, 869–876, 878, 880, 907, 910, 924, 927, 958, 982, 1039, 1045, 1111, 1153, 1213, 1335, 1342; clothing worn by, 85, 115, 448, 910, 927, 1017, 1032; duties of, 263, 389, 390, 396, 399, 475, 479–480, 487, 499, 505, 507, 519, 625, 653, 756–757, 861, 865, 868, 990, 996, 1006, 1012, 1021, 1321; effigies of, 87, 100, 109, 114, 118, 647; high, 95, 261, 416, 465, 674, 680, 707, 767–768, 820, 869–870, 892, 929, 980, 984, 1018, 1020, 1027, 1047–1048, 1054, 1066–1067, 1104, 1109, 1122, 1212, 1220, 1248, 1302; payment of, 90, 118–119, 191, 234, 260, 490, 503, 510, 525, 526, 861, 873, 989, 990, 997, 998, 999, 1000, 1003, 1006, 1007, 1013; political power of, 201, 202, 385, 395, 505, 869–870, 874, 988, 1016, 1025, 1026, 1027, 1034, 1060, 1065, 1066–1067, 1104, 1198, 1236, 1292, 1309, 1365; prayers said by, 95, 103, 117, 118, 192, 411, 421, 444, 448, 489–490, 510, 512, 519, 647, 784, 886, 960, 1051, 1248, 1267, 1268, 1307,

PLACE INDEX

NAME INDEX

ABOUT THE AUTHOR

DOUGLAS L. OLIVER is emeritus professor of anthropology, Harvard University, and presently occupies the Pacific Islands Chair in Anthropology, University of Hawaii. He obtained the degree of Ph.D. in Ethnology from the University of Vienna in 1935, and subsequently held a number of positions, both academic and governmental. He was a consultant on Pacific island affairs for the Department of State from 1948 to 1951 and for the United Nations in 1949. He has, during his career, carried out a number of ethnographic field studies, including one of Bougainville in the Solomon Islands and two of the Society Islands. He also planned and directed the postwar Economic Survey of Micronesia for the Naval Military Government to provide for rehabilitating the native economy in the Trust Territory of the Pacific Islands.

As a scholar on the Pacific islands, Professor Oliver is among the most distinguished. His writings are numerous, and include the following books: *A Solomon Island Society* (1955), *The Pacific Islands* (1951, revised ed., 1962) a classic in its field, *Invitation to Anthropology* (1964), and *Bougainville: A Personal History* (1973). He edited *Planning Micronesia's Future* (1951, reprinted 1971).